Library of Congress Cataloging-in-Publication Data

How public organizations work : learning from experience / edited by
  Christopher Bellavita.
          p.   cm.
    Includes bibliographical references.
    ISBN 0-275-93387-3 (alk. paper).—ISBN 0-275-93391-1 (pbk. :
  alk. paper)
    1. Public administration.
  JF1351.H68   1990
  350—dc20   90-32291

Library of Congress Catalog Card Number: 90-32291
ISBN: 0-275-93387-3 (hb.)
       0-275-93391-1 (pbk.)

First published in 1990

Praeger Publishers, One Madison Avenue, New York, NY 10010
An imprint of Greenwood Publishing Group, Inc.

Printed in the United States of America

The paper used in this book complies with the
Permanent Paper Standard issued by the National
Information Standards Organization (Z39.48-1984).

10 9 8 7 6 5 4 3 2 1

To
Cynthia J. McSwain
Teacher, Colleague, and Friend

Contents

Tables and Figures

TABLES

FIGURES

Preface

Public administrators wrote this book to describe how public organizations work and how they can be improved. Some chapters describe how the authors use theory to be effective at work. Other chapters discuss how their experiences have led them to develop personal theories about public organizations and human behavior. The book seeks to encourage other practitioners, especially those enrolled in education programs, to rediscover the part they play in the creation and use of public administration knowledge.

The authors write from experience. Collectively, they have spent more than 250 years working in, managing, and leading complex public organizations. Their ideas have emerged, in part, from their practice. The authors are also what one of them calls closet scholars. While they are full-time administrators, they have also received, or soon will receive, a doctorate in public administration from the University of Southern California. Consequently their ideas reflect contemporary theoretical understandings about the purpose and functions of public organizations.

The book is a product of an informal seminar that started because the practitioner-scholars who had completed their degree or their course work wanted to continue their study of organizations. They came from different agencies, backgrounds, experiences, and philosophies. They met for about two years to discuss what they knew about how public organizations worked.

Four ideals governed the book's development: (1) an emphasis on including people's ideas, not excluding them; (2) a desire to integrate disparate ideas, not necessarily to select the best ideas; (3) a tolerance for differences in concept, methods, and subject matter; and (4) an effort to show how theory can inform practice and how practice can contribute to theoretical advancement.

It should also be pointed out that the thoughts expressed in each chapter are the author's. They do not represent the policy or views of any government agency.

HOW ADMINISTRATORS LEARN
ABOUT PUBLIC ORGANIZATIONS

I have talked with several hundred public administrators over the last ten years. I found that most of them learned what they knew about organizations through a combination of books, courses, role models, and experience. It will come as no surprise to readers who have worked in organizations that their most significant knowledge came from experience.

Taking a course, reading a book, or listening to a lecture will tell you what other people know. These provide one level of knowledge about how organizations work. Watching managers and executives at work is a second way to learn about organizations. Role models can provide many ideas about what to do—and what not to do—to be successful. Observing people and coming to your own judgments about what works is another level of knowledge. Managers have told me that they learned much from this method, especially early in their careers.

The third way of learning, through experience, forces you to put what you think you know to the test. For example, it may be fashionable to believe in participatory decision making, or to think that it is possible to integrate individual goals with organizational goals. But what do you do when no one wants to participate, or when people only want participation on their terms, or when a powerful person's pursuit of individual goals threatens the ethical integrity of the entire organization? Working in an organization means that you continuously use your knowledge to make decisions on these and other issues every day. Taking an action, and living with its consequences, gives you knowledge *of* instead of knowledge *about* public organizations. It is a level of knowledge that you gain only from experience.

HOW PUBLIC ORGANIZATIONS WORK

With that said, how do public organizations work? The simple answer is that you have to discover this for yourself. That is the way most effective public administrators I know learned. You can read all the books and articles you want and listen to all the lectures you have time for. But unless those words resonate with something inside you, something that grew from your experience or from your passion, the words will have little meaning.

Words can help, however. They can be the start of a conversation that triggers insight. That is one reason this book was written. It seeks to communicate through each level of organizational knowledge: through vicarious experience, through direct experience, and through examples.

This book can be used for vicarious learning. Each chapter describes what a public administrator knows about an aspect of life in public organizations. The authors have something to say that they believe other practitioners and those who are interested in public organizations will find interesting.

The book can also teach through example. The authors illustrate what it means to be a reflective practitioner, someone who integrates theory and practice. The authors have been successful in organizations, as evidenced by their positions and their accomplishments. They are also able to reflect on their experiences, to learn from these experiences, and to tell other people about their points of view. You are invited to agree or disagree with what they have to say, and to take from the chapters practical and theoretical ideas you can explore for yourself, as you would with any role model.

Engaging the chapters in that spirit provides a third way to use the book. You can learn from this book through the experience it creates. Obviously the book does not replicate the operational reality of public organizations. But in reading it, you can participate in the same method the authors used to learn for themselves how public organizations work.

TRANSFORMATIONAL DIALECTICS

Transformational dialectics is the method of inquiry used in this book. In its basic sense, the dialectic is a method of analysis in which one person expresses a point of view and another person states an opposing view. The result, in the ideal case, is the emergence of a third viewpoint that embraces the best of the first two. The third view becomes the new thesis, and the dialectic continues.

The "transformational" part of the methodology refers to what eventually happens to the ideas and to the people who participate openly and authentically in the dialectical process. They are changed, and the change—as some authors in this volume demonstrate—can be striking. Rarely is the change instantaneous, however. Learning, like the dialectic, is continuous. Thus the chapters are portraits of ideas in progress.

Nearly all the chapters describe transformations that have taken or can take place. Sometimes the changes are in people, sometimes in organizations. But each new idea that is offered is contrasted with an opposing perspective.

In using the transformational dialectic the authors sought to provide approximate meanings for the terms used; to offer evidence that is illustrative; and to define truth as the plausibility of the description or analysis, and the interest generated by ideas. The authors tried whenever possible to write in ordinary language rather than in jargon. Their intent is to facilitate communication. The evidence that they offer in support of their arguments is illustrative rather than conclusive. Each author is explaining a point of view, not trying to convince the reader that his or hers is the only good way to explore the topic. The truth of what each has to say should be judged by its plausibility instead of its statistical certainty, for the ideas in this book are maps of experience, not the experience itself. Finally, truth is also related to the reader's reaction to what is expressed (White & McSwain, 1983).

Not every author necessarily subscribes to the point of view, organizing assumptions, or the specific way the dialectic was used by the other authors. But they all respect the intellectual adventure that underlies the perspectives in each chapter.

A CONCEPTUAL GUIDE TO THE BOOK

In teaching practitioners, I have found it useful to offer a conceptual framework they can use to organize their experience. The idea is not to tell them what works or what they should know but to provide a vocabulary they can use to share their ideas about what their experiences mean. I will outline the general features of that framework here as an interpretive guide to the chapters that follow.

The framework has four broad elements: the nature of organizational reality; how you can gain information about that reality; how you can learn from the information obtained; and where you can apply the knowledge gained.

Organizational Reality

Reality is what cannot be wished away. Some people maintain that organizational reality is as objective and tangible as a table, car, or any other item in the material world. Other people assert that organizational reality is subjective, created by the contents of people's thoughts. Some of authors in this book write mainly from the "reality-is-objective" perspective. Others assume a more subjective stance. But they all recognize that organizations are a mix of both realities.

Information about Reality

You can use everyday events, concepts, theories, metaphors, and paradigms to direct your inquiry about organizations. Most chapters contain examples of more than one technique.

Everyday events include the concrete things that administrators do when they go to work: for example, attend meetings, make phone calls, write reports, and so on. Almost all the authors refer to everyday events when describing their point of view about organizations.

Concepts are generic ideas derived from specific instances. For example, concepts like values, personality, consciousness, roles, power, and leadership each represent a particular way of thinking about aspects of organizational experience. Some chapters use concepts—such as "learning," "evil," and "archetypes"— as their basic unit of analysis.

There are many ideas about the meaning and uses of theory. For a starting point, theory refers to a coherent, integrated group of ideas intended to describe, explain, prescribe, or predict something. Several authors in this volume have developed theories that are based on their organizational experiences.

Metaphor is a way to understand one phenomenon in terms of another. Metaphors appear in many of the chapters. Spider webs, gods, goddesses, heroes, demons, and meditations are offered as ways to understand some part of the public administrator's world.

Paradigms, or basic patterns, is another way to gain information about organizations. Again, several of the authors refer to and use the idea of paradigm to explain their views about organizations and administration.

The Learning Process

Learning is a theme in every chapter. Undoubtedly that is due, in part, to the academic interests of the practitioner authors. But learning is also the activity that helps make sense out of all the everyday events, concepts, theories, metaphors, and paradigms you see once you start looking for them.

The model of learning that I find most appealing to practitioners was developed by David Kolb. One of the authors (Waldo) described Kolb's work in detail, so I will only say a few words about it here. For Kolb, learning is the process of transforming experience into knowledge. One learns through a variation of the scientific method: have an experience, think about the experience, generalize from the experience, and test the generalization the next time you encounter an applicable situation. The new experience gives you more data to think about, thus continuing the learning process.

The Application of Learning

In my view, there are four main areas that contribute to your organizational knowledge and effectiveness: who you are as a person, your relationships with other people, the structures that influence your behavior, and your skills. These are the areas in which the knowledge you have acquired can be applied and tested. The chapters in the book are grouped according to the four domains, so there will be more to say about each.

CONCLUSION

One conclusion that emerges from many of the chapters is that effective practitioners do not rely on external authorities to tell them what works in public organizations. They discover for themselves what works, communicate what they find to other people, and listen to the response their point of view stimulates. Through this process of reflective learning, their ideas are strengthened, as is the discipline of public adminstration.

The practitioners who contributed their ideas to this book continue an intellectual tradition that began at the dawn of public administration. Periodically, the tradition is forgotten and needs to be revived.

Acknowledgments

The editor gratefully acknowledges Alison Bricken, sociology editor at Praeger, Bert Yaeger, project editor, Mary Lou Masey, copy editor, and Frank Nice for their help during the preparation of this book.

1

The Role of Practitioners in the Intellectual Development of Public Administration

Christopher Bellavita

Public administration is a practical discipline. Its aim is to help solve government problems. The discipline's history has been written as the story of events, ideas, and literature (McCurdy, 1986; Burke, in press; Henry, 1988). Another way to view its evolution is to examine the changing relationship between theoretical and practitioner knowledge.

While public adminstration draws from many fields, organization studies are a core element of its knowledge base. Usually, theorists have ideas about *why* things work the way they do in organizations. Practitioners, the effective ones, are more interested in *what* works. But practitioners also have ideas about theory. The purpose of this chapter is to set the context for the book by reviewing the role practitioners have played in public administration's intellectual life, and by suggesting what role they might play in its future.

Public administration has gone through three eras: the Age of Principles, the Age of Science, and the Age of Deconstruction. During the discipline's early years, there was little distinction between theory and practice. Most of the founders had substantial experience working in organizations. They preached to others what they practiced. At about the time of World War II, academic theorists challenged the conventional knowledge of the practitioner theorists. They raised questions about accuracy and utility, about the nature of truth in public administration, and about the standards that should guide the search for new knowledge. Eventually they also introduced administrators to ideas from a variety of academic disciplines.

By the early 1960s, public administration had lost any semblance of intellectual unity. The 1970s and 1980s added more voices, offering confusing and contradictory advice about how to be effective as a public administrator.

Some public administrators responded to the cacophony by continuing to search for that definitively practical idea, the theory that works, usually interpreted to mean a set of ideas that enable the user to exercise control. Other administrators react as E. F. Schumacher did when he wrote, "It's amazing how little theory you need once you start to work" (1975). A few practitioners confront the proliferation of knowledge by seeking their own way to link theory and practice.

THE AGE OF PRINCIPLES: PUBLIC ADMINISTRATION: 1880s–1940s

The movement to develop public administration as a field of study was led by practicing administrators and university professors. They were united by a belief that reason and science could replace partisan politics as the arbiter of how to manage government organizations (Mosher, 1975). Woodrow Wilson established the tone for the practical foundation of public administration by asserting that government was like a business, so the principles that proved successful in business could be applied to government (Wilson, 1887). Other people followed Wilson's approach to inquiry and to the application of knowledge. Their strategy was to identify what worked in practice, and then to codify the results into a set of principles that other administrators could use.

Early Theorists Had Practitioner Experience

Considering the utilitarian nature of the profession, it is not surprising that practitioners were the first intellectual leaders in public and private administrative studies. Frederick Taylor (1911) founded scientific management. He worked for the Midvale Steel Works in Philadelphia during the 1880s. Frank Gilbreth (1912) and his wife Lillian were early advocates of motivation theory and humanism in the workplace. Frank Gilbreth was a management consultant. Henri Fayol (1916) described the general principles of management as a process that other people could follow. His organizational knowledge came from managing coal mines, steel mills, and other industrial activities.

Mary Parker Follett was among the first theorists to write about the importance of interpersonal processes in organizations (Fox & Urwick, 1973). Her practical experience came from community service activities and from consulting. Paul Appleby (1949), who wrote an important public administration textbook toward the end of the era, spent twelve years as an administrator with the Department of Agriculture.

Lyndall Urwick, coeditor of the 1937 work *Papers on the Science of Administration*, had been an officer in the British military, a manufacturing executive, and an industrial engineer. Chester Barnard, who described how organizations functioned as social systems (1938), was the president of New Jersey Bell Telephone for more than twenty years, headed the USO during World War II, and was president of the Rockefeller Foundation.

Activist Scholars Also Played a Role

Besides Wilson, other scholars contributed to the early development of public administration. Many of them had close ties to government or business. Luther Gulick (1937) was a professor at Columbia University. He translated Fayol's management principles into the "PODSCORB" acronym, was a member of the Brownlow Commission, and was the first City Administrator of New York. Leonard D. White (1926) was a professor at the University of Chicago. He wrote the first public administration textbook (aimed, primarily, at practitioners), and was the Chairman of the United States Civil Service Commission.

Frank Goodnow, a Columbia University professor and the author of the 1900 text *Politics and Administration*, was a major force in the progressive reform movement and was the first president of the American Political Science Association. William Willoughby (1918), an early budget expert, was the director of the Institute for Governmental Research (which later became part of the Brookings Institution), and a member of the 1912 Taft Commission that led to the creation of the Budget Office and the General Accounting Office.

Education Reflected a Bias for the Practical

In each era, educational institutions helped spread administrative ideas. The first education programs for public service had a strong practitioner focus. The New York Training School was founded in 1911 and later merged with the New York Bureau of Municipal Research and the National Institute of Public Administration. The school's focus was to help students learn by doing. The program placed students in municipal agencies and put them to work on projects to observe what they and their coworkers were doing "freshly, critically and optimistically" (Stone & Stone, 1975, pp. 268–69).

Universities, too, aligned themselves with public administration's intellectual development. From the first decade in the twentieth century through the mid-1930s, the Universities of Southern California, Michigan, California at Berkeley, Cincinnati, Minnesota, and Chicago, along with Stanford, Syracuse, and Columbia, established practitioner-oriented, multidisciplinary professional programs in public administration (Stone & Stone, 1975).

Early Science

The people who initiated public administration were being "scientific," as they understood the meaning of the term. Their science was a mix of observation, measurement, codified experience, and common sense (Waldo, 1984; Chandler & Plano, 1986, p. 35). Their intent was to systematize the knowledge administrators needed to be effective. Later, critics called their methods unscientific, raising an issue that remains alive today: what is the correct way to develop knowledge about public administration?

THE AGE OF SCIENCE IN PUBLIC ADMINISTRATION:
1940s–1960s

In a 1946 *Public Administration Review* article, Herbert Simon, an academic, criticized the knowledge and mode of inquiry that characterized the Age of Principles. In "The Proverbs of Administration," he argued that what had passed for administrative science in the early decades of the century was fatally flawed. The accepted wisdom was contradictory, inconsistent, and often irrelevant to administrative problems. Dwight Waldo (1984) also questioned the scientific nature of the culture-bound principles that had passed for the logic of orthodox administration.

People who defended the principles approach to administration maintained that what Simon called "proverbs" were heuristic guides to action that had meaning to people with a basic understanding of how organizations operated. Fayol once described administrative principles as "the lighthouse fixing the bearings, but it can only serve those who already know the way to the port." The principles were for practitioners, not for administrative neophytes (Koontz, 1961, p. 184). But the defenders were not heard, at least not in the increasingly powerful academic administrative science communities.

Simon's critique, and his major subsequent writing, *Administrative Behavior* (1947), were the harbingers of the Age of Science in public administration. They were also the symbolic beginning of the second-class status that practitioner knowledge would assume in the intellectual life of public administration.

Science Expands the Core of Public Administration

The 1940s through the 1960s removed any doubt about the practical value of science. From the atomic bomb that ended World War II, through the massive growth of the consumer society, to the moon landing, the often arcane work of scientists provided symbolic and material benefits to Americans. It was not the ingenuous science of a Gilbreth, whose "Therbligs" described the seventeen basic movements of work (1912), or of a Hawthorne experiment that discovered "halos" where later analysis (Franke & Kaul, 1978) suggested systematic feedback. It was, instead, the science of Einstein, Fermi, Freud, Plank, and Salk.

Public administration, during the two decades after World War II, was marked by an effort to apply the cannons of normal science to the problems of government. Simon argued that before it would be possible to discover the unchanging laws of administration, it would be necessary to describe exactly how an administrative organization looked and functioned. Objective description, not stories of experience, was the first step in a scientific approach to administration.

The shift from practitioner heuristics to scientific truth opened public administration to knowledge from a variety of academic disciplines. Simon applied cognitive psychology to the study of administration (1947). Argyris (1964), McGregor (1960), Maslow (1943), Likert (1961), Presthus (1962), and Katz & Kahn (1966) contributed ideas from social psychology and group studies. Gouldner (1954), Parsons (1960), Blau (1955), and Merton (1949) brought the concepts and methods of sociology. Downs (1967), Buchanan (1962), Cyert & March (1963), and a former State Department official turned scholar, Tullock (1965), provided an economist's perspective to administrative studies. Luce and Raiffa (1957) contributed the mathematical insights of game theory. Professors had become the intellectual leaders of public administration.

Science Encounters Social Reality

The physical scientists' success in controlling material reality was not easily duplicated in the world of people. The initial hope was that the scientific method could be used instrumentally to mitigate administrative problems. In the ideal case, scientific findings would help organizations increase productivity, develop leaders, motivate subordinates, or improve communication.

Administrators tried using the ideas developed by Maslow (1943), Selznick (1949), Argyris (1957), McGregor (1960), Herzberg (1966) and a host of others. The results were mixed. The applications derived from social science did not work with the certainty and reliability of, say, a television set or a refrigerator. As Wallace Sayre (1958, p. 105) explained it, management techniques had a high obsolescence rate. The contribution that each new idea made to administrative rationality declined as people found ways to get around the requirements it imposed.

The problem administrative scientists faced—and that they continue to face—was summarized by T. C. Miller (1984). Many interesting aspects of an administrator's life are qualitatively different from the subject matter of natural science. Unlike physical reality, administrative reality is largely made by humans, and is not consistent over time and space. Administrative behavior is a fundamentally different phenomenon than the behavior of matter, so the modes of inquiry appropriate for discovering the laws of matter are not automatically suitable for explaining human behavior.

Like their predecessors in the Age of Principles, almost all the intellectual leaders of public administration shared the unexamined assumption that whatever the truth was about administration, it existed "out in the world." During the Age of Science, administrative truth was waiting to be discovered, described, analyzed, and explained by people who were skilled in the techniques of positivist, fact-based, objective science. Only a few people questioned that assumption (Waldo, 1984, p. 21).

The Effects of Science

Two consequences of the Age of Science deserve mention here. First, the knowledge base of public administration expanded from its initial focus on law, political science, and business administration to include economics, sociology, psychology, and math. The expansion enriched the store of ideas available to administrators, but the contributions the ideas made to administrative practice were problematic. Donald Schön (1983, p. 308), among other analysts, concludes that practitioners have gained little from the theories developed in management and other administrative sciences. The expansion also meant that a discipline once concerned chiefly with budgets, personnel, and management lost an intellectual axis that it never regained. It became much harder to say with certainty what public administration was.

The second consequence was that in sharp contrast to the Age of Principles, practitioners in the Age of Science played almost no direct role in developing the ideas that came to dominate the intellectual agenda of public administration. The prominent ideas of the era were developed by people who had limited practical experience of working in public organizations.

THE AGE OF DECONSTRUCTION IN PUBLIC ADMINISTRATION: 1960s TO PRESENT

The current era can be called the Age of Deconstruction because public administration has ceased to be a unified discipline. Contemporary analysts have divided the field into a variety of categories (for example, McCurdy, 1986; Shafritz & Hyde, 1987; Harmon & Mayer, 1986; Henry, 1988), but for my purposes, public administration presently has three broad factions: the traditional public administration, the lineage of the New Public Administration (NPA), and the policy studies group.

The traditional public administrationists concentrate primarily on budgets, finance, personnel administration, and the technical issues that have commanded attention since the days of Woodrow Wilson. Authors such as Schick (1966, 1971), Mosher (1968), Krislov (1974), Levine (1980), Newland (1984), Volker (1989), and others bring a mix of scholarly and practitioner perspectives to the field's orthodox concerns.

Other members of the traditionalist community continue to apply mainstream social science techniques to the problems of public organization and management (for example, Golembiewski, 1979; Kaufman, 1981; Mosher, 1979). They have not abandoned a faith in systematic inquiry, or in what Chester Newland terms the "search for reasonableness" in public administration.

Throughout the 1960s, traditionalists contributed practical techniques and ideas to the discpline. However, their work generated comparatively little intellectual excitement. As a result, mainstream public administration became a languid discipline, disowned by political and administrative scientists, and by many students. Its claim as the source of practical solutions to government problems was challenged by two groups: the new public administrationists and the public policy scientists.

THE NEW PUBLIC ADMINISTRATION

In 1968 a group of young public administration professors met in Minnowbrook, New York. The meeting symbolized the start of a radical examination of the meaning and direction of the field.

The professors questioned the social relevance of what passed for public administration (Frederickson, 1971). They envisioned that the field could be concerned with something more than managing the public's business and carrying out assigned tasks. Many agreed with Todd LaPorte's view that public administration should be concerned with "the reduction of economic, social and psychic suffering and the enhancement of life opportunities for those inside and outside the [public] organization" (1971, p. 32).

Another concern of the NPA group was the overreliance on positivist methodologies. They acknowledged the value of traditional ways of gathering knowledge (Marini, 1968, pp. 363–364), but they also asserted that the modes of inquiry associated with existentialism, phenomenology, humanistic psychology, and other philosophical perspectives could provide new insights into what had to be done to improve the way government operated (White, 1971; Kirkhart, 1971; Harmon, 1971).

Practical Applications of the New Public Administration

Although the New Public Administration challenged many taken-for-granted ideas that had been shared by administrative theorists since the 1880s, the movement had little immediate impact on the practitioner community. Practicing public administrators were not well represented at Minnowbrook. According to a participant, there were so few practitioners present that their workshops could have been held in a phone booth (Marini, 1968, pp. 5-6). Some members of the NPA insisted, in defense, that the distinction between academics and practitioners was a false one (Marini, 1968, pp. 364–65).

But the movement did hope to affect administrative practive. Their strategy was the same one that had been used in the other eras of public administration: NPA ideas would be introduced into government by university students trained by NPA faculty. However, as those students entered government in the 1970s, the age of an activist federal government began its decline.

Poverty, racism, and other social problems were recognized as endemic and not amenable to quick fixes by the infusion of federal funds. Government began to experience fiscal constraints, and there were few new social initiatives. The public became suspicious of government and, eventually, of public servants. An increasingly distrustful citizenry told government to do less with less. Accountants, economists, and systems analysts were more in demand in public organizations than action researchers, phenomenologists, and social activists.

The Intellectual Legacy of the New Public Administration

But the New Public Administration should not be dismissed as a short-lived aberration of the social turbulence of the 1960s. The movement planted seeds that are still growing.

The NPA's philosophical challenge to positivism opened consideration of a wide range of methods of administrative inquiry (Morgan, 1983; Lincoln and Guba, 1985; Harmon, 1981; Denhardt, 1981b). The concern articulated at Minnowbrook that administrators should be seen as whole people and not simply as an organizational role matured into the humanist stance of such scholars as Herman and Korneich (1977); Ingals (1979); Denhardt (1981a); White & McSwain (1987); and Theobald (1987). The challenge to traditional ways of organizing opened a reexamination of the meaning and structure of bureaucratic action (White, 1969, 1983; Thayer, 1973; Gawthrop, 1984).

The NPA also nurtured and gave credence to the notion that reality could be understood as a subjective as well as an objective phenomenon. The idea was not original with the New Public Administrationists (Waldo, 1984; Berger & Luckman, 1966). But they did give it an intellectual respectability that other administrative theorists have benefited from (Staw, 1982; Culburt & McDonough, 1985; Suarez, Mills, & Stewart, 1987, pp. 215–38).

In 1989, Minnowbrook II was held to consider what changes had taken place in the public administration that Minnowbrook I examined (Frederickson, 1989). The expectations about what could be done were significantly more modest than they had been twenty years earlier. But many of the same issues surfaced, colored by "constrained hopefulness" (Frederickson, 1989, p. 100; Mayer, 1989; Guy, 1989; Holzer, 1989; Porter, 1989; Bailey, 1989; Cleary, 1989).

Minnowbrook II resembled its predecessor in another respect: practitioners did not play a central role in the deliberations. While several more nonacademics participated in Minnowbrook II (Frederickson, 1989, pp. 98–99) than in Minnowbrook I (Marini, 1971, pp. 2-3), the practitioner perspective was voiced primarily by academics who had been practitioners in the 1960s (for example, Radin & Cooper, 1989). It is as if there are still two intellectual domains in public administration. One is the province of theorists, researchers, and other academics. The other is the realm of the working public administrator.

PUBLIC POLICY AND POLICY ANALYSIS

While the New Public Administrationists were challenging the intellectual foundations of the discipline, another group of academicians and practitioners were completely abandoning public administration. The policy studies approach to government began in the 1960s, largely in response to the perceived failure of public administration (Wildavsky, 1976).

If the NPA represented the left wing of public administration, policy studies were the right wing. Members of this group were unconcerned with questions of epistemology and ontology. They were interested in the practical issue of what government could do within existing political and institutional frameworks.

The Origins and Evolution of the Public Policy Perspective

Universities again played a central role in the growth of the policy movement. When public policy schools began in the 1960s, their objective was to help make government more effective by improving the quality of the information that decision makers received (Quade, 1975; Haveman, 1987). The schools were to be different from what many people perceived to be the moribund schools of public administration. Unlike the eclecticism of public administration, policy schools would have a core curriculum of microeconomics, operations research, and political and organizational analysis. In time, policy analysis became synonymous with applying economic rationality and quantitative methods to public problems (Weimer & Vining, 1989).

As the policy approach to government evolved, it became apparent that good decisions did not automatically translate into good actions. Policy theorists came to appreciate the limited role that analysis played in shaping public policy. They recognized that improving the policy process meant understanding what happens after a decision has been made. This awareness led the schools to develop implementation as a field of study (Pressman & Wildavsky, 1973). Other scholars maintained that "implementation" was what public administrators had been doing for one hundred years (Jones, 1977). But few people in the policy studies community were persuaded.

Government cut back on social initiatives, and policy analysts refocused their attention on improving the operation of existing programs. They became interested in public management (Lynn, 1987b; Bardach, 1987; Behn, 1987).

Like implementation, public management arguably had been a concern of public administration since the start of the discipline. And as the policy community's interest in management evolves, they encounter many of the same issues about groups, leadership, control, and politics and organization design that have engaged public administration scholars for decades (Lynn, 1987a; Heymann, 1987). The policy community's concern with public management continues their interest in finding ways to help improve government practice. But it also underscores the historical link between policy and public administration.

The Role of Practitioners in Policy Studies

As with traditional public administration, practitioners played an important role in the initiation and development of policy studies. Many of the seminal public policy works were written by people with significant experience in government (for example, Quade, 1975; Rivlin, 1971; Wholey, et al., 1970).

And as with public administration, academicians have influenced the subsequent intellectual development of the policy field more directly than practitioners.

Sometimes the scholars have had substantial experience in public organizations and public service before joining university faculties (for example, Meltsner, 1976; Radin, 1973; Thayer, 1973; Cooper, 1986; Lynn, 1987a; Heymann, 1987). Other scholars who developed and advanced ideas about public organizations had minimal, if any, experience working in those organizations. While one can, like Mary Parker Follett, contribute valuable ideas about administration without having been an administrator, knowledge gained from daily experience is qualitatively different from knowledge acquired through research or consulting (Schön, 1983; Pirsig, 1974; Dooling, 1979). Not better, just different.

PUBLIC ADMINISTRATION AS INTELLECTUAL CHAOS

Much of public administration's history has been a search for the best way to understand the field, motivated by the belief that right understanding would lead to right practice. In the Age of Principles, truth was in the experience of practice. In the Age of Science, answers were sought through positivist scientific inquiry. The Age of Deconstruction has brought a chaos of ideas that some people believe is an inherent feature of administrative science (Astley, 1985), and that others see as the consequence of careless research (Lynn, 1987b). Whatever the cause, contemporary public administration offers practitioners an abundance of ideas, and little agreement about which ones will be useful.

For instance, theorists have developed several dozen ways an administrator can model and analyze organizations (Harmon & Mayer, 1986; Burell & Morgan, 1979; McKelvey, 1982; Boleman & Deal, 1984; Morgan, 1986). To help practitioners understand themselves and the people they work with, scholars offer fourteen major theories of personality (Corsini & Marsella, 1983), sixteen types of personalities (Keirsey & Bates, 1978), and more than sixty different concepts of the human mind (Hampden-Turner, 1981). People who work in organizations can be rational in at least five different ways (Diesing, 1976), cogitate in one or more of five separate styles (Harrison & Bramson, 1982), and perceive sense data in four different ways (Laborde, 1984). Moreover, there are at least ten ways to think about decision making (Dye, 1975; Allison, 1971), a dozen motivation theories (Staw, 1982; Manz, 1986; Evans, 1986), and numerous ways to lead an organization (Yukl, 1981).

The Age of Deconstruction has also challenged some fundamental assumptions that have shaped understanding and inquiry throughout public administration's history. For example, there has almost always been an unquestioned belief in a single reality, a reality that was both tangible and external to an observer. Reasonable people could discover the objective truth about administrative reality, using the eyes of experience or, later in history, the techniques of science. Most public administration and public policy scholars continue to accept the single reality hypothesis, and to maintain that theorists can help improve practice through "the usual tasks of scholarship": systematic theory-based research, supported by factual evidence (Lynn, 1987b, p. 183; McCurdy & Cleary, 1984).

Today, there are thoughtful counterarguments by theorists who claim that administrators live in multiple realities (Boleman & Deal, 1984; Morgan, 1986) that are individually and socially constructed (Staw, 1982; Suarez, Mills, & Stewart, 1987; Culburt & McDonough, 1985). Moreover, many scholars maintain that there can be no objective truth about those realities. Instead, administrative truth is "ultimately a matter of socially and historically conditioned agreement. Social inquiry [can] not be value free, and there [can] not be a 'God's Eye' point of view—there [can] only be various people's points of view based on their particular interests, values and purposes" (Smith & Heshusius, 1986, p. 5).

To people who believe that knowledge about public organizations can only be interpretations of reality, research "is a never-ending process . . . of interpreting the interpretations of others. All that can be done is to match descriptions to other descriptions, choosing to honor some as valid because they 'make sense,' given one's interests and purposes" (Smith & Heshusius, 1986, p. 9).

To me, the central point is not which administrative ideas and modes of inquiry are correct, but that academic experts do not agree among themselves which views are correct. Consequently practitioners cannot rely on external authorities as arbiters of truth about, for example, what theories should be used to motivate workers, to lead, to organize, or, for that matter, to interpret the history of public administration. The "authorities" are, at best, advisers, people who have a point of view about the world, and whose ideas may be considered when establishing one's position. To make effective use of that advice, practitioners have a responsibility to become more conscious of their roles as creators and users of theory.

THE INTELLECTUAL ROLE OF PUBLIC ADMINISTRATION PRACTITIONERS

I do not wish to leave the impression that I believe practitioners have been intellectually quiescent through much of public administration's history, patiently waiting for theorists to reveal the truth. Effective administrators have always had ideas about what works in public organizations. Sometimes those ideas were not articulated; other times they were not heard. After a decade of teaching public administrators, I have yet to encounter a practitioner who could not, under the appropriate circumstances, construct a theoretical explanation of his or her actions.

Academic theories affect how administrators think and behave at work (Astley, 1985). What has been less appreciated, I think, is that the way workers, managers, leaders, and other administrators behave has also infleunced what theorists think. Practically all the ideas about administration in currency at a particular time— from Gulick's PODSCORB (1937) through Cohen, March, and Olson's "garbage can" (1972) through Peters and Waterman's "search for excellence" (1982)— originated in the observed behavior of working administrators.

Selznick (1949) studied the people involved in the TVA project and described how administrative politics led to cooptation. Kaufmann (1960) studied forest rangers at work and described how administrative agencies construct an environment that promotes conformity. Wildavsky (1964) studied how administrators put budgets together. Mintzberg (1972) observed how managers actually spent their time. Argyris and Schön (1974) studied leaders and how they talked about and used theories. Meltsner (1976) identified how policy analysts behaved. Behn (1988) looked at patterns of effective management in public organizations.

Practitioners are the lifeblood of the public administration theorist. Without the data their working lives provide, academic theories would be vacuous. But why, as public administration and policy studies evolved, did the important ideas appear to come from academics and not practitioners? And must the division of intellectual labor remain that way in the future?

Barriers to Theorizing

There are three reasons why practitioners play a nominally secondary intellectual role in public administration. First, ideas become notable in a field only after other people are aware of them, through books, articles, or conferences. The incentive system of the academy rewards building and communicating theory; public organization incentive systems usually do not.

Second, it is typically not enough simply to have an idea. Appropriate authorities must accept the idea. Certain skills are required to conduct authoritative inquiry (for example, clarifying assumptions, formulating hypotheses, collecting data, and applying evidence). Those skills are developed through the training and experiences available primarily to the people with the interests and temperament to be academics.

Third, there are opportunity costs associated with theorizing. For the practitioner, time spent formalizing theories means less time for practice, for family, or for other pursuits. The desire to engage in the systematic process of reflective scholarship may not be a major compulsion in many action-oriented administrators.

Again, none of this is meant to suggest that practitioners do not theorize. By definition, effective administrators know how to take the appropriate action at the right time. Their short-term effectiveness might be explained by luck. But it is the rare administrator who succeeds solely through good fortune. Usually, conceptual thinking is going on, either before or after action.

Formal and Personal Theories

Two general models explain the relationship between thinking and action. One approach assumes that thought precedes action. In public administration the model translates into the norm that theory should be used to guide action, whether it be budget theory, management theory, or ideas about how policies are to be designed. In this model, theoreticians identify what works (or what should work) and provide practitioners with ideas that they can use to guide their practice (Behn, 1987; Bardach, 1987).

A second model suggests that thought follows rather than precedes action (Weick, 1979). Administrators act before they think, with action based on their experiences and on their "feel" for a situation (McCall, Lombardo, & Morrison, 1988). They learn through what Weick calls "retrospective sensemaking," reflecting after the fact on the meaning and lessons of experience. What they learn is added to their store of knowledge, to be used in another situation. Instead of being guides for behavior, formal theories and models become mental templates that practitioners use to frame and to interpret their experience. Looked at this way, formal theories are but one among several resources for reflection. Practitioners can also use the personal theories that emerge from their experience.

Donald Schön (1983) described reflective practitioners as people who can consciously use theory to inform action, and who can use action to construct theories that can be applied to future action. Reflective practitioners are not cryptoacademics in the sense that they prefer to think about acting than to act. They are people who can, if required by the situation, generate knowledge through traditional and nontraditional methods of inquiry. They can learn from books, role models, and from their own experience. Also, as the authors in this book demonstrate, they can teach others what they know.

Reflective practitioners have always been a part of public administration. Appleby, Urwick, Barnard, Schultz, McNamarra, Heymann, and many other people mentioned in this chapter have contributed to the field's theoretical knowledge and have been effective as people of action. I believe than in light of the challenges and uncertainties that government faces, public organizations would be more effective and public administration would be more dynamic if there were more reflective practitioners.

AN AGE OF COMMUNITY: PUBLIC ADMINISTRATION IN THE TWENTY-FIRST CENTURY

The spirit motivating this book is that in the next century public administration can have an Age of Community. As in an ideal democratic community, the disparate elements of public administration would exhibit tolerance for difference, include instead of exclude inconsonant ideas, and base membership on what is held in common, not on distinctiveness.

Practitioners and scholars from traditional public administration, the new public administration lineage, and public policy specialists already share a common bond. Each seeks to improve the way government will manage the problems that it encounters now and in the coming decades.

Reflective practitioners can be the nucleus of a new public administration community. They want to be effective at what they do. They want to understand what influences effectiveness, to improve their practice, and to guide others. Their desire creates an incentive to bridge the varied parochial interests in the deconstructed discipline. There is little evidence of a similar incentive elsewhere in public administration.

During its history, public administration has relied for truth sometimes on the authority of practitioner experience, and at other times on the authority of science. But experience unmediated by understanding and theory unconnected to day-to-day experience are inadequate guides to behavior. Ideally, the relationship between practicing administrators and those who theorize about public affairs should be a partnership. In practice, the two groups live in separate worlds. Many administrative theories seem arcane and irrelevant to the concerns of practitioners. Many details of the practitioner's life are of limited interest to the discipline's most creative theorists.

Reflective practitioners can link the worlds of theory and practice. The chapters in this book illustrate what that can mean to the intellectual life of public administration.

PART I

THE INDIVIDUAL AND PUBLIC ORGANIZATIONS

One part of understanding public organizations is to understand oneself. We all carry in our minds a unique perception of our organization and our role in it. Our perceptions are shaped by such factors as personality, values, attitudes, skills, experiences, and education. The three chapters in part I describe ways of understanding who we are and what we can learn about ourselves in a public organization.

In chapter 2, Patrick Sheeran describes how he learned to manage. More specifically, the chapter shows how Sheeran learned to think about management. Like many managers, he began this first assignment without having been trained. He had to make up as he went along, what it meant to be a manager, using for guidance role models and his philosophical predispositions. While he was effective as a manager, it was not much fun.

A new job exposed him to a different style of management. He began to question his own taken-for-granted assumptions about people and organizations, and he started to read books and to take courses on management. Organizational theories provide a framework to help people organize their experiences. In Sheeran's case, reading about Theory X and Theory Y gave him concepts he could use to understand something about his career. The theories also gave him ideas about what he needed to do to become a different manager.

The chapter describes the origins of Sheeran's organizational philosophy and what happened to encourage him to change. The chapter illustrates why it is important for public administrators to be aware of what they believe about human nature, about management, and about themselves.

Sheeran is currently a program specialist at the Office of Population Affairs, U.S. Department of Health and Human Services. He has been a public administrator for over twenty-five years and has served in the Office of the Secretary of Defense and in the United States Air Force. He received his doctorate from the University of Southern California in 1986.

In chapter 3, Nancy Eggert writes about how to stop thinking like a manager, or at least like a traditional manager. Her chapter introduces an innovative way to think about the relationship between human potential and public administration.

Eggert begins with an incident that led her to question whether organizations have to be governed by norms of power. The question led her to develop an alternative image of how a public administrator can behave. The image links her understandings of paradigms, participatory group methods, and meditation.

Eggert contrasts the dominant organizational paradigm, based on control, with what she calls the "contemplative paradigm." There are four paths to the contemplative approach: "affirmation and gratitude," "letting go and embracing the darkness," "birthing and creativity," and "transformation and compassion." Eggert believes that describing the contemplative experience is "somewhat similar to trying to experience the fragrance of a rose by reading about it." She closes her chapter with suggestions that readers can use to experiment with the contemplative paradigm in their own organization.

Eggert has been an attorney with the National Labor Relations Board since 1973. She has also worked with many organizations involved with adult literacy, community development, and organizational transformation. She is completing her doctorate in public administration.

Some psychologists suggest that the stories we tell about who we are, what we are doing, and how we should behave eventually become what we are and what we believe. Stories and metaphors influence how we interpret reality and plan strategies for changing that reality. In chapter 4, I use the metaphor of "the hero's journey," developed by Joseph Campbell, to describe ten administrators who have helped to revitalize the public sector.

Heroes in public administration are people who find ways to improve the public sector, in spite of attacks, harangues, sabotage, indifference, and cutbacks. Their journeys follow a predictable pattern. They leave the world of everyday events and enter an unfamiliar land to change some aspect of their organization. They undergo an ordeal, aided by allies and hampered by enemies. After some adventures, they return a changed person; and their organization are also changed. The chapter illustrates how administrators can use stories and metaphor to structure, interpret, and give meaning to their behavior.

2

Managers Are Learners and Teachers

Patrick J. Sheeran

As a former Catholic priest, I was schooled in theology and philosophy. I lacked management training per se and had spent a considerable time as a student, which involved doing things on my own. The managers with whom I came into contact were chiefly clergymen, parish priests, chancery office officials, and bishops. Some of them were not very good managers, and some were excellent. They served as role models and mentors for me, and contributed significantly to the type of manager I would become.

When I was appointed to my first parish, I was responsible for the management of a school and several parish groups, including the Catholic Youth Organization and the altar boys. Since I had had no training, I jumped into my new role totally unprepared to be a manager.

My theological and philosophical backgrounds gave me a foundation for understanding human nature. I was familiar with the teachings of St. Augustine, Thomas Hobbes, and John Locke. Augustine and Hobbes had a dismal and pessimistic view of human nature. They perceived man as essentially predisposed by nature toward evil. According to Hobbes (Scott & Hart, 1976, pp. 241–55), man will do evil because of two psychic forces that dominate his behavior, the fear of death and the drive for power to protect himself from others.

Working within a hierarchical institution, it was easy for me to adopt a managerial style that assumed human nature was evil, that people cannot be trusted, and that they must be controlled, directed, and driven to get desired results. My mentors generally exhibited the same philosophy and style. Sometimes, I considered it easier to do things myself rather than to work with or depend on others to get them done.

I followed that imperialistic style for several years. I shaped the school program with all kinds of rules to ensure compliance. I acted in a Hitlerian manner toward the Catholic Youth Organization and the altar boy group. Usually we got things done correctly and on time. But everybody functioned like robots, and nobody was very happy. In fact, many people were scared; not of being fired but of the anger they would incur from me for noncompliance.

Although my organizations were productive, I really had no training in or understanding of management. Later I came to understand that the false premises upon which I built my view of management shaped my style. I was using a particular management theory and using it well, but at the time, I lacked a consciousness that there was even such a thing as a theory of management.

HOW MANAGERS LEARN TO MANAGE

Most people become managers after developing expertise in another professional field, as I did. It has been my experience that many public sector managers were former engineers, teachers, social workers, physicians, psychologists, nurses, or analysts of one kind or another. William Oncken (1984, pp 66–71) refers to those other professional fields as "vocational." They are disciplines that professionals have studied, are trained to work in, and that require the application of one's own skill. Management, however, involves getting things done not with one's own resources but with the help of other people.

Becoming a manager is like beginning a totally new career. Managers learn about management from trial and error, on-the-job training, or imitation of other managers. Occasionally they learn from studies and courses in management or from a combination of these (McCall, Lombardo, & Morrison, 1988). The management styles that follow from inadequate on-the-job training in less than optimal managerial settings, or from imitating managers with poor managerial skills, cannot be expected to produce good managers. While mentoring is a useful way to improve managerial skills, the wrong kind of mentor can do more harm than good to a management novice. In many respects, the novice is left on his or her own to learn how to manage.

THEORY INFORMS PRACTICE I

I eventually discovered that the approach I used to manage in the church had a name, Theory X. I found out that it is a philosophy often attributed to the School of Scientific Management and to Frederick Taylor. Further research enabled me to trace the ideas that make up Theory X back to Sir James Steward, who lived in England more than one hundred years before Taylor. However, the assumptions upon which Theory X were based go back to my old friends Thomas Hobbes and Saint Augustine.

While the ideas expressed in Theory X may be unfashionable today, they are far from being outmoded. Variations of the theory can be found in various federal government agencies and in some parts of the private sector. Chandler and Plano (1986, p. 31) state that this theory "contains the potential for tyranny."

In essence, Theory X is based on a philosophy that I heard often in the church, and later in the military: "people are no damn good." Frederick Taylor believed in that philosophy. He was dedicated to productivity and efficiency, and he saw antiorganizational acts as evil, a notion with which I identified while bearing responsibility for organizations in the Catholic church. Taylor (1911) opposed the "loafing" of workers, which he called "soldiering"—and so did I and many of my colleagues.

While the theory is well known to most students of organization and management, it is worth summarizing its principal characteristics. They are:

1. Employees do not like to work, and they will try to avoid it.
2. To meet the needs of the organization, managers must control workers.
3. Employees will avoid assuming personal responsibility.
4. Workers care more about security than ambition.

This theory has enabled managers, including myself, to act in an autocratic manner, directing, forcing, controlling, threatening, and punishing subordinates.

PRACTICE CHALLENGES THEORY

After several years as a tyrannical manager, I joined the United States Air Force as a chaplain. I was now operating in a double zone of hierarchy, the military and the church. That made it easy for me to maintain the Theory X managerial style. The behaviors of the generals and colonels who were my new role models reinforced my style. I frequently heard that "A good manager should be . . . [angry] about half of the time."

After four years of duty in the United States and overseas, I was reassigned to Travis Air Force Base in California. As I entered the base, a sign caught my eye: "The Friendliest and Finest." The Commanding General at Travis was Maurice F. Casey, (now Lieutenant General Maurice F. Casey, USAF, Retired). From officers and enlisted men alike, I heard what a wonderful leader this man was. Morale on the base was high, the troops were happy and prepared to undertake willingly any task the general would assign. I had to meet this man.

I eventually did, and we became friends. His method of running an organization was one that I had not encountered before. He traveled around the base. He visited the mechanics, mostly enlisted men working on airplanes. He visited the men loading airplanes. He flew missions with pilots. He was always talking to the troops, to the junior officers, and to enlisted men in particular. There was an esprit de corps among the troops that I had not seen before.

He had a different assumption about people than I did. He believed that they were good, that they could be trusted to be productive, and that they needed recognition and appreciation. His approach was obviously working effectively at Travis AFB.

One day I asked the general what the difference was between him and an autocratic general for whom I had previously worked. He said that "The two of us want the same thing: to get the job done well. His style is to drive people to get the job done; mine is to lead people, to motivate and entice people to get the job done." I recognized that I had a new role model, but more important, I understood that I needed to know more about management.

We had a joke in the Air Force that we would not feel very secure flying with a pilot who boarded his aircraft with a book entitled "Ten Easy Lessons in Flying." I realized that I did not have even one easy lesson in management. So I decided to enroll in an MBA program at a local university and eventually in a graduate program in Public Administration to learn about management and to improve my management skills.

THEORY INFORMS PRACTICE II

I learned about the formal assumptions of Theory X in graduate school. It was there that I also discovered a name for the type of management that General Casey practiced. It was called Theory Y and it was developed by Douglas McGregor (1966, pp. 3-10 and 1967, pp. 79-80).

Theory Y is based on assumptions about human nature that are the opposite of those of Theory X. According to Theory Y, human nature is basically good. People view work as natural and enjoyable. If they are committed to an organization's goals, they will take responsibility for doing what they can to see that the job gets done. The theory assumes that the ability to make good decisions does not rest solely with someone called a manager. Anyone properly trained or experienced can make a good decision.

Theory Y invites a management approach that creates opportunities for workers, develops their potentials, removes absolutes, provides guidance, and stimulates growth. The theory owes much to the work of A. H. Maslow on human motivation, published in 1943. The assumptions of Theory Y, however, go back much farther than Maslow and McGregor. For example, Saint Thomas Aquinas also saw goodness in human nature and the existence of needs that must be satisfied.

Theory Y has been criticized because there is little empirical evidence to support a hierarchy of needs. But the approach has generated many people-oriented approaches to management, such as management by objectives, participative management, and management excellence. There is hardly a contemporary piece of management literature that is not rooted somehow in Theory Y. Nevertheless, finding out about Theory Y provided me with the foundation for discarding a Theory X approach to management, and a rationale for following General Casey's style.

THE MEANING OF MANAGEMENT

After I had developed a consciousness about management, I wanted to know more. What is management anyhow? Does it involve dealing with people or things, such as budgets, paper work, files, or both? Does it involve decision making and, if so, by whom? Is it a profession or is it a combination of many professions? Is being an effective manager something that is innate, or is it something that can be learned? Is there a difference between management, administration, and leadership, or are these just different names for the same thing? Is there a difference between management in the public sector and management in the private sector? I began my inquiry with books on management.

Peter Drucker (1974, pp. 390–95) notes that the terms *manager* and *management* are "slippery." He discards the traditional definition of a manager as someone who is "responsible for the work of other people" and looks at management as an activity that involves "planning, organizing, integrating and measuring." While this definition may hint at a departure from a Theory X definition of management, it is also a slippery one.

Gerald Caiden (1971, p. 232) provides a useful definition of management, and a distinction between management and administration. He writes that both terms can be used interchangeably to refer to the activity and the people who run bureaucracies. Caiden says that "Management is the term preferred in business, . . . administration is the term preferred in public administration. Both terms refer to the process—the way people get things done through other people in organizational settings."

William Oncken (1984, p. 54) defined management in much the same way as Caiden, except that for Oncken, management involves getting things done "through the active support of others." This definition is broad enough to cover the approaches of both Theory X and Theory Y.

After reflecting on these and other ideas about the meaning of management and about what managers do, my task was to develop my own definition. I came to recognize that management involves two things, administrative processes and working with people. For me, administrative processes were the activities that need to be carried out by the manager and by the people who work with the manager. I see management, then, as responsible for getting things done in an organization *with* the free, voluntary, and active support of other people to achieve organizational goals.

Management activities include everything related to the organization's mission, from goal setting and implementation to evaluation and termination. The words "with the free, voluntary, and active support of other people" mean that the manager may participate with other people within the organizational unit to get things done, but the manager is not forcing or coercing those other people. My definition of management assumes that the organization's members are voluntarily participating in the organization.

My definition may not be especially innovative. But the point is that I developed it myself, after reflection. I believe that it is important for each manager to go through the same exercise, and to come to a personal understanding of what a manager does. It need not be strikingly creative. Although the authors of modern management literature may claim that their works are innovative, in my view the literature is frequently nothing more than Theory Y (and sometimes Theory X) dressed in new clothes. The two most popular management books of the 1980s, *In Search of Excellence* and *The One Minute Manager*, are examples.

THE MANAGEMENT MOLECULE: USING THEORY TO LEARN MANAGEMENT

A reflective manager ought to be clear in his mind about what theory of human nature to use as the foundation for a management style. For me, the answer was Theory Y. I think it is helpful also to have a conceptual framework to organize management experiences. William Oncken (1984) is an underrecognized theoretician whose work I have found to be particularly instructive, practical, and useful. He developed "The Management Molecule" as a Theory Y approach to management (1984, p. 41). Oncken's ideas contain two basic principles that can help someone become an effective manager.

The First Principle of Management: Identify Key People

Oncken conceptualizes the organization as a molecule, signified by a circle. The circle represents the core echelon of the organization, and the manager is in the center of the circle. On its rim are the people with whom the manager has relationships (for example, superiors, subordinates, and internal and external peers, who may be customers or clients).

The manager does not need everyone's help to get things done. Oncken suggests that managers use the 80/20 principle (Lakein, 1975, p. 84) to identify the people on the rim who are most critical. The 80/20 rule states that 80 percent of the value of an activity is in 20 percent of its elements. For example, 80 percent of the value of this book is in 20 percent of the pages. Oncken believes that the first principle of management is to identify the 20 percent on the rim on whom the manager must rely to get things done.

The Second Principle of Management: Use Mechanical Advantage

Once a manager identifies the key people, the next step is to apply the organizational equivalent of Archimedes' principle of mechanical advantage (Oncken, 1984, pp. 196–98): a small effort, properly applied, can be used to achieve a large result. A ten-pound weight, resting on a lever, can be lifted with a pound of effort, provided the fulcrum is located correctly. The person who lifts the weight must apply the effort in the opposite direction from where the weight is to be moved. Applied to organizations, this principle means that the manager must do two things: (1) learn to get things done with the help of other people (the significant 20 percent), and (2) give those people room to operate.

I have heard managers frequently say that they would prefer to do things on their own, rather than relying on other people. That approach is not management, it is being "vocational" (Oncken, 1984, pp. 66–71). Many people became managers because they were good at doing their professional or vocational job. Managers who follow the vocational route often claim that they can perform both vocational and managerial tasks. But the number of hours they spend on the job will increase, and the members of the organization who are not being used will become dissatisfied. The organization is neither effective nor efficient when a manager continues to do both vocational and managerial activities. As managers, they have to learn the difficult lesson of allowing other people to get done what must be done.

The second step the manager must take is to apply leverage at a distance from the people whose help is needed to get things done. The manager can leave people alone once they have been given a task and also be near enough so that if subordinates need guidance or support, the manager is available to help. In this way, a manager begins to work in the opposite direction from the way managers normally tend to work.

This is a difficult lesson to learn for managers who want to do everything themselves or who want to be "on top of" everything. It calls for managers to trust the members of their organizations. It also assumes that the subordinates are adequately trained, so that the manager has confidence that the people can do the job and do it right.

USEFULNESS OF THE MOLECULAR
THEORY OF MANAGEMENT

The molecular theory recognizes that both the organization and its members have needs that must be met. The manager is the key to satisfying those needs. The manager must be able to see that the organization is a lever to get a job done. The tools that the manager needs to use the organization effectively can be summarized in three sentences: The manager must know the difference between management work and vocational work. The manager must understand the organization, its culture, and its key people. The manager must know himself or herself.

Any manager, from the lowest to the highest organizational level, can begin to use this theory by identifying his or her own "molecule," and the key agencies or people on the rims of the molecule. The next task is to identify the behaviors the manager needs to exhibit toward the key people in their molecules, and the kinds of behaviors expected from these people.

The organization's culture will dictate how much of and how quickly the theory can be implemented. Organizations generally resist planned change. The status quo is frequently considered safer and more desirable than change. As it is said, the devil you know is better than the devil you do not know. My advice is to start small and to implement what you can. When you and others see what I expect will be positive results, then you can expand your activities.

THE ILLUSION OF OBSTACLES

The molecular theory, indeed no theory, is a panacea. In the process of getting things done with the support of others, many obstacles will continue to confront managers. However, some of what may appear to be obstacles are actually part of the manager's job.

Oncken describes three kinds of apparent obstacles (1984, p. 129). The first group includes the tasks handed down by superiors. Sometimes what the boss wants done gets in the way of what the manager needs to do. However, these are not obstacles, but rather assignments that must be complied with.

The second group are obstacles associated with organizational maintenance, such as attending meetings and conferences, preparing budgets, and so on. Most of the time these are not obstacles either but are what must be done if the organiza-tion's needs are to be met. Admittedly, meetings, phone calls, and the like can be a waste of time, but in principle they are part of the managerial role.

The third and largest group are obstacles imposed by subordinates. Included in this category is time spent by managers in coaching, teaching, counseling, and motivating subordinates. A manager who neglects these tasks is not a manager. On the other hand, the manager who accepts a "monkey" (or problem) that really belongs to the subordinate is also not acting as a manager. The manager must recognize that coaching and training subordinates is an intrinsic part of the managerial role. An important part of that training is to teach what problems subor-dinates should bring to the manager and what problems they should handle themselves.

THEORY Y MANAGEMENT IN PRACTICE

The above, in summary, is the approach to management that I have found to be useful. Earlier in this chapter, I discussed my management background and style, and how I set out to learn more about management. Because of my search, and through observing many managers in both the public and private sectors in action, I decided to change from a Theory X to a Theory Y orientation. The tran-sition was not easy. It required a change in my view of the nature and purpose of man. As an unintended consequence of that change, I eventually altered my views about society, government, organizations, people in organizations, and my view of a manager's role.

All the talk in the world about the value of Theory Y or Oncken's molecule would not have persuaded me to make the change. I had to see the results for myself. Some years ago I became the Executive Director of a voluntary health agency in California. I used that opportunity to experiment with a Theory Y management system, similar to the molecular theory, and to see the organiza-tional results firsthand.

Some members of the organization resisted the change; they were content with the status quo. But I learned that there were many employees who wanted the chance to develop and to advance. They were enthusiastic and eager to be part of the change. They were willing to be taught and to learn. They wanted to participate in organization development, program planning, and implementation; in budget development and execution; in goal-setting and evaluation. They were hungry to learn more about management and teamwork. They were willing to come to work an hour earlier to participate in training and staff development. I was willing to serve as teacher and coach, and it worked.

We began with what may seem a simple act. We changed the organizational chart from a model consisting of lines and boxes to one of circles. This gave us a better picture of the key people and departments in the organization, and their overlapping areas of responsibilities. It also provided opportunities to engage in better communication and coordination.

Staff members decided to develop a program budget for each department, with a series of objectives. Department managers and their workers developed job charters (instead of job descriptions) to correspond with program objectives. The charters consisted of a series of objectives against which the employee would be evaluated.

Over the course of several years, the agency's program improved significantly and the agency expanded. Employees developed more self-esteem, were happier, and were more productive than they had been. I no longer felt the need to be "on top of" everything. I had developed trust and confidence in my subordinates and a respect for them. Employees had the latitude to do their jobs. Work was more fun for them and more fun for me. Managing at a distance and providing guidance and support were easier on my ulcers than being "mad" half the time, and harassing employees the other half.

My transition from a Theory X to a Theory Y management style was a change from a product to a process view of the world. In the past I had been concerned with getting the job done. I now paid attention to how the job was done. The process of working under Theory Y assumptions made my job and the jobs of my subordinates more interesting. The process was often time-consuming, tedious, cumbersome, and inefficient. Sometimes I wished for the bad old days, when I considered myself infallible and gave direct orders that warranted obedience and compliance from subordinates. But the net results were clearly superior to my old way: the organization was more productive, and employees were more satisfied.

CHANGING STYLES OF MANAGEMENT: SMALL VERSUS LARGE SYSTEMS

To implement any new managerial system, whether it is something as established as Theory Y or as untried as Total Quality Management, the manager and the organization must be willing to experiment. If the willingness is lacking, the status quo will persist. It is also important that the change be supported, if not implemented, by the organization's leadership.

It has also been my experience that smaller organizations are more open to change, including trying a new managerial system, than larger, bureaucratic organizations. When Joseph Califano became Secretary of the Department of Health, Education and Welfare in 1977, he noted that the Department had not so much been mismanaged as not managed at all. The statement may be a reflection on the poor skills of previous managers or it may, as I believe, be questioning whether an agency of such magnitude ever can be managed.

My experience during more than ten years with the U.S. Department of Health and Human Service (DHHS) in Washington, D.C., testifies to the difficulty of implementing change in large systems. DHHS is a sprawling bureaucracy, the largest agency in the federal government, with the fourth largest budget in the world. The agency has many units ranging from bureaus, offices, and divisions to individual work groups.

DHHS has had many competent and well-trained employees. Some of them have been career civil servants, others have been political appointees. Because of the vastness of the agency, its hierarchical structure, and the mixture of Theory X and Theory Y managers operating within it, the organization will not quickly adopt Theory Y methods as the agency-wide management style. However, small units within the agency have the latitude to experiment with managerial change.

A few years ago, I was director of a small division in DHHS whose mission it was to give grants to about eighty different kinds of health, education, and social service agencies nationwide. The division was also responsible for monitoring how the grants were used, which included visiting grantees. At the time, I had four employees assigned to me. Since it would have been impossible personally to monitor all the grants, I depended on those four people to help me get the job done.

None of them had previous experience with reviewing field programs, and there was little guidance about what our jobs and roles were. I relied on the ideas in the molecular theory and on Theory Y assumptions to teach, coach, and guide my subordinates. Together we developed program objectives, monitoring procedures, and reporting mechanisms to ensure accountability for the grant programs.

Most of the time I had to work at a distance from the subordinates, because they were traveling to the various grant sites. I was available by phone to provide teaching and guidance whenever they asked for it. But I never tried to do their jobs for them. Sometimes I had to work in the opposite direction. Instead of giving them direct orders on what to do, we had to develop together reasonable and workable procedures that would not be too burdensome to ourselves or our programs in the field. I was totally dependent on them to get the job done.

CONCLUSION: THE MANAGER AS TEACHER

By attending graduate courses in both public administration and business administration, I became familiar with the theories and practices of management. They helped me make sense of what I had observed as a priest, an Air Force chaplain, and in my other organizational roles. The courses also taught me two important lessons: first, that I had no training in management; and second, that the type of management I practiced was a Theory X style. Later, I was fortunate to be in organizational settings that allowed me to experiment with alternative ways of managing. In my case, I developed an affinity for Theory Y and for Oncken's molecular theory.

A different person, exposed to the same courses, might have come away with different ideas than I did. The point, however, is that people who enter management from other fields, where they learned to get things done by their efforts, should have some formal and on-the-job management training. At a minimum, training will provide a conceptual framework that can be used to guide a manager's subsequent learning. But training will also highlight one of the least acknowledged parts that managers play in organizations.

O. Glenn Stahl (1971, p. 42) noted that "The managing role is very much a teaching role; this does not mean that all good teachers are good managers; but it does mean that all managers had better be good teachers." Stahl's words accurately describe my experience. One way that I learned about the utility of Theory Y and the molecular theory was to teach it to other people. I have since begun to teach management courses to graduate students at two universities.

Other authors in this book have noted that one is never finished learning how to be an effective manager. My career has taught me that a good manager is someone who can teach and who can learn. There will always be new organizational problems to solve and new challenges to meet. Managers may use Theory Y, the molecular theory, or another approach to train their subordinates. But clearly they must teach, coach, and support; otherwise their subordinates will not know what the manager expects or what the manager is thinking.

3

Contemplation and Administration: An Alternative Paradigm

Nancy J. Eggert

A few years ago I had a heated discussion with a close associate in a national literacy organization. I was supposed to lead the board of directors in a series of strategic planning meetings to help the organization get a sence of where it had been and where it was going. I was using participatory group techniques that attempted to evoke and articulate the latent vision that was shared by the organization's leadership. My role was to be a facilitator, and not to push my own agenda.

Tom, my associate, was also on the board of directors, and it was his goal to become a major leader of the organization. In the car on the long drive to the site of the directors' meetings, Tom grilled me about the philosophical underpinnings of the planning process I used. I explained to him that the techniques allowed ideas to bubble up from the group, so that we could all set aside for a time our preconceived notions of what we needed to do and allow some new thoughts to emerge.

My explanations did not convince Tom. "This is just like any other tool you can use to take control of an organization and get them to do what you want them to do," he said. "I want power. You want power. You are just being more subtle and sophisticated in exerting control."

I was unconvinced by Tom's point of view. But I did begin to question whether Tom was right in assuming that acquiring control and power were simply the raw, fundamental facts of human existence, especially in organizations. I wondered whether there honestly could be an alternative perspective on organizational life.

The disquieting incident with Tom launched me on an odyssey of inquiry. I do not have a definitive answer to the question of whether human behavior in organizations must be governed by norms of power. But I do have some answers that work for me and that have proved successful in managerial situations I have found myself in. In this chapter I would like to tell you how I have arrived at my answers.

THE JOURNEY TOWARD THE
CONTEMPLATIVE PARADIGM

Paradigms have been an important part of my journey as a public administrator. I first became aware of paradigms in an encounter with Thomas Kuhn's work, *The Structure of Scientific Revolutions* (1970), in which he explores the concept of paradigm shifts in the natural sciences. As explained by Willis Harman, a paradigm consists of "basic ways of perceiving, thinking, valuing, and doing associated with a particular view of reality" (1988, p. 10). Sometimes societies change and paradigms shift.

A favorite example many people have used to illustrate the concept of paradigm shift concerns a sixteenth-century "heretic" called Copernicus who had the audacity to suggest that the Earth revolved around the sun. Before Copernicus, everyone who subscribed to conventional wisdom knew with certainty that the Earth stood in a fixed and changeless place in the center of a fixed and changeless universe, and that the Earth was the epitome of creation. Human beings, as the central figures on the earthly stage, were central factors in the universe. Earth was the seat of mortal decay and Christian redemption, while the pure and unchanging planets and stars moved by divine spirits, "signaling and influencing human events by their locations and aspects" (Harman, 1988, pp. 7–8).

These were the fundamental assumptions shared by anyone with "common sense" about our place in the universe, the significance of our behavior, and the nature of change. The paradigm generated by these assumptions affected what people in the sixteenth century valued, how they related to one another, and how they went about their daily lives. When Copernicus dethroned the Earth as the center of the universe he began a revolution that eventually shattered the pattern that had governed human life for centuries.

In the last two decades, a number of writers have argued that a new paradigm (or paradigms) are emerging in our own time (Harman, 1988; Capra, 1982; Harman & Rheingold, 1984; Schaef & Fassel, 1988; Thayer, 1981; Beam & Simpson, 1984; Eisler, 1987; Fox, 1983; Theobald, 1987; Lenz & Myerhoff, 1985; Ferguson, 1980; Schwartz & Ogilvey, 1979). These authors suggest that we are in a time when basic understandings about what is real are undergoing a shift as revolutionary as the one sparked by Copernicus.

It is of secondary importance to me whether any of the writers have accurately grasped the direction or significance of changes in our present age. Their importance is in suggesting that life could be apprehended in a manner that is contrary to our current "common sense." The reality that governs our shared understandings has become, in the language of science, a dependent variable. No matter what the dominant reality is in contemporary organizations, there now exists the possibility that there could be an alternative paradigm that influences behavior.

Harmon and Mayer (1986) have indirectly applied the idea of alternative paradigms to their study of public organizations. As public administrators, we live in an environment that is shaped by certain taken-for-granted understandings about values, authority, goals, and related elements that shape organizational reality. Harman and Mayer identify seven alternative conceptualizations of public organizations (for example, systems, markets, and emergent realities) that reveal distinctly different assumptions about the public administrator's environment. Each theoretical perspective provides administrators with a template they can use to identify their current pattern for understanding "what makes sense" in organizations, and to experiment with the implications of operating under different perspectives.

EXPERIMENTS WITH PARTICIPATORY GROUP METHODS

A second series of events that fueled my reflections on alternative paradigms was my experience, beginning in the early 1970s, with nontraditional planning processes used by some businesses, community groups, and nonprofit organizations. For example, a few years ago I was participating in a gathering of representatives from community projects. We were trying to understand the root causes of persistent problems we had encountered and to formulate some strategies for addressing those issues. In a traditional meeting, there might be a formal agenda, driven to completion by the political undercurrents of the participants. But in this room, there was a large wall filled with clusters of index cards, each with a short phrase written in big letters that described some aspect of the situation.

We all stared intently and silently at the cards. Our attitude stemmed in part from our interest in the individual contributions and collaborative conversation that had generated the cards. However, by the time we were staring at the cards, individual ideas had become the collective creativity on the front wall. After a few minutes, brief comments emerged from the silence. "I see something there about. . . ." Or, "There seems to be a relationship between. . . ." Then more silence.

Suddenly there was a burst of creativity. One participant stood up and spat out a full sentence describing what she thought the underlying issue was. The group took her ideas and the conversation continued. Eventually a consensus emerged from the configuration of data about the meaning and implications of the issues that had brought us together.

The technique was surprisingly quick and usually resulted in a group consensus that had a comparatively long half-life. Anyone coming in to the group with a pet idea would soon find his or her favorite insight becoming lost in a sea of index cards. Rationality joined hands with intuition to break loose creativity and insight. Compared with other group processes and meetings, there was more waiting and watching, and less talking. There was the sense that the "truth" would eventually make itself known if we learned to listen carefully to our collective insights and experience.

Another example: I was in the Midwest headquarters of a staid and established Protestant denomination. A dozen committee members were sitting around the polished oak table, about to begin their quarterly deliberations. The cassette player in the corner was emitting the halcyon sounds of New Age composer Daniel Kobialka. Most of the people in the group had their eyes closed as they listened. The tape came to an end, the committee members shuffled their vinyl folders and ballpoint pens, and the meeting was called to order.

The relaxing music and the absence of talk before the meeting helped the participants let go of the extraneous concerns they had brought to the room. By the time the meeting began, everyone was ready for the day's agenda, being able to "listen softly" in the same way one listens to music, rather than having to "concentrate" on the work at hand. Unlike many meetings in contemporary organizations, these participants enjoyed the gathering and each other's company. And their work was completed.

A final example took place in an old mansion in a southern Virginia town. A service organization had gathered for its annual New Year's Eve party and planning conference. There was a fifteen-foot strip of white wrapping paper on the wall of the parlor. Old magazines, rubber cement, and scissors were dispersed around the room. There was merriment and cheer as the party-goers renewed acquaintances and began to build the "Wall of Wonder." Each person recalled some significant happening from the past year and found a way to symbolize it by cutting a picture from a magazine and adding it to the collective montage.

Later in the evening the revelers gathered in front of the wall and relived the experiences of the past year. Although the previous year's planning retreat ended with specific plans for the next twelve months, the question at this year's gathering was not whether all the goals had been reached. The focus was on what *did* happen, how the direction of the organization had changed, and what the present circumstances revealed about what needed to happen next. People with a highly developed verbal ability are sometimes so good at using words that they neglect to listen. Thus the use of "arts and crafts" for the Wall of Wonder helped the group move beyond the linear and rational processes enforced by language to begin to understand with greater power and depth the significance and direction of their mission.

Although the methods depicted in these scenes are not widely used, and at the time raised more than a few eyebrows, I found them to be effective, and I incorporated them into my methodological tool kit.[1] There were even opportunities for me to use these techniques with the team of attorneys I supervise at a federal agency. Over the years these nontraditional group process techniques have become second nature to me. Maybe I had unwittingly absorbed some of their underlying assumptions about human nature, but I did not lie awake at night thinking about which paradigm they were grounded in.

There was a growing sense within me, however, that these different ways of working with groups somehow "smelled differently." It is like living with the background scent of Pinesol all your life and then experiencing the fragrance of roses—but not recognizing what was different.

ENCOUNTERS WITH CONTEMPLATION

I recognized the "fragrance of roses" in other unexpected contexts: a Tai Chi class at the YMCA, and an accelerated learning workshop that used meditation as a preparation for study. It is difficult to identify the first "aha!" of recognition. Over the past decade our society has been inundated with a variety of books, classes, and workshops with variations on the theme of How to Use Meditation for Fun and Profit. Bookstores have a special section for titles advocating The Right Side of the Brain or the New Age for business, health, or other topics. The phenomenon has extended into courses in public administration and organization behavior, where students have discussed consciousness, brain functions, and alpha waves along with the more traditional Madison, management, and motivation.

I was intrigued by the results of my own experiments with these ideas, and guided by personal interests, I began to explore some of the classical mystics of the West, such as St. Teresa of Avila (Kavanaugh & Rodriguez, 1985), St. John of the Cross (Kavanaugh & Rodriguez, 1979), and Meister Eckhart (Fox, 1982, 1983). I experimented with the contemplative practices they taught, and eventually shared my experiences with other people in meditation groups.[2] After listening to people's accounts of their experiences, becoming aware of my own, and reading what others had to say, it dawned on me that meditation, rather than being simply a set of techniques, is a way of living. There seemed to me to be a contemplative lifestyle—and it smelled like a rose. I wondered if there could also be a "contemplative paradigm"? If so, could it have any meaning for public administration?

DEFINING PARADIGMS

If there is a paradigm that embodies the values, assumptions, and understanding of the contemplative life, then how can it be defined and described? One difficulty encountered with paradigms is that they usually go unnoticed. A paradigm is like the air we breathe: essential, ever-present, but usually invisible. One way to "see" a paradigm is to contrast it with another way of looking at the world. What I would like to do for the remainder of this chapter is to compare the major features of what I believe is the dominant paradigm of contemporary public oganizations (indeed, private and nonprofit organizations as well), with the central features of the contemplative paradigm.

The descriptions of the paradigms will be sketches rather than detailed portraits. The picture of the dominant paradigm will not be remarkable or novel. It is so well known that I anticipate that the briefest of clues will bring recognition.[3] But the contemplative paradigm is another matter. I am still exploring the meaning of the contemplative paradigm for myself, so I consider that my task here is to "conceive" something that I can subsequently develop further.

There is of course the temptation to ridicule the dominant paradigm and to hold the contemplative as an ideal to be achieved by enlightened public administrators.

That would be inappropriate for a number of reasons. First, the description of any paradigm can be distorted and perverted, especially if it has been around for a long time. It may be fun to highlight the corruptions and ignore the gifts of the dominant paradigm, but there are indeed benefits that we as a society have reaped from the ideas imbedded in the present paradigm. The contemplative paradigm would also be subject to warpings and excesses.

Second, I question whether anyone really *chooses* his or her paradigm. One can be open to it or explore it, but one probably cannot, by sheer force of will, enter into it. In this respect a paradigm is startlingly analogous to the meditative state: it is a gift rather than an accomplishment. I believe that a dominant paradigm, whether at the social or individual level, operates as a "default mode." It is what we revert to when we do not make a choice to behave consciously.

The Dominant Paradigm of Organization

Control

Control is a central theme in common sense understandings of organizations. Someone who does not have the situation under control is not considered to be a good manager. As a result there are a variety of managerial techniques to control people and to get workers to do more. It is inimical to the idea of organization to have people following their own agenda. A good bureaucracy has written rules and procedures, and a hierarchical structure where someone is always "on top of" someone else.

Managers rely on coercion and "power over" to get things done. Sometimes, as the chapter in this volume by Frank Nice describes, the coercion can be quite subtle. But it is still there. People have power in an organization because somebody higher up gave it to them, or allowed them to exercise it. The concept of empowerment is frightening in the framework of the dominant paradigm.

In organizations definition and clarity are preferred to ambiguity and uncertainty. Things need to be pinned down. The mystery of organizational life is squeezed out. Managers want theories that will fit specific situations, explain what is going on, and predict what will happen. Surprises and aberrations are nuisances. Even knowledge is controlled, as information is hoarded and parceled out as a precious currency.

Good managers "make things happen." They get things done by sheer force of will. Waiting and watching are signs of reactive managers. There are time lines to be followed, and situations have to be pushed to adjust the world to the demands of these time lines. If it appears that work is behind schedule, the manager has to discover what is wrong, correct it, and take steps to see that nothing interferes with achieving goals. Managers do not have the luxury of seeing how a situation evolves. One must set limits on the gestation period for an idea or project. From this perspective, managers are like gods whose task is to control their piece of the world.

Attachment

Managers in the dominant paradigm need security. The successful manager acquires a variety of roles, positions, ideas, principles, powers, theories, and relationships that provide meaning and significance. Good public administrators develop their own theories from their own experience, but they may become very attached to their way of looking at the world and be willing to blindly defend their point of view as "the right one." When any of their possessions are threatened, managers suffer anxiety and insecurity and must take steps quickly to shore the foundational pillars of identity. It is as if managers are longing for a resting place or haven they never quite find.

Appearances are important. Admitting weakness, vulnerability, or dependence is viewed as a sign that a manager's empire is crumbling. The sense that not everything is quite nailed down or under control fuels the desire to possess more, to fix one's desire on a specific object (such as a new theory, bigger budget, or better people) that will help secure the manager's place in the organization. Within certain bounds, the overriding emphasis is to take care of one's own interests. To look out for number one and to get what you want are the battle cries of the dominant paradigm.

Efficiency

Organizations, according to the logic of this paradigm, have clearly defined purposes. The manager's job is to see that the purpose is achieved in the most efficient way. Nothing—time, budgets, personnel—should be wasted, and waste is defined as activities that do not have a straight line relationship to goals. Utility is the keynote of action. Human beings are valued on the basis of what they contribute to achieving the mission. They have no intrinsic worth outside of their organizational role; they can be replaced. The world, its many gifts and resources are commodities to be developed, used and put into production for the goals of the organization. Hurry up! Get it done! Just do it! These are the cultural rallying cries of the dominant paradigm.

Rationality

Rationality includes not only the valuing of a machine-like logic over other mental processes but a preference for the objective, the measurable, the predictable. Logical positivism, empiricism, and the scientific method occupy a central position in the methodology of organization. Causality is the assumed model for explaining how and why things happen. Rules and procedures undergird the desire for certainty and safety.

Managers governed by norms of rationality live in their heads, not their hearts. Spontaneity and chaos are considered to be dangerous. Outer appearances are the focus of attention, and inner, subjective workings are ignored. Time is a linear commodity that can be budgeted and parceled out. Actions must be motivated by purpose. Questions must be answered. Ambiguity must be removed.

The Contemplative Paradigm

What I wish to present about the contemplative paradigm reminds me of Frederick Hart's stone carving, "Creation Tympanum," above the main entrance to the Washington Cathedral. The background is a dynamic swirling sea from which human figures are emerging. None are yet complete. The viewer does not have the whole picture, but the human form is easily recognized. One has a sense of mystery, rather than confusion. The work makes an impression, but it does not supply all of the answers. That is the effect I wish to convey in my description of the contemplative paradigm.

To provide some form to the swirl of this paradigm, I have borrowed Meister Eckhart's imagery of four paths spiraling into and out of a center (Fox, 1980, 1983). The Contemplative Administrator can be found on any of the four paths at different times.

The Path of Affirmation and Gratitude

The contemplative receives life first as a gift, innocently and with gratitude. She waits patiently for the wonder of life to unfold and to reveal itself. She listens quietly to the deep undercurrents of life that surge below surface concerns. The contemplative is sensitive to the mystery in life. Not everything has to be explained.

There is a profound appreciation of life as it is, a savoring and tasting of each experience. Sights and sounds are absorbed first without abstraction or judgment. They are experienced on their own terms without any intervention or effort. A simple yet difficult exercise to illustrate this path is to sit and listen to the sounds in one's environment, but without naming or judging them. The twittering of a bird or the howl of a siren are simply absorbed and noted. There is no need to react to, categorize, or treat these waves of energy in the air as distractions.[4]

Neither is there any need to use, sell, or develop the beauty that one encounters. Flowers, people, and experiences are appreciated for what they are without concern for their utility or for how one thinks they ought to be, or how one would like them to be. There is no need to pick the flower, sell it, or to find a use for it. The manager's world can be embraced without the need for manipulation or domination. Coworkers have inherent value as human beings first, without regard to what they can do or produce. Human dignity is respected. There is a deep love of life.

The contemplative can take pleasure in the mundane moment and be open to the deep sense of joy and wonder that can well up in the midst of ordinary organizational experiences. It is acceptable to stop and celebrate for no reason at all. A "Thank Goodness It's Tuesday" party would be in accord with this perspective. Time becomes something beyond fungible little packets of existence that tick away in regular intervals.

The contemplative manager is fully present to life as it is in each unrepeatable moment. Awareness replaces numbness. There is no other place to be right now. While participating in a meeting, the manager is fully present to the meeting.

While writing a report he or she is fully present to writing the report. Whatever activity the manager is doing is worthy of his or her life and attention now. There are no unimportant or insignificant moments. Impatience, tenseness, and anxiety are replaced with a relaxed, open awareness—as are lethargy and unconsciousness. A contemplative manager lives deliberately and sensitively.

The contemplative public administrator is attuned to the depths and listens with the "third ear." He or she takes time to go beneath the swirling turbulence on the surface of life and touches the deep undercurrents in which all people participate. Self-knowledge is an important theme on the journey. The self-knowledge helps tune the third ear to the suffering and pain of coworkers and to the world at large.

The Path of Letting Go and Embracing the Darkness

Silence causes discomfort. Words are generated to fill up the empty space. We also are often not comfortable with the silence within. Radio, television, or books are used to control the restlessness of being alone. Days and vacations are filled with activity. It is as if there were an innate fear of silence, of emptiness, of the dark.

The contemplative allows himself or herself to drop into the deep silence and emptiness of the void, secure in the protection of what Tantric Buddhists term the "no-thing." The fear of losing oneself is relinquished with the knowledge that there is no permanent self to lose.[5] Self-image is released and new concepts are allowed to emerge, only to dissolve again back into the deep darkness when their journey is completed.

Contemplatives do not abandon the use of structure, operating modes, and management styles. But they are not what provide security. The contemplative public administrator is comfortable in the empty space between the dissolution of the old and the emergence of the new in organizational life. There is no need to cling to principles, concepts, emotions, or thoughts in the way a manager might who is operating under the dominant paradigm. The contemplative can refrain from psychological projection since there is an awareness that ideas are helpful representations of reality, and not reality itself. This path concerns the "art of letting things happen, action through non-action, letting go of oneself. . . . [T]his actually is an art of which few people know anything. Consciousness is forever interfering, helping, correcting and negating. . . ." (Jung, 1962, p. 93).

As an exercise, take time in the silence of the day to watch your thoughts, ideas, and emotions. Where did they come from? Follow them back to their source. Before long they dissipate like ripples on a pond. A contemplative manager is not defined by any characteristic, role, goal, or accomplishment. There is nothing for him or her to defend or protect.

Pain is recognized and acknowledged as a part of organizational life, whether it be one's own or a coworker's. It is met with neither denial nor stoicism. One can mourn what once was but is no longer. However, the contemplative does not cling to pain in any of its forms, does not glorify it, and does not wallow in it. Pain too is let go. There is no room for rose-colored glasses or for masochism.

Finally, the contemplative has nothing to lose because ultimately there is nothing to be had, nothing to possess, nothing to cling to. The contemplative does not have to be in control. With this understanding comes freedom born of a trust of life itself and of the nothingness at the center of being. This does not mean that a contemplative manager simply sits in a chair and stares out the window at the clouds. The nonattachment of the contemplative path allows one to engage where and when it is necessary. But nonattachment permits one to take a new perspective when that is required, to have a change of heart, to let a new idea or a new structure take form. The contemplative way is anything but victimized nonaction or passivity.

The Way of Birthing and Creativity

Creativity emerges from the nothingness. Conception and birth take place in the dark. When ideas and images are held loosely and then let go, something new can break forth. When we allow ourselves to sink into the darkness that is at the center of our being, we tap into a deep wellspring of creative energy. It is in allowing our old images of life to die that we can be open and receptive to an utterly new conception. We have the possibility of an "aha."

Creativity is a gift we can ask for but cannot manufacture. We, as managers and leaders, can gain access to new insight and creativity by ceasing to do the things that block them. We can be silent. We can listen. We can entertain new ideas. We can play, be silly, be wild and crazy. Dancing, painting, singing, joking, and writing poems can all be vehicles for the creative spirit to come into our organizational lives. These activities can spring loose deeper insights than words can convey. Meetings need not be dull, controlled, overformalized situations that never touch on what is truly important to the participants. There is a time for telling stories, sharing visions, and celebrating our organizational life together. We are all artists.

For the contemplative, our play and dance need not be utilitarian. Simply being alive is a celebration. Life exists for its own sake. One can live for the sheer joy of being in history. Meister Eckhart observed, "[T]he only way to live is like the rose which lives without a why" (Fox, 1982, p. 30).

Creativity is not for ourselves alone but for all who share the organizational universe with us. The gifts that we give birth to are to be shared with others, to enable them to participate in the mystery of life and to get them in touch with their own depths and creativity.

Creativity does not mean unfocused frenzy. Good art requires discipline along with inspiration. Tapping the wellspring of creativity demands that difficult choices be made. The contemplative administrator/artist is free to choose from the entire spectrum of images available, but he or she must choose. When the choice is made, the contemplative can trust the images, the ideas that are revealed, and can embrace them and their guidance with the passion reserved for the administrator as artist.

The Way of Transformation and Compassion

Not all creativity is helpful. It can be coopted for purposes of destruction, ego-fulfillment, and power-grabbing. Dictators, drug dealers, and despots often do not want for creativity.

In the Western tradition, the fruits of contemplation include wholeness, justice, and love. The clarity and breadth of awareness, the responsiveness to situations, and the greater self-knowledge that are the psychophysiological effects of contemplation could be used for any purpose (May, 1987, pp. 29–30). But without growth toward wholeness and love, the journey remains incomplete.

A contemplative is not a navel-gazer, isolated from and indifferent to the injustice and suffering that surrounds. Compassion is a necessary element in the contemplative life, and compassion means action. Sometimes the action requires moving in a new direction, away from old habitual patterns, beyond the things, relationships, roles, structures, and attitudes that bring comfort and security, but that also negate and destroy the new.

The contemplative public administrator identifies with the poor and suffering of the world, in all their forms. The identification is an integral aspect of working in the public's interest. The administrator acknowledges that we live in one world, one universe, and that we all share the wellspring of life that nurtures and sustains us. The brokenness and suffering of one is the pain and grief of us all. There is no compartmentalization of life into ''me'' and the ''rest of the world.'' Neither is there a natural ordering of one person or group over another. Power is a reality, but (to respond to my associate Tom's assertion) it is ''power with'' rather than ''power over.''

Compassion involves risk and vulnerability for the sake of making justice. There are no guarantees or safety nets on the contemplative's journey. The human transformation that makes possible the willingness to take risks and to be vulnerable in the cause of justice is aided by the rewards of the other three paths: the sensitivity and the depth of awareness, the trust of nothingness, the willingness to surrender cherished ideas and concepts, the acknowledgment of pain, and the nurturing of creativity combine alchemically to bring about the radical transformation of the contemplative administrator.

AND NOW IT IS YOUR TURN: AN INVITATION

So far I have shared my journey. If what I have written resonates with you, then you are invited to choose a direction and continue the adventure. The territory to be explored is broader than what I have hinted. Although you need only attend to the guidance of your internal compass and follow your passion, I do have a few additional strategies to suggest.

There is something silly about describing the contemplative experience. It is somewhat similar to trying to experience the fragrance of a rose by reading about it. Why not lay this book aside and sense for yourself the contemplative experience?[6] Find a quiet, comfortable place where you will not be disturbed. Stretch a little to get relaxed. Sit in a straight chair with your feet flat on the ground and hands gently resting in your lap. Take a few long, slow breaths. Form an intention to sink deeply into your depths. Gently turn your attention to the subtle sensation of the breath leaving your nose. Do not try too hard. Just watch. As your mind begins to wander, gently return your attention to your breath.

All right, so nothing happened the first time. Start with five minutes and increase to thirty minutes daily over a few months. *Then* reflect on what you have experienced. The fragrance is very subtle.

A second strategy is to field-test for yourself some of the methods of the contemplative paradigm and see if they are in any way helpful. One relatively safe technique is to listen, without immediate response or judgement. For example, focus on the sound and the meaning of what you are hearing during a meeting, rather than how you will respond. Listening with your third ear may help you pick up what is not being said but which is of critical importance. Another suggestion you might experiment with at your next meeting is consciously to wait before speaking, not jump in impulsively simply because there is a brief pause in the conversation. Ask yourself, "Will this comment be helpful? Has it been said already? Will it move the dialogue along? Or is what I plan to say simply for my own satisfaction or need for power?" Try to discern the depth issue in the meeting.

Ludwig Wittgenstein said that what cannot be spoken about must remain unsaid, and in the East, Lao Tzu noted that the Way that can be spoken of is not the true Way. While it is difficult to accurately represent in language something as transcendental as the contemplative paradigm, there is room for theorizing, all the while remembering that language points to, but is not, reality. Apply the heat of inquiry to the description of the paradigm and see how it can be improved upon. How would you restructure it? How would you communicate the ideas more effectively?

It is also appropriate to ask, "why bother?" Of what significance for the world of public administration and organization is the contemplative paradigm? Will it help us deal with a world of increasing complexity, chaos, and ambiguity? Does it shed light on more mundane problems of employee motivation, managing for quality improvement, or organizational change? Will the contemplative paradigm improve decision making? Must the paradigm be functional to have a role in public administration? Could the contemplative way be an end in itself, independent of organizational context and utility? These questions and more can be recast as testable hypotheses, subjects for what Jacob Needleman has termed "inner empiricism" (Young, 1976, p. xvii).

I will close here with the words of St. Teresa of Avila, one of the original contemplative administrators, who offers guidance for all who seek to act thoughtfully and effectively in the world: "The important thing is not to think much but to love much, and so do that which best stirs you to love" (Campbell, 1985, p. 35).

NOTES

1. Many of the methods described were developed and used by the Institute of Cultural Affairs, an international nonprofit organization working with grassroots community development and education.

2. I am using the terms "meditation" and "contemplation" interchangeably here, although they can be used to refer to distinct phenomena.

3. For more technical descriptions of organizations designed under the dominant paradigm see Thompson (1976), Gortner, Mahler, & Nicholson (1987), and Boyatzis (1982). For another critique of the paradigm, see Denhardt (1981a).

4. This is similar to the "concrete experience" pole of David Kolb's learning cycle (1984). See Paul Waldo's chapter in this volume for further discussion.

5. One does not have to be a mystic to hold this position. See, for example, Gazzaniga (1985).

6. Although a book is not the best way to learn contemplative techniques, there are a number of good texts that describe contemplation and meditation from a variety of traditions. I have found Edwards's book (1987) a good place to start.

4

The Hero's Journey in Public Administration

Christopher Bellavita

The classic hero myth begins with the kingdom in trouble. Crops are not grow-ing. Babies are not being born. Sickness, alienation, and despair are rampant. Life is vanishing from the land. Some claim it is the fault of a sinful and despotic king. Others blame a dragon that roams the countryside, destroying everything in its path. The elders meet to decide what to do, but their ideas have been heard before and no longer have any power. Hope is disappearing from the kingdom. Into this slough of despond comes the hero, the man or woman who takes on the task of bringing new life to a dying land (Pearson, 1986, p. 151).[1]

PROBLEMS IN THE KINGDOM
OF PUBLIC ADMINISTRATION

The public administrator's world is very much like the kingdom in the ancient hero myth. Respect for government service has been declining for years, and the prestige of government jobs has fallen dramatically. According to the 1989 Volker Commission report, "Too many of the best of the nation's senior executives are ready to leave government, and not enough of the most talented young peo-ple are willing to join" (Preface). Annual turnover for senior executives is 10 percent, and among executive winners of the Presidential Rank award, 20 per-cent a year are leaving government (Vukelich, 1988). Only 13 percent of the federal executives said they would recommend a career in government to young people (Levine & Kleeman, December, 1986). Less than 4 percent of 1,500 Har-vard graduates in 1985 planned to enter federal service after graduation (Karp & Renesch, 1986). Of 1,200 students who recently received engineering degrees from prestigious universities, only twenty-nine students took a job in government. Seventy-five percent of presidential management interns surveyed said they would not make a career of government (Volker, 1989, pp. 3-4).

The federal government has a difficult time attracting qualified people. The National Institutes of Health have been unable to recruit a senior scientist in ten years. In the first six months of 1989, forty people turned down jobs in the Bush administration (CBS, 1989). NASA, the Department of Defense, the Environmental Protection Agency, and other organizations also report difficulty in hiring qualified employees; in 1988, the government was unable to fill 35,000 high-skill jobs (Levine & Kleeman, 1986, pp. 5-12; Havemann, 1988). Some people maintain that government can hire only the "best of the desperate" (Johnston, et al., 1988, p. 29).

Analysts offer many reasons for public-service ills. Political officials have campaigned against bureaucrats and government for two decades. Executive pay is not commensurate with that of private industry. Personnel practices make it difficult to learn about and apply for available jobs. There is limited room for career advancement and individual initiative. Many offices are drab, equipment is antiquated, and jobs are monotonous. Motivated workers see that there is little penalty associated with being an unproductive worker. Corruption and incompetence are depressingly commonplace: among them, savings and loan abuses; defense procurement scandals; safety violations at nuclear weapon plants; hazardous waste dump leaks; influence pedaling in HUD, Congress, and the White House; and impeachments of federal judges.

Futurists predict that public service problems are going to get worse. Government workers will be required to do more complex tasks. Competition with private industry for highly skilled employees will intensify. Changes in civil service rules will make it easier for experienced workers to leave government for better opportunities (Johnston, 1988).

Many solutions have been offered to resolve the myriad problems facing the public sector: enhancing the image of the public service; changing the structure of government organizations and encouraging more decentralization; increasing the pay and other rewards of public service; improving the training and the skills of public employees; and so forth (Volker, 1989; Rogers, 1988; Johnston, 1988; Levine & Kleeman, 1986, pp. 13-29; Newland, 1984, pp. 36-43; National Academy of Public Administration, 1983). Obviously no single remedy will resolve the problems faced by the public sector. The approach emphasized in this chapter is to reexamine what a public servant is and might be.

THE STRUCTURE OF HEROISM

My initial intention was to contribute to the debate on improving public service by focusing on the nature of successful work experiences in the public sector. I reasoned that even in the midst of a troubled environment, some public administrators do have positive and rewarding experiences. If I could identify what features, if any, these experiences had in common, I could identify what had to happen before they could be replicated by other people.

I asked forty-five public administrators to complete a sixty-six-item, open-ended questionnaire, eliciting information about the best organizational experience they had in their careers.[2] All the people I asked to complete the questionnaire had at least five years' experience as public sector managers, and many respondents had substantially more experience.

After analyzing the returns, I noticed that practically all the stories that people told were structurally similar to what Joseph Campbell called "the hero's journey" (1949, pp. 245–51). I designed the questionnaire to elicit data about the organizational nature of individual experience. What emerged instead were stories about people overcoming forces to bring new vitality to stagnant systems.

According to Campbell, stories about heroes follow a similar pattern in all the world's cultures. The hero leaves the realm of everyday events and enters an unfamiliar land. The hero undergoes an ordeal, aided by allies and hampered by enemies. The hero returns from the ordeal a changed person and with the power to bestow a boon on humanity.[3]

Applying Campbell's structure to the questionnaire data provided a framework for describing the hero's journey in public administration. The journey consists of three main episodes. The hero first gets the call to adventure, which may come from duty, opportunity, or an internal drive. The second stage is the ordeal. The hero enters the threshold of the journey and has one last chance to say no to it. The ordeal involves planning, organizing, and implementing a specific vision of the future. During the ordeal the hero encounters helpers and enemies. The third stage of the journey is the hero's return. The hero receives a material reward, is changed as a person, and some part of the hero's world is also transformed.

The hero challenges, and in the process revitalizes, the status quo. I believe that the hero metaphor can be used descriptively by administrators to interpret what happes to them in public organizations. The metaphor can also be used prescriptively to suggest how an individual can help to improve public service (Morgan, 1986; Boje, Fedor, & Rowland, 1982; Lakoff & Johnson, 1980).

To offer support for the utility of the hero metaphor, I have selected ten stories to tell of public administrators who have taken the hero's journey.[4] I will first identify the ten administrators and summarize what they did. Then I will describe the hero's journey, using selected parts of their stories as illustration.

1. Anita Boles redesigned the Victim/Witness Assistance Unit of a United States Attorney's Office.

2. Rudolph Ehrenberg created the United States Army's "Organizational Review Activity," whose mission was to locate and eliminate inefficient operations in the Army's European operations.

3. Gary Misch was responsible for negotiating the shipment of 155 million dollars worth of wheat to a Middle Eastern nation.

4. William Driver found a way to end a shortage of qualified C-141B instructor pilots in a Military Airlift Wing of the Air Force Reserve.

5. "Karen Mendoza" designed and implemented a drug prevention and health promotion summer camp for minority children.[5]

6. Clayton McDowall coordinated an effort to form a coalition of nonprofit social agencies in Anchorage, Alaska.

7. William Kastner created, at no cost to the government, a school to train naval reserve officers.

8. Joe Coffee expanded executive and management development in the Department of Treasury.

9. Larry Geri was the primary author of a report that helped change the way the Department of Agriculture organized its program for ensuring compliance with animal health and welfare regulations.

10. Charles Cabell revised the way the Defense Department's Defense System Management College trained program managers.

THE CALL TO ADVENTURE

What motivates a public administrator to undertake a hero's journey? Why are they not content to accept things the way they are? While there no doubt are many, I found three reasons why the administrators I am calling heroes heeded the call to adventure: duty, opportunity, and the drive to achieve something.

Duty

Sometimes duty calls the hero to adventure. Duty refers to the action required by one's profession or position. Rudy Ehrenberg was an Army officer assigned the job of figuring out how the Army could improve its efficiency in Europe. Gary Misch was the Associate Administrator for Marketing of the Department of Transportation's Maritime Administration (MARAD). It was his job to make sure that federal agencies used U.S. shipping when possible. Larry Geri was a program analyst for the Resource Management and Evaluation Staff of a unit in the Department of Agriculture, and was assigned to lead the team of analysts investigating compliance with animal health and welfare regulations. William Driver was the new Assistant Deputy Commander for Operations in an Air Force Reserve wing faced with a shortage of pilots. His boss told him, "You've got it."

Duty does not imply that one's heart is not in the job. Navy Engineering Duty Officers (EDs) have to complete a two-year training program to advance in their careers. The Navy provided a school for active duty officers, but in 1982 there was no school for reservists. William Kastner, a civilian employee of the Navy, was directed by his boss to make the school "happen." But there was no money to start and operate a school. Kastner was also an ED officer, and he believed he had a responsibility to his fellow reservists to "remove the stigma of second class from a group of reserves. . . . I was one of them, and I could not turn back from my obligation to get this done."[6]

Opportunity

Heroes are also motivated by the opportunity to test an idea or to act on a belief. Charles Cabell came to the Defense Systems Management College (DSMC) in 1985. Based on his military experience and other evidence, he did not believe that DSMC's curriculum and instruction methods accurately reflected the reality of defense program management. A group of people at DSMC agreed with Cabell and were "aching to make a change." As the College's new commandant, Cabell was in a position to "tap into that feeling" and to bring about change.

Clay McDowall was trying to find an alternative to institutionalizing eight severely disabled men in Anchorage, Alaska.[7] While he and his allies managed to obtain some money to buy a lift van and to pay for overnight trips, he realized that creating an alternative to nursing homes required more resources. After surveying the area's other small nonprofit and advocacy organizations, he believed that he could accomplish his goal and they could accomplish theirs if they worked together. He began to frame and manage the task of creating a coalition of agencies. His efforts provided an opportunity "to see if the concepts of win-win cooperation and power-building through joint effort would really work."

Drive

Responding to duty and taking advantages of opportunities also imply the presence of a drive to, in one respondent's words, "achieve something tangible and meaningful." Heroes want to make something happen. Before Joseph Coffee arrived at the Department of Treasury's training branch in 1976, the Internal Revenue Service was the only one of the fifteen agencies in the Department that paid significant attention to executive development. Coffee's predecessor "had seen her function as mainly processing requests to go to training, e.g., F[ederal] E[xecutive] I[nstitute], Executive Seminar Centers, Brookings." Initiating a department-wide executive development program was "a mechanism to improve organizations" and a way for Coffee to satisfy his "high need to influence the direction of individuals and organizations."

In 1985, the Chief of the Victim/Witness Assistance unit of a U.S. Attorney's Office resigned. Since she was an attorney, and the Office needed the attorney slot in another division, her position in the unit was not filled. The Victim Assistance unit was responsible for providing new services to crime victims and witnesses, but it lacked leadership. People hoarded information, single tasks seemed to take forever to accomplish, and conflict was hurting the unit's mission. Boles, who at the time was a Presidential Management Intern, offered to help the unit by designing a new program. She was motivated by the chance to aid crime victims, but she recognized that her efforts also could lead to "the possibility of obtaining the permanent Chief's position." However, "the position of Chief was a well sought after position." To earn what she wanted, Boles had to prove that she had the drive and skill to win.

THE HERO'S JOURNEY THROUGH
A STRANGE LAND

The hero's journey is an ordeal: a test of skill, wisdom, and fortune. While the hero has helpers along the way, the journey is fundamentally an individual and voluntary undertaking. No one can command another to heroism, and there is much to dissuade the hero from taking the journey. At the threshold of the experience the hero encounters many reasons why the adventure cannot succeed. During the journey, the hero clashes with enemies who want the quest to fail.

At the Threshold of the Journey

Before the ordeal begins, the hero encounters what Campbell calls a "shadowy presence" that guards the entrance to the passage. In the hero's journey of the public administrator, the shadowy presence in one of the "good" reasons why what the hero has in mind to do cannot be done. I identified six guardians encountered by the heroes I studied; they are illustrated in the examples that follow.

Credentials

Having the right credentials makes it easier to initiate change. Not having the proper credentials means the hero has to use a different resource to get past the threshold.

In Anita Boles's organizational culture there were two types of people, lawyers and nonlawyers, and "all non-lawyers are considered clerical." Many people in the Office "expected and wanted the [Victim Assistance] program to remain status quo. . . . Attorneys and attorney supervisors . . . showed little interest in the program and foresaw little value in its services." Boles thought that "the only way to have a chance at succeeding with this program was to establish another 'professional' group within the office." She believed that this could be done by earning the respect of the other offices, especially the attorneys, rather than by complaining about the lack of respect. Since "respect came from expertise," one of her goals became to make the program "indispensable to the attorney staff."

Boles talked to people throughout the organization and "took an interest in their personal lives and their professional goals." She wanted to find out what her unit could do to make the other units' work easier. She used the information to develop a proposal for the Victim Assistance Unit that would meet the needs of the entire organization, rather than concentrating solely on the population the Victims program was supposed to serve. In particular, her proposal included "ways in which the program would save attorneys time during trials. . . . The line attorneys recognized the time saving attributes and offered numerous suggestions to further this cause." Heroes may need to create credentials to get over the threshold.

Rules

Rules can conspire against the hero. In bureaucracy, rules establish the terrain within which public servants can function. William Driver became the Assistant Deputy Commander of Operations for an Air Force Reserve Wing in 1986. His job was to manage and train reserve pilots, who make up most of the U.S.'s airlift and aeromedical wartime capability. Driver had fewer than 50 percent of the instructor pilots he was supposed to have, and the ones he had stayed only an average of eighteen months. In his agency, the entire force of more than 450 pilots turned over every three years. All the pilots who resigned said that inadequate compensation was the primary reason for leaving the reserves.

Driver knew that as a civilian, a pilot could earn in excess of $50,000 after three years, and work less than 80 hours a month. The Air Force would not provide equivalent hours or compensation. According to federal regulations at the time, a qualified pilot leaving active duty for the reserves could only be offered a GM-13 salary, about $39,000. Driver's organization had never before "even considered a special salary rate for any of its employees."

Driver was not content to accept the status quo. He discovered that another personnel rule provided for special rates to help recruit and retain people in hard-to-fill jobs, if the difficulty was a direct result of private sector compensation that significantly exceeded civil service pay. But before this rule could be used to increase pilots' salaries, Driver had to follow still another rule. He had to provide a salary survey of airline pilots as evidence of the wage disparity. Heroes in bureaucracy must be able to navigate a sea of rules.

Politics

Sometimes the hero's path is blocked by political barriers. The job of the Department of Agriculture's Animal and Plant Health Inspection Service (APHIS) is to protect crop and livestock producers from pests and diseases. One part of the organization, Veterinary Services, has the responsibility for guarding against the spread of certain livestock diseases across state lines, and monitoring compliance with animal welfare regulations. The Service uses a nationwide group of investigators, known as compliance officers, to enforce Department regulations. Officers were hired by and reported to the Area Veterinarian in Charge (AVIC) of each state.

In the early 1980s, parts of the compliance network showed signs of being ineffective. Allegations surfaced that violations of animal health regulations were not being addressed. A significant group within the agency, including Larry Geri, an APHIS analyst, believed that the compliance system was in need of change. But the political dynamics of the agency prevented change.

Veterinarians were the strongest occupational group in the agency, and the agency's administrators traditionally were veterinarians. The AVICs resisted efforts to modify the compliance system because adopting the suggested changes would have diminished their influence with state officials, the industry, and practicing veterinarians. Area veterinarians and livestock owners who believed that stronger enforcement was needed to protect gains in animal disease eradication and control programs were in the minority.

In 1983, the political environment changed. Ronald Reagan named two cattle industry figures (who were not veterinarians) to lead both APHIS and the Marketing and Inspection Services component of the USDA. One of their primary objectives was to "strengthen the . . . compliance network" of Veterinary Services. This change opened the door for Geri to begin a hero's journey.

Money

The absence of money can prevent a hero from starting on an adventure. In 1982, a Navy Department study estimated that it would cost 1,079,000 dollars to begin a school to train reserve Engineering Duty Officers. The school also would require 107,000 dollars to operate and process sixty students each year, assuming the government provided the facilities at no cost.

Although William Kastner had been told in 1982 to start the school, there was no money in his organization's budget, "Command A," to pay for it. The school for active duty engineers did not want to run a reserve school. "Command B," whose job was to operate schools, did not have funds for a reserve school and did not know how long it would take to plan such a program. Another organization, "Command C," agreed to run the school, but they too did not have the money, the facilities, or the personnel to start the school within the next three years.

Besides having over thirty years in the reserves, Kastner had been in sales and marketing for twenty-five years. He saw his task as "just another show. . . . I like to get the elephant to stand on its tail." He told "Command B" that "Command A" and "Command C" wanted the school. He told "Command A" that he would operate the school with the help of "Command C," and he told "Command C" that "Command A" would do all the work. Consequently everyone agreed that the school could start.

Kastner discovered that the Xerox Training Center in Leesburg, Virginia, was renting space. Reserve officers received $75 per day for thirteen days' training a year, no matter where that training took place. Kastner used this money to rent the Xerox facilities, including meals that were "unlimited in size, of great quality and quantity and better than a resort." He persuaded two reserve captains into taking a leave of absence from their civilian jobs and running the school for the first thirty months. He helped a reserve petty officer to return to active duty and to be assigned to the school. The first class of the school that had been created out of thin air began October 24, 1983.

History

Historical forces may prevent a hero from undertaking a journey. Karen Mendoza worked in the regional office of a federal agency that had responsibility for minority health issues. Mendoza was responsible for substance abuse treatment and prevention programs for the region, but she was especially interested in improving primary prevention services for children.

As she reviewed prevention programs throughout her region she "was disappointed that people thought showing a film or giving a talk about the dangers associated with drug abuse were sufficient for drug abuse education." In 1985, she proposed that as an experiement her agency should host a three-day summer health fair for minority children. She believed that the fair, designed to be entertaining and educational, would demonstrate to the minority community that an innovative drug prevention program would be more effective than lectures on helping children avoid substance abuse, stay in school, and develop personal achievement goals.

Recommending a new direct-service program ran counter to the historical trend of her agency's federal-local relationships. The minority community strongly believed that services initiated and provided by local groups were more satisfactory than federally provided service. The regional office actively encouraged the community to manage as many health programs as they could handle. Mendoza also supported local control, but she had been unsuccessful in her previous attempts to convince the local health providers to test her ideas about drug prevention. Adding to her problems, the regional office lacked a budget for prevention services.

Mendoza's initial efforts were rebuffed by her agency. But in many parts of the region, 90 percent of the minority children are affected by alcoholism and other drug abuse in their families or communities. So Mendoza continued trying to convince people to support her idea. The agency, regional staff, neighborhood health directors and interested adults from the minority community finally agreed that it was appropriate to at least experiment with a new approach. So after "some lively discussions" about conflicts between the proposed health fair and the policy goal of encouraging local initiatives, Mendoza was told that she could organize the fair.

Failure

Heroes take risks, and risk-taking can lead to failure. F. Scott Fitzgerald wrote, "Show me a hero and I will write you a tragedy." Many classic hero myths do end in the death of the hero. Several of the heroes I studied were conscious of the risk of failure.

Joseph Coffee's first executive development programs at Treasury involved taking four executive teams off-site for a week of twelve-hour days. "If it failed," he said, "I would lose all my credibility and probably would not be able to have any influence or take risks for years to come in Treasury."

Larry Geri felt that his primary risk was failure: "Inability to complete the [report] assignment on time or at an acceptable level of quality probably would have doomed my APHIS career." Boles believed that her "direct approach with the attorney personnel could have backfired. It may have increased their resistance." For Karen Mendoza, "Anything short of a smashing success would have reduced the probability that my recommendations would be seriously considered in the future, and might have impacted negatively on future proposals for prevention programming.''

The Hero's Ordeal

Once the hero is past the threshold, the ordeal begins. Each journey is unique, because what the hero must do to be successful is specific to the situation. However, the structure of the ordeal can be outlined. It consists of envisioning what is to be accomplished; planning, organizing, and implementing actions to achieve the vision; and having the faith and courage to believe the adventure will succeed.

The journey is an ordeal because it tests the hero's ability to accomplish something beyond the normal range of experience and achievement. But it is not an ordeal in the primitive sense of pain and agony (although those moments may be present). Larry Geri best expressed the nature of the ordeal:

As I sat . . . working from dawn to midnight, I was having *fun*. I was playing, . . . feeling creative, spontaneous, and happy that I was going to accomplish something worthwhile. The hours and hours I worked on the project seemed compressed into minutes. It was a paradoxical experience, effortless hard work. This was fun . . . in a way that Ayn Rand [meant when] she wrote: ''Joy is the goal of human existence, and joy is not to be stumbled upon, but to be achieved.''

Vision

Each administrator I studied had a clear idea of what was to be accomplished. For example, Mendoza wanted a summer fair. Cabell wanted to change the way Defense Department program managers were educated. Kastner wanted to start a school. McDowall wanted to form a coalition of nonprofit social service agencies.

Sometimes the vision, once articulated, did not change. For instance, Driver wanted to increase pilots' salaries, and that is what he did. At other times the vision evolved as experience dictated. Joe Coffee initially wanted the headquarters level of the Treasury Department to help that organization's bureaus build model executive development programs. But within a few years, ''I had altered this vision and decided that a Departmental role was unrealistic,'' and he worked more with individual bureaus. Boles's original vision was to develop a comprehensive Victim Assistance program that affected all the divisions in the U.S. Attorney's Office. Boles modified her objectives after deciding that ''my vision for a successful program was unrealistic.''

Planning

All the administrators had a plan for achieving their vision, although the plans varied in the amount of detail they contained, in the number of other people involved in the planning process, and in the time available for the endeavor. Joe Coffee's general strategy was to achieve credibility, respect, and trust in the organization. "I had a very specific goal to shoot for—which I established. And I had a series of incremental successes which were required to achieve the goal." He believed that bureau chiefs at Treasury had to see some benefit before they would get involved with executive development, and his bosses had to see some early successes before they trusted him to expand his activities. So he planned to spend his first efforts conducting team-building sessions around specific bureau problems to demonstrate how executive development could improve organizational performance. He then built on his accomplishments and expanded the programs available to bureaus, formed advisory groups of executives to help institutionalize executive development, encouraged (with other people) the Secretary of Treasury to approve the group's recommendations, and then helped implement the group's ideas, specifically to establish a Treasury Executive Institute.

While Coffee planned his strategy primarily on his own, Charles Cabell involved his entire organization. After concluding that the DSMC Program Management Course "did not really capture the 'essence' of program management," he conducted a brainstorming session with his faculty and staff of 115 people. Using the "Crawford Slip Method," a technique for generating written ideas, Cabell asked his faculty to answer the question: "What would you do if you were going to be Commandant for the next couple of years?" Within 45 minutes he received 1,400 responses. "Multi-level, cross organization committees, made of deans, directors and people with authority, were then formed to turn the raw ideas into well-shaped recommendations" that led eventually to a plan for a competency-based program management curriculum.

Organizing

Organizing means bringing together the people, money, and materials needed to execute the plan. Rudy Ehrenberg started his organization "with a blank sheet of paper," four million dollars, and the formal authority to "locate and eliminate inefficient operations." His first priorities were to "recruit, form and train the organization; develop operating procedures, standards, values; and establish credibility of the organization." He recruited sixty professional staff with experience in efficiency reviews and management studies, and brought personnel from an existing manpower survey team and from a typing pool into his new organization. Ehrenberg formed six investigative teams, and the first group immediately began an analysis of the Armed Forces Recreation Center.

Most of the administrators I studied, however, were not given many resources to use. They relied primarily on their skills. As described earlier, Boles interviewed the people already working in the Victim Assistance unit and the people who would be affected by the unit's work, and used that information to design an organization that everyone would support. Kastner transformed his talents as a salesman and a $75 per diem into an engineering school.

Implementation

Implementation is the last phase of the ordeal. The main elements in the implementation processes were negotiating, meetings and phone calls, attending to details, and patience and stamina.

Negotiating. A hero needs to be adept at bargaining and negotiating. Gary Misch's job was to insure that at least 50 percent of the wheat the United States sold to a Middle Eastern country was transported on U.S. flag ships. His team included a Department of Agriculture representative, whose main interest was to make sure the sale was not disrupted; a State Department official, who wanted to make certain that the "fragile" relationship between the United States and the foreign government was not damaged; five U.S. steamship company representatives, each concerned that their company received the maximum of the 50 to 60 million dollar market at stake; and officials from the foreign country, who were looking for additional concessions from the U.S. government. Because of competing interests between the United States and the foreign government, and within the United States negotiation team, Misch quickly recognized that "cohesion was not going to be our strong suit."

There were many other examples of negotiation. For example, McDowall attempted to "build a broad-based consensus group among individualistic program entrepreneurs through negotiation processes." Rudy Ehrenberg had to negotiate resolutions to conflicts between his unit and the organizations it reviewed, and between investigators and clerical staff. Kastner had to negotiate with the Navy Personnel Support Office to make it easy for engineering students to be paid while they attended school.

Meetings and Phone Calls. While the hero's journey is a solitary venture, other people are involved. From the start of his efforts to bring social service groups together, Clay McDowall "had made it a firm policy that the tasks of consensus management—seeking input, sharing current information, and addressing objections or concerns of members—although exceedingly time consuming, would assume top priority." This led to "near endless telephone calls . . . [and] constant meetings." Anita Boles used similar words to describe how she "sat in endless meetings listening to [people say] . . . what little room they saw for improvement."

Attending to Details. Clay McDowall noted that "attention to detail" was a key to building consensus among social agencies. One difference I noticed between leaders and heroes is that heroes pay attention to details, instead of delegating them to a subordinate. For example, Joe Coffee ran the first four executive development seminars at Treasury by himself. Boles wrote the Victim Assistance unit proposal herself. Larry Geri, as team leader for the APHIS compliance report, "edited my co-workers' submissions, and wrote, then retyped, the report."

Details can be unpleasant. Rudy Ehrenberg described how he "was frustrated with the amount of time and energy I had to spend on administrative details—office layout, furniture disposition, telephones, automation, parking, security, hiring, travel, pay, etc."

Patience. Clay McDowall noted that his efforts to create a coalition of social agencies exerted "demands on my patience." Karen Mendoza also had to move deliberately to ensure that her plans for a summer fair did not conflict with her agency's policy and her desire not to undermine community self-determination. Joe Coffee is the best exemplar of patience in the sample of administrators. He began his efforts to expand executive development to the entire Treasury Department in 1976 and continued until 1983, when the Treasury Executive Institute opened.

Stamina. Being a hero takes much time and effort. For Bill Driver, finding a way to increase pilots' salaries "took a lot of twenty-hour days to fit this project into my regular workload, and sifting through all the research data was extremely time-consuming." Cabell observed that the most difficult part of changing the DSMC curriculum "was building stamina for keeping the consensus" that had been achieved among the school's staff. Geri described how "In order to meet our . . . deadline, I worked 12 hour days . . . rewriting . . . and editing [the report], and then typed a draft of the 50 plus page report into a portable computer. Over the next 1½ days I retyped the report into our agency word processing system [because] . . . our lead secretary was sick."

Faith and Courage

At the threshold of the journey, the hero has to face the risk of failure. The risks never vanish, and during the ordeal there are moments when the risks are especially pronounced. At these times it helps to have faith in the rightness of the vision and to have the courage to act on that belief.

During Gary Misch's negotiations with the Middle Eastern country, the discussion reached an impasse on what Misch believed to be an important issue. Members of his team thought he should give in to the other nation's requests. Misch disagreed. Because the discusssion was going nowhere, Misch "took a calculated risk that we had the stronger position and that [the country] would yield. . . . I broke off discussions and informed [their] representatives that the U.S. government representatives were going home for consultations." His action was unpopular within his team, and he received much personal criticism for taking it. Within a week, however, the other nation accepted the U.S. position.

There are other examples. Cabell, an Air Force general who believed in experimenting with styles of leadership, stood in front of his new command and, in essence, said "OK, what should we do?" Joe Coffee took executives away from their offices for a week of 12-hour days. Boles asked people who were competing for the job she wanted as Chief of the Victim Assistance unit what kind of organization they would like to work in.

The Hero's Friends

I have emphasized the individual nature of the hero's journey. But the hero rarely succeeds without receiving substantial help along the way. Sometimes aid comes from people. At times it comes from the hero's own resources. I identified five allies that were especially significant to the the heroes I studied: the Informed, the Committed, the Positioned, Skills, and Ideals.

The Informed

William Driver needed to prove that pay for civilian pilots "significantly exceeded" the General Schedule of civil service pay. A civilian pilot who was also in the Air Force Reserves suggested that Driver contact the Air Line Pilots Association (ALPA), the civilian pilots' union. Driver met with an ALPA representative who gave him the salary of every major airline pilot in the industry. Analyzing these data, Driver discovered that in 1985 the *average* pilot's salary was over $106,000. Armed with these figures, Driver wrote a proposal to allow the Reserves to offer pilots a base salary of $50,000 with an additional $15–$20,000 in other flight pay. While still short of the $100,000 private industry could offer, the Air Force Reserves "can now give a pilot coming off active duty something to think about."

The Committed

Heroes are helped when they have or can gain the commitment of other people to their vision. Joseph Coffee, Bill Kastner, Clay McDowall, Karen Mendoza, and Anita Boles were all able to find people who could support, nurture, or otherwise protect them. Coffee demonstrated that executive development could improve organizations, and through his actions he gained the trust and commitment of powerful people in Treasury. Kastner and Mendoza convinced their bosses that there was a different way to, in one case, start a school, and in the other case, teach children about health promotion. McDowall, Cabell, and Boles gained the commitment of coworkers to their ideas by involving people in the decision-making process.

Rudy Ehrenberg was faced with an especially difficult problem. His study teams, staffed by civilians, were making recommendations about how military units could function more efficiently. Commanders often came to Ehrenberg asking "for redress from the 'arbitrary judgments of an uninformed civilian.' " To be effective, his Organizational Review Activity needed the full cooperation of the unit being studied. Ehrenberg established an "open decision meeting" near the end of each team's study process to surface objections and allow rebuttals. In addition, he involved the study teams in implementing their recommendations. "We did not want to issue a report and walk out the door." He also developed a policy that the organizations his group analyzed could use 50 percent of the people and money saved as a result of the study. Because of these strategies, most of Ehrenberg's clients eventually "gave us high marks in key areas: validity, credibility, objectivity, and implementability." The Organizational Review Activity soon became known as "Europe's Management Consulting Group."

The Positioned

Sometimes the hero finds help from people who, while not especially committed to the particular quest the hero is on, are in a position to be useful. After the Pentagon approved William Driver's proposal to increase pilots' salaries, it was sent to the Office of Personnel Masnagement for their approval or disapproval. The father of one of the pilots in Driver's reserve unit was a senior official in OPM, and he "assist[ed] us in assuring the package [did] not get lost down there."

Skills

Besides courage and faith, the hero also needs substantive skills to carry out the vision. Ehrenberg needed to understand organizational and management audits. Cabell had to know about Defense program management and education. Boles, Geri, and Driver needed knowledge about, respectively, criminal justice, compliance programs in the Department of Agriculture, and U.S. personnel regulations. They also needed the research, analysis and writing skills to investigate technical issues. Coffee had to have command of organizational and executive development technologies to demonstrate why the Treasury Department should allocate more resources to that function. Mendoza, McDowall, Kastner, and Misch had to be sufficiently persuasive to convince people with contrary viewpoints about the merits of their visions.

Ideals

The hero in public administration sacrifices some part of self for an ideal that is bigger than self. The sacrifice may be time, friendships, reputation, family, career, or on rare occasions, life. Ideals provide support that sustains, during times of stress, the original motivation for taking the journey.

McDowall believed in the time-consuming, inefficient, frustrating, but indispensable ideal of democracy. "Although some members [of the coalition] challenged our management style on efficiency grounds, no one ever challenged the process integrity and dedication to inclusion of [our] group." For Misch, "My prime motivation was one of perhaps patriotism." Boles believed that it was not necessary to accept the guarded and contentious atmosphere in her organization, and that it was possible to create "a healthy and harmonious work environment."

The Hero's Enemies

Heroes also encounter enemies, the people or forces that do not want the journey to succeed. The pathologies of bureaucracy can be the most pervasive enemy. One administrator characterized explicitly what many other heroes referred to: "the wasted human resources (particularly the failure to train or retire employees who fail to adapt to new needs), the petty vendettas on the part of upper and middle management, the manipulations of the 'merit' personnel system." While the enemies work against the hero, they can be countered, and at times used to the hero's advantage. I identified five specific enemies of the heroes I studied: warlords, terrorists, the anxious, the incompetent, and time.

Warlords

Warlords are people whose territory, resources, or other interests are threatened by the hero's actions. When Cabell took command of the Defense Systems Management College, curricula were organized into business, technical, and policy blocks, each the responsibility of three teaching departments. Under this arrangement, the departments "had . . . achieved warlord status," a subject matter power base that would make it difficult to make any significant changes in the curriculum.

Rudy Ehrenberg's first study team concluded that the Armed Forces Recreation Center (AFRC), an organization that managed hotels and recreation facilities for U.S. soldiers, could cut fifty positions and reduce their budget by more than a million dollars. AFRC staff members "could not accept [the] recommendations" and fought to prevent implementation of the team's findings.

When it became apparent that William Driver's pay proposal would be approved by OPM, a senior officer in Air Force headquarters sought "to stop implementation for 'further study,' since no one really thought the proposal would be approved." The officer was angry that the pilots from Driver's unit would "retain the pay [level] no matter where they moved in the agency." Instead of seeing what Driver had accomplished as a model that other reserve units could emulate, the officer emphasized that it would be "a gross inequity that only [Driver's] pilots will receive the much higher salaries." Although the officer was unable to stop the pay proposal, one of Driver's superiors was "denied one promotion as a direct result of our success."

Anita Boles best expressed the challenge warlords present to heroes. "I felt as if I were in the center of a . . . battlefield and [I] somehow had to find the right approach or ingredient to end the battle but keep everyone in the battlefield."

Terrorists

Terrorists try to impede the hero more subtly than warlords. In several cases I studied, coworkers actively tried to sabotage what the hero was doing. In one instance, "two [staff members] tried to disrupt the efforts of others to implement the process. . . . I was surprised and disappointed that [they] were so strongly opposed to the project that they would try to sabotage it." In a second case, the administrator noted that some participants were "behaving in a manner designed only to promote abandonment of the enterprise, and actually made concrete efforts to sabotage the enterprise."

In both the above examples, the hero's allies helped overcome the enemies. In the first case, the saboteurs' "behavior was systematically ignored by those committed to the project; it eventually ceased." In the second case, "the group membership took charge—encouraging their departure, ignoring their interruptions, and forging ahead with agenda items."

Another administrator described how "bureaucrats, and I use that in the worst sense of the word, used passive-aggressive tactics to sabotage what we were trying to do." The people who opposed the administrator's plans "would promise to do whatever I asked of them, but somehow when it came performance time they always had a reason why they 'never quite got around to it.' "

In one case, the terrorists were not metaphorical. Early in the life of Rudy Ehrenberg's organization, there was "a flurry of terrorist attacks in Europe, including one earmarked for our building." The armed soldiers stationed inside and around the building "caused . . . distress to many civilian personnel and a potential morale problem." To keep people informed about the terrorist threat, "we started daily meetings that initially focused on security . . . but soon included organizational issues." After the threat receded, Ehrenberg continued the daily security meetings, "and found them invaluable in keeping people informed and involved" in the substance of the organization's work.

The Anxious

Sometimes the hero has to overcome other people's fears of the new and untested. Joe Coffee introduced the Myers-Briggs Type of indicator to Treasury in 1979. It caused much resistance because "it was new and some people saw it as involving psychological testing." Almost 80 percent of the students at the Defense Systems Management College during Charles Cabell's tenure preferred "structure, answers, and closure." They were suspicious of a curriculum that emphasized "flexibility, possibilities and open-endedness . . . , wondering what 'that kind of stuff has to do with running a [defense] program.' "

The hero may be able to turn fear into an ally. Larry Geri's unit in the Department of Agriculture was responsible for conducting compliance reviews and evaluations. This provided the unit with "an element of fear which works in our favor." People who have "something to hide are frequently a little nervous when we come around."

The Incompetent

There are incompetents in government, as there are in private industry. Incompetents can obstruct the hero's path.

One of the administrators worked on a team with several people senior to him who had neither the ability nor desire to work on the project. The "information they collected [for the project] was gibberish. I had to rewrite [two people's] segments. . . . I knew these 'older and more experienced' analysts . . . wouldn't like my judgement that their work was inadequate, and I would have to deal with their anger eventually." One of the employees quit six months after the project was completed and moved to another agency. The second employee lasted a year before going to a different government job.

Time

Time can be the hero's ultimate enemy. It stands ready to vitiate all that the hero has accomplished.[8] But time also serves other functions in the journey. It sometimes presses the hero to act. Gary Misch had less than four weeks to organize, brief, develop strategy, and complete negotiations with a team of virtual strangers. Larry Geri had less than three months to complete the study design, data collection, and analysis of the veterinary compliance network. Rudy Ehrenberg had to establish credibility quickly for his new organization, in part to minimize Congressional involvement in detailed oversight of the military budget cutting. His first study was completed in ten weeks. Cabell had three years to implement a new curriculum at DSMC, but, as he observed, three years is not a long time in a bureaucracy, and the advocates of the old curriculum "could out wait the new commandant."

Time also can be used to the hero's advantage. Joe Coffee's evolutionary approach to establishing executive development took eight years to unfold. Public organizations are transformed slowly, and with the average political appointee staying little more than a year, it is difficult to get public managers to think in long time frames. Coffee "learned early in my career that bureaucracies do not like long term goals and strategies. They are often perceived as too complex, cost too much and involve too many risks. Thus, everything I do is short term. In other words, I never revealed that the short-term steps were part of long term goals."

Driver started his effort to increase pilots' salaries in November 1986, and OPM approved his final 1,000-page proposal on June 7, 1987. Eight months is a brief time for this type of bureaucratic change to be adopted. The process took place too quickly for effective opposition to develop.

RETURN TO THE KINGDOM

After successfully completing the ordeal, the kingdom and the hero are changed. I observed four consequences of the hero's journey in public administration: the hero received a reward, the hero was changed, the status quo ante was transformed, and in some fashion the world was improved.

The Hero's Rewards

The public administrators in this study received five types of rewards for their efforts: career advancement, money, increased recognition, more work, and satisfaction.

Anita Boles became Chief of the Victim/Witness Assistance program. She and most of the unit's staff received merit awards. McDowall gained the recognition and respect of the political and social services community in Anchorage. William Driver was promoted to a GM-14 and awarded a cash bonus and a certificate of recognition. In the eight-year history of Joe Coffee's organization development work, he received several cash awards from the Treasury Department, promotions, and a Trainer of the Year award from the American Society for Training and Development.

Because of the health fair's success, Karen Mendoza received requests to contribute to projects outside her agency's region, which gave her more experience and more visibility within her agency. Rudy Ehrenberg's success resulted in increased demand for the services of his Organizational Review Activity. Larry Geri received a substantial cash award, a promotion to GM-13, and enhanced status in his organization.

All the administrators mentioned the personal satisfaction they gained. One person expressed it especially well:

I had attained a mastery of the skills needed to perform the assignment . . . I was living up to my potential, and I was about to achieve something important and worthwhile. . . . It is the feeling a baseball player has when that tiny baseball, approaching at 90 miles-an-hour, appears to be the size of a beach ball, and you know you are about to hit a home run. I was 'in the zone.' And I knew . . . following the success of this effort, I would have the chance to . . . benefit from the organization's reward structure, and be able to try to reform it when the opportunity arose.

The Hero's Transformation

The hero's journey changes people. The glamor of money, promotions, and other external rewards eventually fades. The knowledge and lessons learned from the experience remain. The heroes I studied learned about organizations, about people, and about power. But they also learned something about themselves. Their strengths were tested. Their weaknesses and potential for growth were revealed.

Gary Misch's experience negotiating wheat shipments "tested my mettle more than any other that I had encountered until then. It was significant, intense, interesting and frustrating, all at the same time. . . . I learned that I could rise to the requisite leadership demands. . . .''

Kastner learned that he "was able to take concepts from industry and use them in government. . . . [Starting the reserve school] was just another selling job. Power comes to those who pick up the baton.''

Joe Coffee discovered that he "could effectively work with large organizations at the highest level and contribute to their effectiveness. I also learned that to accomplish anything significant, I had to stick to it over a long period of time. And I found I had the tenacity to do that.''

Larry Geri's experience was "a major boost to my self-confidence; it made me feel highly confident as both an analyst and a leader. . . . I realized . . . that . . . I needed to become more extroverted in order to be a more effective . . . leader.''

Rudy Ehrenberg found that creating, developing, and leading a new organization "was similar in many ways to being a parent, in that it involved pride, satisfaction, frustration, humility and joy." Ehrenberg came to the organization "with a dominant Theory X leadership style from twenty plus years of leading soldiers." His journey taught him how to modify his leadership. "I proved to myself that I could effectively lead and manage people while allowing them an active voice in decision making. My previous efforts at collabortion and group participation had been shallow or paternalistic. Increased self confidence and greater respect for my subordinates allowed me to remove barriers that had previously blocked me from changing my style. The result was a relaxed work/ organizational environment, greater cohesion, and a more productive group."

Karen Mendoza came to recognize "more about my personal interests, skills, and needs for additional development. . . . I learned the importance of balancing my concerns for people and the project . . . ; I have some good ideas; I do not always express myself as well as I would like to; I still have work to do in some areas, such as dealing with conflict, but I am creative."

William Driver is "clearly a stronger leader/administrator for the experience. . . . I learned that I could put together a fairly complex proposal encompassing several staff disciplines and sell it all the way through three large organizations." The experience reinforced his belief that "one can use the 'system' if the game is carefully played. . . ." He also "developed a greater appreciation of conflict as a positive force for change. . . . It does not seem that many really significant changes take place in an entrenched bureaucracy without conflict. . . ."

Clay McDowall learned that he had "the ability to see 'the best possible,' in terms of desired outcomes, and to plot and pilot the course . . . to attain the planned ends." He also learned that to be more effective in organizations "I needed to build skills in establishing rapport."

Cabell learned "how powerful my intuition is. I learned to listen to that 'inner bell' from among the noises and crises of conflict and agreement" that told him something was not quite right. Cabell then "temporized until what was bothering me became clear. In all but a few cases that small bell turned out to be ultimately right." Sometimes he dismissed his intuition, and "I later regretted or had to alter my decisions if I ignored it."

The Transformation of the Status Quo

The hero concept is important to public administration not simply because it is a way to describe how individuals can understand their behavior but because it is through the heroic actions of individuals that organizations and society are improved. Because of the work done by the administrators I described, problems were solved; ideas were developed, tested, and disseminated; new systems were created; and the future took shape.

Through William Driver's efforts, the pilot-staffing crisis his unit faced is virtually eliminated. "Since the implementation of the [pay increase, we have] never been more than one pilot under authorized strength, and only one pilot has departed for an airline job since August 1987. . . . We have now attracted a much higher caliber applicant than previously when we were perceived to be an employer of last resort for marginal pilots." His work "has also . . . [created] a demand across the agency for a nationwide special rate for all [reserve] pilots to solve similar problems in other locations."

Mendoza's main success was that "We finally got the message across that effective prevention entails more than drug education." The health fair was conducted again the next summer, and the idea was adopted by minority communities in other regions of the country. "I believe we may have spared . . . [minority] children from the experience of sitting in the same long 'drugs can be dangerous' talk year after year."

In 1984, before the Victim/Witness Assistance program was changed, the unit helped 982 people. In 1985, under the program that Anita Boles developed, 7,865 civilian victims and witnesses were helped.

In Anchorage, McDowall's program "accomplished nearly everything that I hoped it would." Social service agencies agreed on a list of needs they would all lobby for. Alaskans became aware of disability issues. Disabled people became empowered by what they had achieved.

Larry Geri's report provided the APHIS administrator with the data he needed to show that the animal health and welfare compliance system had to be changed. The administrator formed a task force of key stakeholders who recommended program changes that were eventually implemented. A new unit, separate from Veterinary Services, was created to manage the agency's regulatory enforcement programs. Field investigators were retrained in law enforcement techniques and given a computer system that allows them to track cases through the compliance process and to improve the allocation of investigative resources throughout the country.

In the Treasury Department, more than 1,500 executives and managers have gone through the seminars that Coffee organized. Executives became more interested in development for themselves, their subordinates, and their units. Thirteen Treasury bureaus now have executive development programs. Bureaus used some of the seminars to make substantive program changes. The Treasury Executive Institute was established.

The Navy report on the feasibility of a school for reserve engineering officers estimnated that it would take seven years to process 630 officers through the school. During the first thirty months of the school that Kastner initiated, 677 officers graduated. The school's staff of three trained 270 reservists a year. In contrast, the equivalent active duty school trains about 140 officers each year with a staff of eight. The reserve school was so successful that the active duty school asked to take it over. Their request was approved. "The active and reserve community are now closer together. The reserves are no longer considered second class citizens."

The Transformation of the World

The world is rarely transformed by the deed of a single hero. None of the people I have called heroes dramatically changed the world. But they all made a contribution, no matter how small, to making the nation and the world a better place. Ultimately that is the mission of public service.

The individual acts of heroism helped "revitalize the kingdom" in one of two ways: by helping people, or by insuring that public resources were used effectively. The public administrators described in this chapter helped crime victims, minority children, disabled people, pilots, naval officers, livestock ranchers, ship workers, wheat farmers, public executives, and managers. They found ways to use tax money efficiently in defense, the maritime industry, agriculture, social services, and criminal justice.

CONCLUSIONS

In this chapter I have described the hero's journey in public administration. I believe that "hero" is an appropriate metaphor for public administration. I think it can be used to interpret the behavior of administrators whose accomplishments exceed the normal range of experience. It can provide a model for other administrators to emulate.

As discussed earlier, many solutions have been proposed to resolve the dilemmas facing the public sector. People behaving in routine and ordinary ways will be able neither to carry out the ideas that have been suggested, nor to discover new answers. Ultimately, it will take groups of people working together to improve life in the public sector. But heroes are the ones who take the first step.

Joseph Campbell describes two ways to undertake the hero's journey (Campbell, 1949, p. 58). One is the unconscious "animal path," so named because of stories in which the hero follows an animal into the woods and blunders into an adventure. The second path is to go on the journey consciously. It requires making a decision not to wait for other people to create change but to take responsibility for doing it yourself.

At one level, no one can teach anyone else how to be a hero. Each journey is as different and as unpredictable as the dream you will have tonight. But there are signs that can be seen, signals that mark the path others have taken (Table 4.1).

I believe that none of the people I have written about in this chapter would agree with my description of them as heroes. It is for others to name the heroes. It is for individual administrators who care about the future of public service to live the hero's life.

Many public administrators have said no to the call to adventure. Some have not heard it at all. Some have turned back at the threshold of the journey for one of many good reasons. Some have been defeated by the enemies the hero must encounter.

Table 4.1
The Hero's Journey in Public Administration

1. Call to Adventure
   A. Duty
   B. Opportunity
   C. Drive
2. Journey Through a Strange Land
   A. At the Threshold
      1) Credentials
      2) Rules
      3) Politics
      4) Money
      5) History
      6) Failure
   B. The Ordeal
      1) Vision
      2) Planning
      3) Organizing
      4) Implementing
      5) Faith
   C. The Hero's Allies
      1) The Informed
      2) The Committed
      3) The Positioned
      4) Skills
      5) Ideals
   D. The Hero's Enemies
      1) Warlords
      2) Terrorists
      3) The Anxious
      4) The Incompetent
      5) Time
3. Return to the Kingdom
   A. The Hero's Rewards
      1) Promotion
      2) Money
      3) Recognition
      4) More Work
      5) Satisfaction
   B. The Hero's Transformation
      1) Strengths Tested
      2) Weaknesses Revealed
      3) Growth Areas Discovered
   C. Status Quo's Transformation
      1) Problems Solved
      2) Ideas Spread
      3) Systems Created
      4) Future Shaped
   D. World's Transformation
      1) People Helped
      2) Resources Used Effectively

The result, in part, is a public sector where "Crops are not growing. Babies are not being born. Sickness, alienation and despair are rampant."

This chapter described the journey of ten people who did not surrender.

NOTES

1. The word *hero* traditionally has been applied to males, and *heroine* to females. That distinction seems as outmoded as *author* and *authoress*. In the myth of Hero and Leander, Hero is a female.

2. Respondents were asked questions in twelve areas: nature of the situation, opportunities and challenges, goals, tasks, people involved, resources and power, decision making, communication, structure, culture, rituals, and lessons of the experience. The catalyst for some of the questions was J. Kouzes and B. Posner, *The Leadership Challenge,* Jossey-Bass Inc., 1987. Respondents were doctoral and masters degree candidates at the University of Southern California's Washington Public Affairs Center and Sacramento Public Affairs Center.

3. Throughout *The Hero with a Thousand Faces,* Campbell emphasizes the esoteric character of the hero's journey. While acknowledging that primary feature, in this chapter I am emphasizing the exoteric nature of the journey. See also P. L. Travers, "The World of the Hero," and E. Edinger, "The Tragic Hero: An Image of Individuation," both in *Parabola,* Volume 1, Winter 1976.

4. While all the questionnaire responses described elements of the hero's journey, I selected the ten that provide the clearest illustration of all the stages of the journey. Written responses, averaging thirty pages per respondent, were supplemented with personal interviews when needed for clarification. Each of the ten administrators were provided a copy of this analysis to insure accuracy and to protect confidences. The names of some organizations have been changed at the request of respondents. In addition, all these stories are told from the point of view of the hero. The stories might be different if told from another actor's perspective, in the same way the story of Prometheus would be changed if told by Jupiter.

5. "Karen Mendoza" is a pseudonym for a woman who asked that her name and agency remain anonymous.

6. Quotes are from either questionnaire responses or interviews with the named individual.

7. McDowall's efforts were in the not-for-profit sector. Although not discussed here, there were other "heroes" who played a part in the Anchorage example.

8. In three of the cases described in this paper, the hero's accomplishments were undone after the hero left the agency.

PART II

OTHER PEOPLE AND PUBLIC ORGANIZATIONS

Understanding how public organizations work means understanding other people and what happens to them when they try to work together. Each person in an organization has a particular view of the world and, in some sense, exists in a unique reality. The effect is magnified when groups of people interact.

Conflict is the central theme of the next three chapters, since that is frequently what happens when people interact over issues they care about. Two of the authors describe how conflict can be used constructively. A third author writes about the dark side of conflict.

Richard C. Sonnichsen, the author of chapter 5, is the Deputy Assistant Director, Inspection Division, of the Federal Bureau of Investigation. He is in charge of the FBI's Office of Planning Evaluation and Audits. Sonnichsen writes that the same problems routinely appear in organizations because there is no mechanism to address their root causes. He suggests that evaluation can help examine root causes, and in the process stimulate organizational learning.

The difficulty, however, lies with people. Evaluation, in spite of the promise it offers organizations, is a judgmental process. Few people enjoy being judged by others. Evaluation may offer learning, but for many people it triggers conflict.

Sonnichsen presents a model of the evaluation environment, focusing on the relationship between the evaluators and the people and programs being evaluated. He describes four generic relationships that he has seen during evaluations and suggests what can be done to increase the likelihood that conflict will be beneficial to the organization and to its members.

Sonnichsen is a doctoral candidate in public administration. He has been a Special Agent of the FBI for twenty-five years, and has held management positions for the past sixteen years.

In chapter 6, Paul B. Lorentzen writes about working with evil people. Organizational evil is a concept that does not appear frequently in organization literature. According to Lorentzen, people have become increasingly willing to acknowledge that evil exists.

The author describes his first contact with organizational evil and the spirit-killing pain that it caused. His efforts to understand the phenomenon took him to the literature on organizational and individual pathologies, where he encountered the idea of narcissism.

Lorentzen argues that at least some evil behavior in organizations is similar to the behavior of people who are malignantly narcissistic. In his chapter, he discusses how to distinguish between evil management and poor or inexperienced management. He also describes how the federal government's political employment process may encourage evil. He concludes the chapter with three ways to deal with organizational evil, and a discussion of two tactics that will probably not work: love and whistleblowing.

Lorentzen has been a public administrator in the federal government for thirty-two years. During his career he progressed from a management intern in the Civil Service Commission through various positions in the Deparments of Commerce and the Interior. He is the past president of the Federal Executive Institute Alumni Association. He earned his public administration doctorate in 1984.

Frank D. Ferris is the Director of Negotiations for the National Treasury Employees Union. In chapter 7 he describes experimental efforts to resolve employee-management conflicts outside the legal framework of the Civil Service Reform Act (CSRA). The experiments were based on the ideas of Mary Parker Follet, an organizational theorist who wrote early in the twentieth century.

Ferris first reviews Follett's thoughts about conflict and contrasts them with the conflict management mechanisms established by the CSRA. The author then demonstrates how Follett's interest bargaining technique helped the Internal Revenue Service and the National Treasury Employees Union to resolve two intractable issues: the productivity and pay of 10,000 data transcribers, and the IRS's quality improvement process. Ferris ends his chapter with some ideas about extending Follett's ideas, and suggestions about how the Federal Labor Relations Authority could make conflict an asset instead of a liability in public-sector labor relations.

Ferris has been a public administrator for eighteen years, in positions with the union, the Internal Revenue Service and the University of Missouri. He is currently completing his doctorate in public administration.

5

Organizational Learning and the Environment of Evaluation

Richard C. Sonnichsen

The central theme of this chapter is that evaluation can be a powerful method for producing information and an effective tool to facilitate organizational learning. However, to achieve this optimum condition for the utilization of evaluation, one needs a thorough understanding of the complex social dynamics that take place between evaluators, line program managers, and top management officials. This chapter will examine the organizational environment in which evaluation takes place and will present a model that depicts the dynamics between the evaluator and the program manager. The purpose is to identify and explicate the behavioral factors that affect the outcomes of the evaluation process, and the capacity of an organization to learn from evaluation activities.

The data and observations in this chapter are based on the accumulated experiences of the author and the Federal Bureau of Investigation's evaluation staff over a twelve-year period. Besides information collected from the FBI's internal evaluations of investigative and administrative operations, data were also gathered from participation in many seminars on public sector evaluation.

ORGANIZATIONAL PROBLEMS AND ORGANIZATIONAL LEARNING

One endemic frustration for career public administrators is the seemingly endless number of meetings called to address recurring problems that defy solution. Many daily crises faced by government decision makers are replicas of predicaments thought to have been previously addressed. Regular participants at these assemblies experience "déjà vu" as the same problems present themselves with monotonous regularity.

Personnel turnover and subtle variations in problems and crises contribute to the repetitious nature of organizational problem solving. However, there is a more significant and generally unrecognized reason for recurring problems.

Organizations are often ineffective at identifying the root causes of persistent problems. As Lindblom observed three decades ago, when confronted with a problem, decision makers limit themseleves to tinkering at the margins or with symptoms (1959). This superficial approach to organizational problem solving ensures problems will recur, since the root cause has been neither identified nor addressed.

Stated differently, organizations are not good learners. Argyris (1982) eloquently argues that organizations have great difficulty in learning, and they seldom question the underlying basis of problems. Organizations have been routinely depicted as resisting change, lacking innovation, stressing conformity over creativity, and needing to develop more adaptive problem-solving structures (Thompson, 1969; Bennis, 1971).

Organizations need to acquire knowledge before they can learn, develop, and grow (Dery, 1986). However, since organizations are incapable of acquiring and digesting all available knowledge, they selectively use the information that is available and disregard the rest. Organizational knowledge gathering depends on its capacity for learning, and for rigorously and routinely examining what the organization does and how it does it. Through self-inspection and reflection, organizations can discover and correct deficiencies, adjust activities, and ensure effective and efficient goal attainment.

Argyris (1982) defines organizational learning as a "process of detecting and correcting error." He differentiates learning in organizations as single or double loop. Single-loop learning occurs when organizations achieve their objectives through uncovering and correcting routine errors. Double-loop learning occurs when the underlying policies, norms, and objectives of the organization are questioned. Organizations can increase their capacity for effective problem solving by striving to migrate from single- to double-loop learning.

Double-loop learning is difficult for organizations since it demands that they function in a continuously questioning mode, tolerating contesting views of operations. If implemented, this process would approach the "self-evaluating" organization of Wildavsky (1979).

Whether single- or double-loop, organizational learning is not an easy task. Learning is usually not a conscious activity, but an ad hoc endeavor used when there is a problem to be solved. The residue of this ad hoc adventure is an unsystematic buildup of rules, operational procedures, traditions, and culture that hampers future decision making.

The learning process, whether applied to public policy or internal organizational issues, involves many entities within an organization, each with differing information, biases, and objectives. A parochial perspective often dominates these viewpoints, reflecting both personal and organizational agendas. It has been my experience that a more effective approach to acquiring knowledge for rational and informed decision making is the formal use of evaluations.

THE PROMISE OF EVALUATION

Evaluation is a management technique that can help organizations learn by examining and questioning organizational activities and goals, and by surfacing alternative viewpoints of agency activities to spark reflection and debate among decision makers. Evaluation can provide the self-correcting mechanism that organizations need to pilot along a desired path. Evaluation also can help an organizational detect and solve problems, survive in hostile and competitive environments, improve performance, and grow and develop.

Organizational learning can be enhanced in environments where evaluation is an accepted concept, where evaluations are conducted in a cooperative atmosphere, and where the results are considered seriously by both program personnel and top management. To operate optimally as a stimulus to learning, the evaluation process must be accepted as an integral, organic part of the organization's administrative operations, and the evaluators must function as facilitators.

For purposes of this chapter, internal evaluators are defined as a permanent staff working within an organization, and program managers are the people who have operational responsibility for the program being evaluated. Before presenting the model that illustrates the behavioral dynamics of evaluation, I will first summarize the purpose and function of the evaluation process, particularly as it pertains to internal organizational settings. This discussion will establish the context that influences the relationships between internal evaluators and program managers in organizations.

INTERNAL EVALUATION IN ORGANIZATIONS

Evaluation's primary value to an organization is in its approach to program review. Stripped of its jargon and fixation with methodological subtleties, evaluation is concerned with the production of useful information about how programs work, and about how effective they are in alleviating the problems they were designed to cure. However, the knowledge about program effectiveness generated through the evaluation process is rarely unequivocal. When properly carried out, evaluation presents alternative views of what affects the target program's performance. Each alternative view described will be subjected to examination and interpretation by each stakeholder, who will draw diverse conclusions.

Evaluators seldom uncover unknown problems or solutions so novel and illuminating that program personnel are surprised (Sonnichsen, 1988). Evaluators do, however, bring fresh insight and new perspectives to problems, and they can redirect attention from routine daily rituals to important program issues. The challenge of evaluation is to identify the germane issues in a program and to elevate them to an appropriate level in the organization, where they will be subjected to critical scrutiny. The visibility thus afforded programmatic issues ensures a proper forum for debate. Illuminating program issues helps to prevent stagnation and the myopia that can affect the viewpoint of personnel charged with the day-to-day administration of a program.

When viewed as a mechanism for furnishing alternatives to problems, evaluation is consistent with the advocacy by Paul Feyerabend (1975) of theoretical and methodological anarchism, meaning that all approaches to gathering knowledge can produce useful insight and understanding. Even candid, off-the-record remarks by persons inside or outside the program can contribute to the creation of various program alternatives that will provide the basis for change and improvement.

Soliciting and scrutinizing divergent viewpoints during an evaluation allow the decision maker the luxury of examining more than one alternative as the solution to a problem. By striving to identify and analyze the pertinent options available to program operators, evaluators will cultivate differences of opinion, thus ensuring the reasonable alternatives are developed for review. A satisficing (Simon, 1947) approach to evaluation only precludes the discovery of optimum program alternatives.

The ultimate goals of an evaluation are to have organizational stakeholders react to and use the findings. To accomplish these aims, evaluation must be viewed by those it serves and those whose programs are reviewed as an essential element in the administrative and operational mechanisms of the organization. To the useful and effective the evaluator must objectively solicit and analyze data about programs, draw inferences, and suggest alternatives when deficiencies are discovered.

Often the failure of evaluation to be productive stems from the detachment of the evaluation staff from the mainstream of organizational life. The evaluator's environment is coterminous with the organization's. To practice internal evaluation successfully, evaluators need a thorough knowledge and understanding of the organization's rubrics, culture, decision-making process, important actors, and political structure.

To enhance their potential for success, evaluators can position themselves as the links between program managers and top organizational management. This process is a people process: evaluators interacting with organization employees to determine operating efficiency and effectiveness. To be effective in the "people dimensions" of evaluation, evaluators have to understand the behavioral characteristics of individuals and the role of group dynamics. Evaluation is also a judgmental process. Success depends largely on the evaluator's ability to overcome the natural resistance of program personnel. So a significant part of the evaluator's job is to persuade program managers of the potential benefits of adopting one or more of the alternatives surfaced by the evaluation process.

RESISTANCE TO EVALUATION

Evaluation is neither mundane nor mystical, evaluators neither nescient nor omniscient. Evaluation is simply a management tool for detecting and correcting errors and deficiencies and for suggesting alternative approaches to administration and operation. However, not everyone views evaluation in this light. While evaluation is gaining acceptance as a valuable diagnostic management technique for judging performance, the acceptance is not universal. There are many impediments that limit the recognition of evaluation as a factor in the administration of an organization.

Wildavsky (1979), for example, suggests that evaluation and organization may be contradictory activities. The typical organization connotes stability. Evaluation, even when operating under ideal conditions, introduces uncertainty and promotes a measure of instability into the routine activities of a program. Evaluation implies change, and change in organizations generally encounters resistance (Katz & Kahn, 1966).

Two conditions exist in most evaluation settings (Sonnichsen, 1988): (1) No program is perfect and functioning at an optimal level; an evaluator will always develop suggestions to improve it. (2) An externally (outside the program) suggested improvement is interpreted as an implicit deficiency in the program and resisted by program personnel.

These conditions have the potential to polarize evaluation participants and generate dysfunctional conflict between evaluators and program personnel. Indeed, the relationship between evaluators and the program managers is often stormy.

There is a tendency by both evaluators and program managers to view evaluation as a sporting event with winners and losers. Evaluators and managers usually reside in different parts of the organization and are separated by the line-staff dichotomy. They have traditionally dealt with each other in cautious terms, each suspecting the other of less than honorable motives. Governed by different ideas about how to further organizational goals, their relationship can run the gamut from hostility to cooperation, and all gradations between. Effective evaluators recognize and counter the potential impediments.

That is easier said than done. Designing and conducting a successful evaluation is frequently treated as a methodological issue. It is seldom appreciated, however, that a successful evaluation depends significantly on the interpersonal skills of the individual evaluator(s). An evaluator's ability to influence and persuade are not quantitative skills but behavioral aptitudes used during encounters with actors, clients, and stakeholders in the evaluation setting. The interaction of the evaluation staff with other organizational entities during the evaluation procedure is a complex social arrangement dependent on internal and exogenous factors. One significant factor is the relationship between the evaluator and the line manager responsible for the program being evaluated.

EVALUATION AS VIEWED BY PROGRAM MANAGERS

The paradox of evaluation is that while it is designed to contribute to organizational learning, it may still cause angst among those it serves, creating conditions unsuitable for organizational growth and development. One reminder of the paradox occurred at a meeting of the University of Southern California's Washington Public Affairs Center long-running evaluation seminar. To better understand the viewpoint of the program manager and to bridge the gap between evaluators and program managers, distinguished public sector managers were invited to discuss their observations on the practice of evaluation (Sonnichsen, 1989). It became immediately apparent that program managers resented evaluators. Program managers traditionally resist evaluation because of perceptions about the purpose of evaluation, disagreements about the way the evaluation is conducted, and because of the way evaluation findings are used and misused. The program managers at the USC seminar echoed these critiques. They confirmed vociferously what most evaluators have experienced; namely, that managers are antagonistic toward evaluation because they believe that it is of little benefit and that it has the potential to harm their careers and alter their programs.

The program managers also viewed evaluators as having greater access to agency executives, and on many federal organizational charts the evaluators are located above the program managers in the hierarchy. They saw evaluation as something imposed on them by forces external to their programs, conducted by evaluators who were not accountable for agency productivity, and used in a judgmental fashion to gauge program performance. In addition, the resources needed to respond to inquiries during the evaluation process and the occasional use of program monies to fund the evaluation tended to breed an animosity between the evaluator and the program manager that hindered a productive evaluation effort. Thus the purpose and use of evaluation may be deemed oppressive no matter how benevolent the actions of the evaluators.

Viewed through the lens of the program manager, evaluation is threatening. Line managers are required to furnish program data to evaluators that may then be used to demonstrate to agency executives and congressional funding bodies that the program is not functioning at an optimal level. Managers at the USC seminar, like managers throughout the government, wanted increased input into the data collection effort, and a voice in its eventual use in judging performance.

A common lament was that easily obtained data tended to obscure a program's real impact and performance, and that numbers generated by evaluation tend to measure program outputs, not results. Program managers were particularly concerned about the superficial analysis of numbers to describe programs and the subsequent use of the numbers by political administrators to advance administration policy, whether or not the program was having the intended effect. When agency executives and congressional committees concentrate exclusively on numbers, it prevents a more in-depth examination of a program's impact and may have the unintended consequence of misdirecting the program.

The difficulty in measuring the impact of government social programs contributes to this problem. Lacking impact data, Congress and the administration tend to focus on easily obtainable numbers. Once started, the routine publication of data of this type is difficult to stop, particularly if an annual incremental increase in the program numbers can be used to show that a political policy is working.

HOW CONFLICT CAN LEAD TO LEARNING

Organizations are social entities created by individuals, and they are the product of the thoughts and actions of these individuals (Sims & Gioia, 1986). Evaluation in an organizational environment is a reflexive encounter between the evaluator and the program manager that usually precipitates conflict. This dialectic has the potential to be destructive. But if it is managed correctly, it can contribute to productive outcomes.

Conflict can serve as the foundation for bridging the difference between evaluators and program managers, resulting in successful evaluations that contribute to organization learning. Opposing views can be reconciled and generate increased reflection by both parties, leading to greater insights into the benefits and dysfunctions of a program. A reduction in anxiety levels between participants in this process must be a part of the evaluation calculus.

The burden for transforming this encounter into a productive expression of collaboration, however, rests with the evaluator, the initiator of the evaluation process. Evaluators can gain the trust and respect of program managers both by demonstrating the benefits of the evaluation process and through actions that show how the manager's perceived risks can be offset by gains in program performance. Mutual recognition of the positive and negative effects of the evaluative process is a major step toward increased utilization of evaluation and its ability to contribute to organizational learning. To aid in that recognition, I have developed a model of the evaluation environment.

THE ENVIRONMENT OF EVALUATION: A MODEL

The interaction between the evaluator and the program manager can be represented at the extremes by two polarizing attitudes: cooperation and conflict. The model depicted in Figure 5.1 represents a set of behavioral conditions experienced by the author and by FBI evaluators during internal evaluations. The model describes four different environmental modes that evaluators must often experience. These conditions are partially under the control of the evaluators but interdependent with and affected by the reactions of the program manager.

The continuum from conflict to cooperation represents the mind-set of either the program manager or the evaluator. It is fluid and many change during the course of the evaluation. At the inception of the evaluation, evaluators can position themselves at any point on the continuum and adjust their attitude according to the reaction of the program manager. Using this mode, the relationship between evaluator and program manager can be characterized by one of four ways: confrontational, contentious, coercive, or collaborative.

One assumption of this model is that the evaluation was requested or commissioned by someone other than the program manager. In other words the program manager is not the primary client. In fact, this is commonly the situation in organizations with internal evaluation staffs. Evaluations, under these conditions, are

Figure 5.1
Description of Evaluation Environment

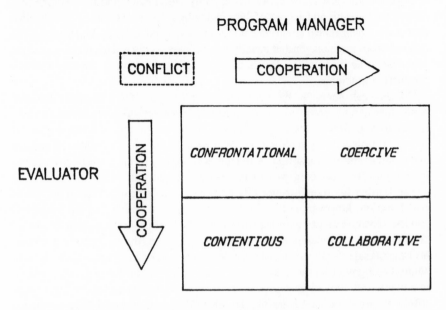

usually conducted on a periodic basis or specifically requested by top management. This method of initiating evaluation activities thrusts evaluators into a potential conflict with program managers. The manager did not request the evaluation, it is probably unwanted, and it is potentially disruptive.

The attitudes displayed by the evaluator and the program manager are subject to fluctuation and continuous adjustment and may sometimes touch all four modes during an evaluation. A program manager, reacting to recommendations, may move the evaluation environment from a collaborative mode to a confrontational mode. Likewise an evaluator acting cooperatively, may, when confronted by resistance to suggestions, became confrontational.

Starting points in the matrix can be affected by many externalities. The source for the request of the evaluation can be instrumental in determining the program manager's initial behavior. An impact evaluation requested by an agency head has far more threatening implications for a program manager than a routine cyclical evaluation precipitated by the evaluation office. The type and degree of influence exhibited by the evaluator and the program manager are pivotal to the determination of the behavioral context for evaluation. The outcome of the evaluation can hinge on the reciprocal influence processes between the evaluator and the program manager.

The four quadrants in the model describe the potential evaluation environment created by the attitudes, interests, and personalities of the evaluator and program manager. The details of these four conditions follow.

Confrontation

Confrontation is a common reaction to evaluation and one of the more significant obstacles the evaluators must overcome. The confrontational condition occurs primarily when the program manager feels threatened and refuses to cooperate with the evaluation team, and they react in kind. Access to program personnel becomes difficult and data collection may be impeded. The uncertainty produced by evaluation will trigger defensiveness in program personnel who view the evaluation process as intrusive. They expect little benefit to accrue to them, and a much greater potential for negative consequences.

Evaluators, on the other hand, can become confrontational out of frustration. When other postures prove fruitless, evaluators may deliberately become confrontational while trying to facilitate change.

Conflict encountered during an evaluation can vary from mild disagreement to open hostility. It may be initiated by either party and become manifest in oral debate, combative memoranda, or resistance to peaceful overtures. Conflict exhibited by the program manager that has not been resolved by the end of the evaluation often resurfaces during implementation of recommendations. Bureaucratic inertia and other resistance strategies are available to the program manager not interested in comforming to suggested recommendations by evaluators.

Effective communications are pivotal to evaluation, and any condition that interferes with the flow of information may precipitate confrontation among the participants. For example, a significant difference in power between evaluators and program managers will drastically affect the flow of information among the parties. If the evaluation office is perceived as a power broker in the organization, wielding influence among decision makers, it may become necessary for the evaluators to attempt consciously to reduce the perceived threat that evaluation and change fosters.

Coercion

The potential for coercion is present when the evaluator exhibits a preconceived bias toward a program. Bias may occur when the evaluator is familiar with the program's activities. It may also happen if the evaluator perceives that changes in the program will be accepted politically in the organization and will enhance the evaluator's image or career.

A coercive relationahip may also result if a program manager surrenders to an aggressive evaluator. A compliant program manager who is either unwilling or unable to defend program operations can become the victim of unscrupulous evaluators. Such evaluators may be operating with preconceived bias and may be conducting the evaluation based on their agenda, or the agenda of a superior.

Of the four conditions described in the evaluation setting, this latter is the one I have encountered the least. Program managers are seldom submissive individuals; most often they are vigorous defenders of their operations. When coercion is encountered, it is usually at the start of the evaluation, when the evaluator has a hidden agenda and the program manager has not detected the underlying direction and intent of the evaluation. The coercive condition will generally evolve into a confrontational mode when the actions of the evaluator become more clearly defined.

Contention

Evaluators find contentious environments to be a ubiquitous condition. Anything else would be unnatural. Few program managers welcome an evaluation of their operations by outsiders and fewer still anticipate that such an evaluation will be beneficial.

A contentious environment develops when program managers are opposed to the evaluation and resist any review of their program, even when cooperative evaluators are encountered. Managers may sense a threat to the stability of their operations and resist the efforts of the evaluator. Since program managers are normally upwardly mobile and concerned about their careers, they can perceive evaluations as critical of their management capabilities, thus placing their careers in jeopardy. Because it is nearly impossible to construct a rigid delineation between a program and a program manager, a criticism of the program is a de facto criticism of the manager.

Collaboration

Cooperation is encountered when a program manager, interested in having a program reviewed by a conscientious and skilled evaluator, works with the evaluator in a joint effort to review program performance. The essential ingredient for this condition is evaluators who are both objective in their pursuit of information about the program and empathetic toward the managers and the conditions under which they operate. The pursuit of a collaborative evaluation environment is a mutual endeavor. Both parties must expend some effort to reach this goal. A collaborative effort requires compromise and an ability to listen to and objectively consider the other person's viewpoint.

Cooperation is antipodal to conflict. In the ideal case, both participants see that the evaluation activity can improve efficiency or effectiveness. The ideal is, however, seldom the case. In my experience, cooperation is exhibited more by the evaluator than the program manager. The evaluator has more to gain during a collaborative evaluation, whereas the manager usually senses little benefit and some potential losses.

A collaborative evaluation environment allows the evaluation process to have its greatest impact. When evaluation is undertaken collaboratively, it can lead to the double-loop learning that is characteristic of effective organizations.

HOW TO USE THE EVALUATION ENVIRONMENT MODEL

The Evaluation Environment model (Figure 5.1) has heuristic value for the evaluator. The two dimensions representing the mental approaches, or attitudes, of the evaluator and the program manager should be viewed as a continuum. The position of either party at any given time is affected by many political, social, and behavioral factors. But it depends significantly on the response of the other participant. The underlying assumption driving a collaborative approach to evaluation is that two persons or groups of persons, recognizing that endemic hostility and conflict are destructive conditions, can act cooperatively and accomplish constructive ends.

Evaluations can be more successful and productive if evaluators recognize not only their behavioral characteristics but also the traits of other stakeholders in the evaluation. By adjusting their behaviors, evaluators can observe the effect on the program manager (and vice versa) and determine whether the adjustment has had the desired effect in reducing hostility, overcoming differences, or approaching compromise on issues. The recognition that movement along the two dimensions of the model may precipitate a corresponding reaction by the other participant can increase understanding of the complex interrelationship between the evaluator and the program manager.

Seldom does an evaluation begin and end in the same behavioral mode. More commonly it flows from one quadrant to another, affected by all the variables common to the evaluation environment. Restraint should be exercised in attaching values or a hierarchical ordering to the four environmental conditions depicted in the Evaluation Environment model. Each of the four conditions has the potential to lead to productive organizational learning experiences.

Although the working environment is more pleasant for both parties in a collaborative venture, the necessary ingredients for this condition are not always present. Sometimes, a confrontational posture may be the most productive approach to initiate needed change. It should be noted also that while the greatest amount of conflict occurs in the confrontational mode, some conflict is present in all four modes. Conflict is an intrinsic characteristic of human nature. Properly managed it can contribute to organizational growth and constructive change.

The model can be used as more than a template for determining and examining behavioral conditions during an evaluation. It can be the basis for altering the behavior of one of the actors in the encounter through a reciprocal learning process. The evaluator might encourage the program manager (or vice versa) to use the model as a basis for explaining their behavior. When this occurs, as Paul Waldo describes in another chapter, the stage for reflection, deliberation, and organizational learning is set.

CONCLUSION

Complicated organizational issues require unbiased, unemotional, and factual data before they can be adequately understood. An evaluation staff can collect, analyze, and present this information in forums to assist in the organizational learning process. One prerequisite for a learning experience is a collaborative evaluation environment. Evaluators working under these conditions, in an organization with an evaluation ethic and a sincere desire to examine and solve recurring complex issues, can facilitate the organization learning process through the conduct of cooperative evaluations with the program managers.

The Evaluation Environment model presented here does not completely describe the immense variety of relationships among evaluators and program managers. The model is designed to capture the more significant features of the encounters I have experienced over twelve years. Most of the input for the model comes from activities of an internal evaluation staff of one federal agency. However, the reactions of colleagues from other evaluation staffs and program managers, and the ubiquitous lament in the literature about the utilization of evaluation results, suggest the dynamics described in the model may be responsible for the nonuse of many evaluation reports. Intuitively the model appears to have applicability to organizational stiuations other than evaluation.

The Evaluation Environment model can raise the awareness of evaluation participants to potentially inhibiting behavioral factors. The behaviors described in this chapter are not unlike the reactions exhibited by any people or group engaged in activities or discussions where there are opposing viewpoints. The model does not identify new human emotions or reinterpret the literature on behavior of individuals in organizations. What the model does do is explicate the conditions encountered in evaluation settings. It is my hope that increased cognizance of the interpersonal dynamics among evaluation actors will contribute to a better understanding of their viewpoints and their attitudes, and speed progress toward more successful evaluations. Cooperative and constructive evaluations can enhance the organization by acting as a self-reflective mechanism, probing core organizational problems and issues, and contributing to the goal of organization learning.

6

Organizational Evil:
Concepts and Practices

Paul B. Lorentzen

Evil, as a concept and a practice, is largely ignored in theories of public organization and administration. A search of standard public administration textbooks did not find the term *evil* in any index (Fesler, 1980; Sharkansky, 1982; Vocino & Rabin, 1981; Gortner, Mahler, & Nicholson, 1987). This chapter proposes a step toward filling this void by:

1. Adapting to public organizations the psychological concept of "evil-in-practice."
2. Discussing the factors affecting the incidence of evil-in-practice in public organizations.
3. Providing guidelines for public administrators to help them identify and contend with evil-in-practice when it is encountered.

While I believe that the phenomenon discussed herein is prevalent throughout public organizations, my experience has been limited to the federal government. Therefore the illustrations used in this chapter to explain the concept of evil are drawn from the federal sector.

The objective of this chapter, then, is to discuss the nature and characteristics of one type of behavior in public organizations that may be termed evil. I make no attempt to catalogue other possible manifestations of evil, although there is a wider range of pathologies that affect organizations and their members that usefully can be assessed through the analytical lens of "evil." But because the effects on organizational members who must live and deal with the particular personality type who displays the evil-in-practice behavior are so traumatic, I expect the limited focus of this chapter to nonetheless have practical value.

A PERSONAL EXPERIENCE

Toward the end of the 1970s, after working in the federal government for more than twenty years, I found myself reporting for the first time to a presidential political appointee. Up until this point I had reported to civil service career public managers. The appointive position was a new one, established after several years' controversy regarding its desirability. The appointee's job was to give direction and increased visibility to the mission and programs of an old agency. The agency had been characterized by great programmatic complexity and a history of managerial ineffectiveness. As is common of many political appointees in the federal government (National Academy of Public Administration, 1985, pp. 7–8, 1988, pp. 17–23; Volker, 1989, pp. 17–19), the person selected as the first incumbent of the new position met the political criteria for selection but possessed little experience in managing organizations in either the public or the private sectors.   My job was to lead an effort to improve administrative (especially human resources) management in the organization. I worked directly for the agency head, the new appointee. My previous experience working for senior administrators led me to recognize the value of mutual candor in communications, open discussion of options, and professional objectivity in designing improvements. But within a few weeks it became evident that my normal way of operating and communicating with the agency head was neither productive nor desired.

Other officials in the agency also recognized that a different set of behavioral norms was now in force at staff meetings and in other contacts with the agency head. Any statement that one made to the appointee was judged according to whether he considered it helpful or harmful to his position and status, not whether it was factual or useful to managerial problem solving. The agency head criticized and denounced people who called his attention to controversial issues and problems, instead of discussing and analyzing the situation to find ways to meet the difficulties. Gaining access to the appointee was based on being a member of a small corps of special aides. One could join the corps not by supporting agency programs and objectives but by offering flattery to the appointee or gossip about those he considered his enemies. He did not acknowledge the value of different opinions. Saying anything that possibly could be construed by the agency head as suggesting the need for a modification or rethinking of his views resulted in prompt ostracism or dismissal.

I was unprepared for the aura of secrecy and subjectivity that pervaded the royal court of the new agency head. To remain on his staff, one needed to accept his self-image (which seemed close to one of perfection), and to be willing to become a sycophant. The agency head's behavior deprived other officials in the organization of the opportunity to exercise autonomy, contribute originality, or participate in the process of trying to improve the agency's programs and its management. To be successful in that agency, one had to become an automaton serving the appointee's personal agenda: self-aggrandizement and increased political status.

The arrival of the new appointee meant that the agency officials who had to deal with him either adopted the behavior of what Lind and Marshall (1987, p. 62) call a "courtier," or they found themselves among those he consider his enemies.[1] Many people did conform to the subservient role, either because of tendencies toward sycophancy or because they too were motivated to increase their status by playing the current political game. Other staff members, motivated primarily by the desire to improve management excellence in agency operations, were unable to make the required behavioral shift and constituted the "enemy" ranks.

Based on my experience as one of the "enemies," and on conversations with many of the other officials similarly labeled, it was clear to me that the agency head's behavior and style had the effect of making us (1) feel isolated in our own work environment, (2) constantly defend to ourselves our orientation toward management, (3) continually be tempted to violate our personal values by using deceit and manipulation to try to accomplish agency objectives, (4) doubt our self-worth, (5) feel that our sense of self-respect was always being assailed, and (6) feel a deepening sense of depression about the evident ineffectiveness of our daily activities.

In summary, my encounter with the political appointee's behavior destroyed the essential elements for personal and professional health and effectiveness: self-respect, independent thinking, valued work contributions, and the opportunity to develop. The impact was killing to the spirit.

During the twelve years since this "spirit-killing" experience, I have reflected often on what causes some individuals to behave the way the agency head just described did. When I presented the ideas in this chapter to some colleagues—all current or former federal government officials—I found them nodding vigorously in recognition. "I know that person," one of them declared. The reaction was not a surprise to me, as I have met many federal managers in the last ten years who found themselves working in a similar environment and who were contending with the same spirit-killing effects.

Until recently, my inclination was to ascribe all conduct like the appointee's to "poor management," by which I meant untrained or inexperienced individuals placed in managerial positions, who are too insecure, immature, or fearful to seek and to listen to advice from those who have more experience. Sometimes the individuals eventually are able to profit from time on the job. They learn how to motivate and use their staff for their own and for the organization's benefit by creating trust, encouraging candor, using participative problem solving, and by developing feelings of involvement. Other people never change.

Now, however, I believe that there is another possible explanation for the spirit-killing conduct. Instead of poor management, we may be dealing with the presence of evil. More specifically, behavior similar to the agency head's can be understood as something that I term "organizational evil-in-practice."

NAMING ORGANIZATIONAL PATHOLOGIES

Many theories and studies have been advanced in an effort to explain the pathological characteristics of modern organizations. One recent contribution uses the concept of addiction to explain many of the behaviors described above.

Schaef & Fassel (1988) contend that organizations frequently function in the same way as an addict. They exhibit the same traits that individual addicts show, such as denial about what is happening, dishonesty, confused thinking, turning all issues into arguments for or against the self, perfectionism, control, frozen feelings, and ethical deterioration.

Another organizational analysis describes five types of neurotic behaviors in top executives: dramatic, depressive, paranoid, compulsive, and schizoid (deVries & Miller, 1984). The character and climate of unhealthy organizations are said to be the result of the influence of leaders' deep-seated neuroses. In essence, the entire organization takes on the personality of the executive.

While society readily accepts the existence of addictive and neurotic behavior, there is less agreement in the secular world about the substantive nature of evil. Often, evil is considered to be a metaphor or myth, a name given to the negation of goodness (Keen, 1988, p. 45). However, the term is beginning to appear more frequently in the popular press in connection with notorious criminal acts and trials. George F. Will wrote about the boys who beat and raped a jogger in Central Park that ". . . the attackers did what they did because they are evil" (1989, p. C7). Amy Schwartz, commenting on the same event, said that ". . . if we can't fathom an act of evil, most of us know it when we see it" (1989, p. A19). Arthur Brodsky, writing about Richard Nixon and Watergate, encouraged people to "Listen to the Watergate tapes . . . and hear the voices of evil as the country is betrayed. Evil isn't a partisan concept, an issue of Republican or Democrat. Evil is an absolute" (1989, p. B5). Concerning the Joel B. Steinberg trial, Richard Cohen wrote of the man accused of killing his foster child that "A Joel Steinberg who once would have been called evil is called a narcissist . . . these terms serve simply to dress up evil, to give it a more contemporary look" (1989, p. 9).

THE CONCEPT OF EVIL-IN-PRACTICE

In psychoanalytic theory, narcissism is a stage of human development characterized by extreme concern for self and a lack of concern for others. Narcissistic people have grandiose self-images; unrealistic notions of their abilities, power, wealth, intelligence, and appearance. They feel entitled to things they have not earned simply by virtue of their inherent greatness. Because this view of themselves is not supported by reality, and hence is very fragile, narcissists need constant admiration and praise from others. They are indifferent to the wishes and feelings of other people, are more concerned with the appearance of things than with reality, ethically empty, emotionally hollow, and exploitative in their relations with others. Since they are interested ultimately in themselves, they are insensitive and lack empathy. Generally, they believe other people are unscrupulous, unreliable, false, and opportunistic—consequently projecting onto others their own characteristics (Maeder, 1989, pp. 44–45).

Some forms of narcissism are malignant (Peck, 1983, p. 78). The distinguishing feature of people afflicted with *malignant* narcissism is willfulness, an overweening pride or arrogance that rejects any judgment premised on inferences of their in-adequacy. They take the law into their own hands, cause others to suffer, ignore the humanity of their victims—all to ensure that they appear to themselves to be continually on top of things, continually in command and control. This appearance of competence, however, is only a pretense, for they live in fear of being exposed to the world and to themselves for what they really are (Peck, 1983, pp. 78–84).

Narcissistic managers bring to organizations a lust for power that is based on willfulness and political self-aggrandizement, the desire to impose their will upon others by overt and covert action, and the use of scapegoats to defend their integrity and preserve their image of perfection. The desire to control other people, to foster their dependency, to discourage their capacity to think for themselves, to diminish their originality is the "evil-in-practice" brought to organizations by narcissistic managers.

Frequently their single-minded behavior gives the appearance of "hard-nosed" management, a trait often sought by those who appoint people to political office. It is a management style that promises to control the bureaucratic ranks without being affected by any human trauma that might result, all the while skillfully maintaining a favorable public image.

The climate established by the presence of evil that the malignant narcissist brings to an organization is the antithesis of the environment required for effective management (Table 6.1). Bartolome (1989, pp. 137–39), for example, has summarized six managerial factors that are the building blocks for the open and trusting environment an executive needs to successfully anticipate troubles and develop innovative strategies. Each factor is negated by the presence of evil-in-practice.

Table 6.1
How Organizational Evil Undermines Organizational Effectiveness

Managerial Factor	Healthy Organization	Evil Organization
Communication	Keep subordinates informed.	Secretive.
Support	Show concern for subordinates; encourage ideas; defend their positions.	Egocentric.
Respect	Delegate to subordinates; listen and act on their opinions.	Disrespectful to subordinates.
Fairness	Objective, impartial appraisals; liberal praise.	Unappreciative; bias and favoritism.
Predictability	Consistent and dependable behavior; keeping explicit and implicit promises.	Dishonesty; arbitrariness and inconsistency.
Competence	Technical and professional ability.	Amateurish behavior; unwillingness to learn.

The concept of evil-in-practice advanced in this chapter does not require reaching a definitive understanding or general acceptance of the nature of evil. I am arguing that some behaviors experienced and observed in organizations are typical of those that are attributed to persons with malignant narcissistic personalities, and that the effect of this kind of behavior on other members of an organization is similar to an act that is generally termed evil, namely the killing of an individual's spirit.

Similar spirit-killing effects may be experienced in organizations as the result of something other than the behavior of a narcissistic administrator. The poor manager, the addict or the neurotic described above, can all enervate an organization. But in the case of organization evil that stems from malignant narcissism, we are dealing with something more than an unfortunate pathology that can be corrected through training or treatment. Evil is a spirit that threatens the fiber of an organization's health.

HOW THE FEDERAL ENVIRONMENT
ENCOURAGES EVIL-IN-PRACTICE

The purpose of a public organization is to provide a service for the public's benefit in accordance with a legislative mandate. Conventional organization theory establishes three instrumental criteria against which to assess the excellence of public management: effectiveness, efficiency, and economy. The conduct of public administrators is evaluated on the basis of how well their actions conform to intended purposes (effectiveness), are competently performed in a "right" manner (efficiency), and expend the minimally needed resources to accomplish the job (economy).

In practice, public administrators are influenced by their personal values and motivations, which can be more or less congruent with the instrumental standards of excellence. Some administrators find substantial agreement between their personal goals and the instrumental values of organizations. They want to see that the programs and projects for which they have responsibility are advanced as intended, and operated in a timely and economic manner. They are motivated by programmatic challenges and strive to meet the standards of managerial excellence.

Other administrators, however, place a higher priority on reaching personal rather than organizational goals. In this respect, the organization becomes an instrument for their own aggrandizement. Such individuals strive for more power, more status, more prestige. Their main preoccupation is not with achieving the organization's mission but with attending to their personal fate (Jackall, 1983, pp. 132–34).

This dichotomy of organizational motivations and behaviors is actually a continuum, with most people displaying some mix of organizational and personal orientations. But in my view there are several characteristics of service in the federal government that encourage personal orientation over more organizationally oriented behaviors.

The size, complexity, and significance of the federal government's respon-sibilities and programs provide many opportunities for attaining national-level power, status, and prestige. There are thousands of executive positions that deal with matters of international and national importance, often in the media spotlight. These can carry such imposing titles as Secretary, Commissioner, Director, Ad-ministrator, Solicitor, Inspector General, and many more. Privileges, perquisites, and wide visibility that accompany power and status redound to those who occupy these offices.

Most of the top positions of government are filled by political appointment rather than through the merit system. Almost 3,000 appointees inhabit the upper reaches of the federal government.[2] Practically all of these people obtain their jobs for the primary purpose of carrying out the current policies of the president and his administration. Given our system of government, they are supposed to (and they do) consider their political mandate to have first priority among their several obligations.

While some of the appointees remain in place for four years or more, the average tenure for a noncareer, political official is 1½ to 2 years. Thus there is continuing influx of new people, most of whom obtain the job's power and status for a com-paratively short time before moving on, now having the impressive federal ex-ecutive credentials as part of their résumés (Brauer, 1987, pp. 174–94).

There are no qualification standards for those political appointees other than the criteria in the mind of the political officials making the appointments. Programmatic and managerial qualifications take second place to political loyalties. For many recent appointees, their federal government job is their first venture into the public sector, into management, and even into the particular substantive field they are responsible for.

The past fifteen years has seen the creation of an atmosphere, established at the presidential level, in which it is fashionable to denigrate the career civil ser-vice. By campaigning against the "mess in Washington" and the incompetence of bureaucracy, Carter and Reagan were in effect stating that political executives were needed to keep career officials in their proper place, to purge their ranks of the many who were not performing as wanted, and generally whip the remain-ing careerists into shape, making sure not to trust any career official in the pro-cess (Sanera, 1984, pp. 458–545).

As the result of these factors, the upper reaches of the federal government pro-vide an arena for many people with minimal management experience or ability to obtain significant power. There are data that suggest the consequences of this environment have been something other than effective management. An October 1989 report described the results of a survey of federal Senior Executive Service (career) members who left the government during the January 1983 to July 1988 period (U.S. Merit Systems Protection Board, 1989). While the most frequently cited reason for leaving government was inadequate compensation (57 percent), a significant number also gave as reasons the politicization of their organization (44 percent), their knowledge and skills were not being used (46 percent), and

the incompetence of their supervisors (38 percent). With regard to politically appointed executives, only 25 percent of the career executives thought that the appointees brought valuable experience to their jobs, only 18 percent felt that they
had good leadership qualities, and only 15 percent said that political appointees
had good management skills or were concerned with merit principles. Finally,
of the career executives whose last supervisor was a political appointee, 50 percent listed the incompetence of their immediate supervisor, 63 percent listed
politicization of their organization, and 46 percent gave ethical concerns about
practices at higher agency levels as important reasons for leaving.

Our form of government depends on being able to fill the thousands of political
positions whose incumbents give direction and control to the executive branch
agencies. One cannot deny that there are persons appointed to high positions in
the federal government who are well qualified for their jobs, who competently
discharge their responsibilities, and who are motivated by the opportunity to serve
the public. But what I *am* pointing out is that given the characteristics of the federal
government and its system of political appointees, it can hardly be a surprise that
some of the people attracted and appointed have narcissistic personalities, and
that some of these people will turn out to be malignant. In short, the federal government provides an ideal environment for attracting the malignant narcissist whose
behavior is one basis for organizational evil.

HOW TO DEAL WITH ORGANIZATIONAL EVIL

The value to public administrators of being forewarned about organizational
evil and being prepared to act when confronted by it is obvious. The evil-in-practice
behavior creates an atmosphere wherein lies and the desire to confuse are rampant (Peck, 1983, p. 66). The adverse effect on one's personal and professional
life of working in an environment lacking in honesty, empathy, and respect can
be dramatic. One's initial encounter with such an environment may lead to profound feelings of stress, depression, and loss. In my own case, having neither
anticipated nor imagined the reality of organizational evil, I felt the need for the
first time in my life to obtain psychological and legal counsel.

Based on my own experience with the phenomenon of organizational evil-in-
practice, I can offer three practical steps one can take to minimize its adverse
consequences. First, I believe that one should be able to *recognize organizational
evil when it is encountered*. The distinguishing features have been recounted in
some detail above. It may be difficult, however, not to confuse the various
manifestations of poor management by inexperienced or untrained officials with
the pathological behavior I have termed evil. Many first-time managers will exhibit ineffective styles of leadership and operation, but they are willing and able
to learn better ways, with the help and support of staff. They are open to suggestions and frequently solicit recommendations and advice about how to function
more effectively.

That is the crucial distinction: an openness to honest and sincerely offered ideas about how to do things better. It is a trait that a person with a malignant narcissistic personality can never display. It quickly becomes apparent whether the official listens to, considers, and values the ideas that others offer, or reacts as outlined above by "killing the messenger" and labeling all those who are not obviously subservient as "the enemies."

Once you determine that you are working for a person who exhibits evil behavior, and not simply a manager who may improve over time, the second guideline becomes operative: *seriously consider removing yourself from the situation.* The feelings that one experiences when confronted with organizational evil, with its lies and its deceptions, is first disbelief, then revulsion, then confusion, and finally the desire to avoid and escape. This, according to authorities, is a healthy reaction to a dangerous environment (Peck, 1983, pp. 65–66). If there are other programs or positions you have thought about as the next steps in your career, this is an excellent time to pursue them and to remove yourself from the spirit-killing environment of your present organization.

The idea of giving up and abandoning one's organization may seem too dramatic or even cowardly by some people. However, it must be realized that when one is dealing with a malignant narcissist, unlike with an addict or a neurotic, there is no chance of changing his or her behavior. Persuasion, suggestions, examples, or kindness do not work. The pride and arrogance underlying the behavior, necessary for maintaining the self-image of perfection, will cause any such efforts to be viewed as personal attacks and to be hostilely rejected. The more you try, the more forcefully the controlling and commanding behavior will be imposed upon you.

If circumstances force you to continue working in the environment of evil, my third suggestion encourages you to *communicate with and seek support from managers in the same predicament.* The primary reason for building a support network is to foster a positive psychological state, not to plot or scheme against anyone. Since you have already been relegated to the "enemy" ranks, your actions will be viewed as hostile in any event, so there need be little hesitation for fear your actions will meet with disapproval.

The difficulty with this third guideline lies elsewhere. Many public managers are not used to talking openly with their peers about their workplace problems. In my more than thirty years in government, I have frequently encountered the attitude that one should stay in control of one's emotions, not admit to any stress, and always maintain a tough image. But when living daily in the midst of organizational evil, it is vital to continued personal and professional health that one combat the sense of isolation and forge sustaining bonds with other victims.

There is another step that one can take at this point, mentioned here more as a matter of caution than as a suggested action, and that is whistleblowing. Few managers who have decided to go public have, upon reflection, felt that the ensuing scenario (often called martyrdom) warrants their encouraging others to do the same. More often than not, whistleblowing has provoked unsympathetic systemic reactions, including delay, recrimination, and blaming the victim (Laurent, 1989, p. 9). It must be remembered that we are not dealing here with poor management or with bad administrative habits that are susceptible to improvement. What I have written about in this chapter is a personality type that uses power to destroy others for the purpose of defending and preserving the integrity of a sick self.

It has been my experience that many people have great difficulty acknowledging the existence of a quality termed evil, hence they cannot accept that it is counterproductive to try to reason with and convert such a spirit-killing person to a better style of management. Take it from someone who has made the effort: it does not work. When one encounters a malignant narcissist, one is not dealing with a management style but with a disease that baffles even psychiatry as to how it may be cured (Peck, 1983, pp. 254–63).

Evil is incapable of empathy and respect for others. That is what makes it difficult to do battle with. Evil ignores the humanity of its victims and is insensitive to the act of spirit-killing. Peck ends his study of the subject with the conclusion that only love can conquer evil (1983, pp. 185–89 and 267–69). But the methodology of love is so difficult to execute in a public organization that it calls for a self-sacrifice of godlike proportions. It does not seem appropriate to me to include such a suggestion as a practical step that one can take when faced with this situation I have described here.

CONCLUSIONS

This chapter was sparked by my belief that the literature on public organizations has largely ignored the idea of evil.[3] My experience has taught me that evil does exist in public organizations. What I have written here is an exploratory effort to understand the causes and consequences of one type of evil, that generated by a malignant narcissist. Obviously I believe that there is much more that needs to be done on the wider topic of organization evil.

The chapter has focused on the effects of evil on the individual. One hardly needs to point out that there also are severe impacts to the organization, including decreased productivity and a reduced ability to accomplish agency missions. In today's public sector environment, team-oriented, participative management is essential to organizational effectiveness (Brown, 1989). Exactly the opposite type of management is guaranteed to public organizations when people are placed in leadership positions who are likely to display the pathological behaviors described in this chapter. The wider organizational impacts should certainly be of major concern to officials making appointments.

The best way to avoid both the personal and organizational damage is to make sure that individuals with malignant narcissistic personalities do not become public administrators in the first place. How that can be done is worthy of another chapter in public administration.

NOTES

1. Lind and Marshall describe a courtier as someone who "knows just how to flatter the boss, project the right image, and manipulate other people for his own gain. He knows how to dress for success, he uses just the right tone of voice, and he is always 'on the inside.' "

2. U.S. Office of Personnel Management statistics show 2,747 political appointees in the federal government, as of September 1988.

3. One could make a similar comment about the lack of attention given to love by the organizational literature.

7

Integrating Interests to Control Conflict: A Critique of Federal Sector Labor Relations

Frank D. Ferris

The 1978 Civil Service Reform Act was designed to increase the responsiveness of the federal bureaucracy to the political leadership of the Executive Branch (Long, 1981, p. 305). Title VII of that law established the labor-management relations system for federal employees. The system is modeled on the preexisting labor relations program that had been established by Executive Orders dating back to 1962. Those orders, in turn, were based on the American private sector system of labor relations, which is derived largely from the 1935 National Labor Relations Act.

It is, therefore, fair to say that the current federal sector labor relations system is based generally on the dynamics and problems the private sector had roughly fifty years ago. This is particularly significant. Whereas fifty years ago private sector labor relations were generally recognized as extremely adversarial, with Marxian class overtones, those conditions hardly characterized the federal sector workplace in 1978, when the CSRA was passed. There was no need to restore peace or regulate economic conflict, and rather than there being overtones of class differences between managers and employees, there was the widespread feeling that these two groups were too close. In retrospect, it seems that the more pressing need was to create a system that would help the employees, managers, and political leaders integrate their needs and talents more efficiently for the benefit of government service. This raises the obvious question: Do we have the appropriate labor relations system in light of today's federal sector needs and management philosophies? What follows will help answer that.

The paper begins with a review of the ideas of Mary Parker Follett (1868–1933) about the criteria than can be used to analyze the management of conflict. Although she wrote almost one hundred years ago, her ideas about how to manage differences or conflict remain fresh, and equally applicable to governments and organizations—public or private.[1] Her criteria are then applied to Title VII of the U.S. Civil Service Reform Act (CSRA), that is, that statutory system for federal sector labor relations (Title 5 U.S. Code Section 7100 et seq.). My aim is to assess how well that system conforms with Follet's theory, thus demonstrating how the lessons of theory can be applied to the practice of administration. Following that section, I will describe what has happened in two federal employee-management conflicts that took place outside the structure of the CSRA. In those cases, activities compatible with Follet's theory were used to achieve ends that were not legally attainable under the CSRA. The lessons of the two case studies suggest how Follett's ideas and the CSRA can be improved.

FOLLETT'S THEORY OF INTEGRATION

As one moves through Follett's vision, it is necessary to keep in mind two important beliefs she held that serve as the foundation of her works. First, she was what can be termed an "emergent" theorist (Harmon & Mayer, 1986, pp. 337–40). She believed that the appropriate action to take is not always apparent when we first enter a situation. Instead, it emerges as we proceed.

The best analogy is that of a tennis match. It is virtually impossible to plan your next shot until you have seen your opponent's last move, which is in turn influenced by your last move. Due to the near infinite number of permutations that can develop in a match as well as the spontaneous nature of reactions, no coach or manager can tell the player in advance what to do at each point of the match. Often, it is only after the game is complete that we can understand why we did what we did. The message to a public administrator is that he or she should not rely heavily on giving orders in advance or manage by imposing rules and regulations. The best course of action is to help those involved in a situation to understand what needs to be done and how to do it. They learn what to do from the emerging situation and you learn from them.

Follett's second point was that true "control" of a government or organization must be built upon understanding the motives of the individual and the group, rather than the more abstract needs of the organization or the power of its hierarchy. Moreover, individual and group interests must be integrated so that all points of view are respected. In this way, individuals will be mobilized to support the activity and, therefore, have little reason to oppose the agreed upon path (Harmon & Mayer, 1986, p. 339).

Stated more plainly, Follett's two foundational principles combine to mean that the best resolution to any conflict situation is to integrate the needs of all involved so that no one works to undermine the resolution. Everyone's energy is used to support the solution. Because these needs are constantly shifting and emerging as people move further into the situation, the solution must be capable of being reshaped as new facts become known. Obviously, Follett's ideas will not sit well with people who like to manage from the top down by giving orders.

Alternatives to Integration

To understand Follett's theory of integration, we need to start with a review of the four conflict management strategies that she believed blocked any movement toward the integration of interests: domination, power balance, compromise, and manipulation.

Follett's first barrier is any attempt to dominate or assert power over a situation (Metcalf & Urwick, 1940, p. 32). Although the dominant party hopes that the subordinated interests will wither and die, Follett believed that rarely happens. Rather, these interests simply become repressed tendencies that undermine commitment to the imposed actions until they are strong enough to rise up and themselves dominate. Lasting control can not be achieved where one party dominates another.

A second approach Follett criticized is the balance-of-power strategy (Metcalf & Urwick, 1940, p. 32). This process is used when two or more parties have nearly equal power over one another and, as a result, choose not to fight but to maintain the status quo. Follett argued that the balance rarely lasts because the interests of all parties remain unresolved throughout the stand-off.

A third process that also fails to satisfy is compromise. This view may be hard for Americans to accept, since it is a method of conflict resolution that is all but revered (Metcalf & Urwick, 1940, p. 32). In compromise, parties are required to give up or modify some of their important needs. The unsatisfied interests do not disappear, although they may be temporarily repressed. The parties simply wait until they can redo the deal under a more favorable set of circumstances.

The fourth process Follett identified as being contrary to achieving true control is crowd manipulation (Fox & Urwick, 1973, p. xxix). This is generally an emotional appeal to prejudices, designed to create an illusion of unity. In reality, it obscures the real differences in a situation lest it be obvious that they can be mutually resolved or integrated and the leader of the emotional appeal lose his or her place at the front of the crowd. This is often the power used by the leader of a single-issue interest group or coalition.

Integration

In contrast to the strategies outlined above, Follett argued that conflicts are not only natural but are good for an organization in the same sense that any basic organizational resource would be. Conflicting interests should serve to unite the members of an organization and, when those interests are properly integrated, to commit the organization to a course of action designed to help each interested party achieve what it needs from the situation (Metcalf & Urwick, 1940, p. 9).

Follett's vision of what she called integration (sometimes coordination) consisted of four parts: direct contact, early interaction, reciprocal relationships. and continuous interaction (Metcalf & Urwick, 1940). First, there must be direct contact among all the responsible parties to an interaction. You cannot learn from an emerging situation if you are not part of it. Any attempt to deal indirectly with one another, including the use of representatives, detracts from the potential to discover and integrate the principal parties' actual interests.

Second, everyone involved in a situation should meet as early as possible so that rigid positions, which inhibit an integrated solution, do not have time to form. Ideally, the parties meet not only before any solutions have been advocated but also before each has developed its own understanding of what the problem is. The sooner the principals interact, the sooner they will know their true needs or interests, as opposed to what they may have felt was a concern before they entered the situation. Moreover, early interaction reduces the chances that one party will distrust the other, or need to remedy some perceived injustice created because the parties resisted dealing with one another.

Third, in Follett's words, there needs to be a "reciprocal relating of all the features of a situation" (Metcalf & Urwick, 1940, p. 194). The group needs to see how the interest of each is related to the interests of all others involved. This increases the likelihood that the parties will become committed to a united course of action. Follett does concede that in some situations interests will be mutually exclusive and integration must give way to one of the other means of gaining control. But she emphasizes that this option works only in the short run.

Follett offered detailed advice as to how to promote a reciprocal relationship. Parties must lay all their "cards on the table" (Metcalf & Urwick, 1940, p. 38). A shared vision of the problem to be solved is just as important as a jointly supported solution. Parties must be honest with one another about their needs, and do so as early as possible, so that everyone knows the dimensions of the problem to be solved. False interests should not be put on the table just to protect other more important needs or to create a fall back position. Beyond this, the parties need to divide their stated interests into their smallest parts. Follett argued that this will help the group discover the true nature of their interest, making it easier to meet the need or discover how it overlaps with the needs of others.

Follett advised that once interests are jointly understood, parties should engage in collective fact-finding. She believed that separate efforts to find the facts of any situation only feed the tendency to look at one another as opponents. Moreover, joint fact-finding gives the parties the opportunity to learn more about one another (Metcalf & Urwick, 1940, p. 75).

Once the interests and facts are clarified, the parties should engage in a discussion in which they "evoke" (Metcalf & Urwick 1940, p. 197), or call forth, one another's ideas as to what might be done to create an integrated solution. By engaging in what is essentially brainstorming, they establish a problem-solving process that is more powerful than separate, distrustful, two-sided efforts. This process not only allows all parties to participate in developing a solution but also encourages the parties to rely heavily on their skills to invent or create new solutions. It avoids the impoverished technique of relying on an "either or," zero-sum, or limited-choice approach, which Follett believed to be a major obstacle to any integration.

The fourth element in Follett's vision is that the coordinating process must be continuous. Parties must always be willing to deal with new interests or the changing situation. This concept is grounded in her idea that nothing remains static; situations are always changing and evolving. As a result, interests or needs will also evolve or become clear where they were once unknowable. Any procedural rule that freezes an understanding or agreement for an artificial period of time will undermine the ability of the parties to remain coordinated and, hence, in control of themselves.

Table 7.1 summarizes the elements of integration. One can see how similar her advice is to that of today's most prominent conflict integration theorists, Roger Fisher and William Ury. In their book *Getting to Yes* (1981), they advocate putting yourself in your opponent's position, focusing on the problem rather than the people or personalities involved, avoiding positions or solutions at the outset, brainstorming options, and looking ahead rather than to the past for solutions.

Intergration and Labor-Management Relations

Follett was not naive. She recognized that interest integration violated many of the habitual ways people tried to resolve conflict. Yet she believed in the fundamentally practical value of her ideas and worked to apply her theories to employee-management situations. She believed that unions would be merely a temporary solution to labor problems as long as collective bargaining relied only on the balance of power and compromise. Bargaining under these conditions would lack any vitality to create and, hence, would be merely a temporary expedient until management found a better way to integrate employee interests and their own (Metcalf & Urwick, 1940, p. 22). Follett criticized both labor and management for having the wrong vision of the purpose of employee representation. Follett felt that a union was not in business to be a separate track of information to management, to be an adjunct to the management process, or even to be a vehicle

Table 7.1
Follett's Elements of Interest Integration

---

1. Direct contact between the principal leaders of both parties to a conflict situation.

2. Early contact between parties before a problem is even defined.

3. A reciprocal relationship.
   a. Open, honest expressions of interest or needs.
   b. Breaking interests into their smallest parts.
   c. Joint fact-finding.
   d. Brainstorming or creating alternative solutions.

4. A continuous relationship between the parties, enriched by experiments and maturing interests.

---

management used to get formal employee commitment to a decision. Instead, she believed that a union was an integral part of management because it represented the interests of a group that management could not afford to ignore or even sub-jugate to its own interests if it wished to achieve control, that is, to satisfy its own interests (Metcalf & Urwick, 1940, p. 173).

Similarly, she urged union leaders to support what was best for bargaining unit employees within the context of what was also best for others involved in their work situation. So long as the union ensured that employees were allowed to par-ticipate in decisions affecting them, then the integration of interests would pro-duce increasing benefits for the workers. Follett believed that increasing the benefit pie, rather than trying to take benefit from others in a zero-sum game, was the real goal of the union or any other group. In many respects, it is this perspective that makes her ideas relevant to contemporary government and organizational dynamics, as I will demonstrate in the following discussion of the Civil Service Reform Act.

HOW PUBLIC UNIONS WORK

Under the federal sector labor relations system, nonmanagement employees can certify a union as their representative by a majority of those who vote. Once elected as the representative, the union is expected to negotiate a labor agree-ment covering employment conditions. Employment conditions are defined in the law as personnel policies, practices, and working conditions. The law also specifies a number of issues that cannot be negotiated (Title 5 U.S. Code Section 7103, 7106, 7117). In addition to the subjects precluded by law, the Office of Personnel Management (OPM) can exclude something from negotiations by is-suing a government-wide regulation (Title 5 U.S. Code Section 7117).

Once a contract is negotiated, the union enforces the agreement, as well as existing regulations and laws related to employment conditions not in the con-tract, by filing a grievance against management when an infraction is committed. Unless the grievance is settled voluntarily, the dispute goes to a private-sector arbitrator, who renders a final and binding decision by imposing his opinion of what the parties originally intended to do when they drafted the contract or regula-tion. The arbitrator does not consider the interests in the situation as it now exists.

In addition to the right to grieve on behalf of the employees, the union general-ly can go to court to enforce laws that are not grievable, lobby Congress to pro-tect or even benefit employees, and use the media to bring pressure to bear on managers. However, in contrast to the private sector, the public union is not per-mitted to strike or to use other economic weapons. Just as significant, the union is not permitted to negotiate for a system that would require employees to join or at least pay dues. Consequently, a union must develop an ability to encourage employees to voluntarily join if it is to remain economically viable.

With this as background, I will now use Follett's theory as a framework for understanding the conflict resolution processes imbedded in the CSRA.

DOMINATION AND OTHER COMPETING BARRIERS

By prohibiting the union from negotiating over certain matters, the law actually requires management to force its will on the employees in these nonnegotiable areas. Management is not even required to get the employees' opinions in advance of deciding these issues, and, if it should err by actually negotiating an agreement covering a nonnegotiable matter, management is required to void the agreement as soon as it realizes this, without any further negotiations with the union. In the federal government, management is not required or permitted to meet with employees and seek agreement as to what their performance standards should be or who should be assigned what work. Clearly, this constitutes a system of domination.

On top of this domination of the union and employees, OPM can impose its will on both parties by issuing a regulation that voids even the agreements that management and the union jointly make. This puts the parties to a conflict in a situation where they have little or no way to have their needs met. Even if labor and management want to try to integrate their interests, in many areas they are prohibited from doing so by law.

Unions are not without the ability to fight back and themselves try to dominate the situation. The CSRA requires agency managers to recognize unions where employees vote for them. The intent is, in part, to balance the power that managers have as a way to protect employees from abuses of managerial power. In the day-to-day operations under the Act, unions can use their power to involve Congress, the press, and the courts to counteract management when the parties are not permitted to negotiate for an integration of their mutual interests.

OPM regulations have at times been tied up for years in this face-off, with the effect that no action is taken by either side while the parties wait for the circumstances to change so one can dominate the other on the issue. In perhaps the most notorious example, OPM was repeatedly stopped from promulgating revised reduction-in-force regulations from 1982 to 1986. In the interim, it had to modify its proposal three times before one was allowed to go into effect (Government Employees Relations Report, 1982, No. 972, p. 14; 1983, Vol. 21, p. 1455; 1986, Vol. 24, p. 358).

The irony of this is that even though the CSRA was passed to increase the control of the Executive Branch leadership (Long, 1981, p. 305), in the labor-management area it actually drives Executive Branch employees outside the Branch in search of allies to help solve their problems. Would it not be preferable for the Executive Branch to have a system whereby the parties are motivated and permitted to solve employee relations problems without the intervention of other branches or powers?

On those issues that are negotiable, the parties are generally encouraged to put concrete proposals on the table as the way to initiate the bargaining process. If they cannot reach a voluntary agreement, the dispute goes to mediation and then to binding arbitration (Title 5 US Code Section 7119). Although the law does not prohibit the use of any dispute resolution technique, the parties quickly learn that success in both the mediation and arbitration process requires that they use compromise. If they have not shown that they have backed off some proposals or made other movement, they are likely to be stopped from moving forward in the process or even suffer substantively in the final imposed decision. There is simply nothing that enables or promotes interest integration as an alternative to compromise in an impasse. But there could be. For example, arbitrators or mediators could be required by regulation to first list the parties' interests on each issue and then certify they are mutually exclusive, incapable of integration. Only at that point could compromise be used to settle a conflict.

Because the union is not permitted to require employees to join or pay dues, it must constantly be persuading employees to join. This reality triggers the "crowd manipulation" strategy that Follett described. Unions persuade most easily by convincing employees that they are subject to the unilateral actions of management, or by telling employees what the union did for them that management would not have done voluntarily. Employees need to be convinced that they will get something for their money in additional to a contract. In the private sector, there is less need to do this constantly. Unions are permitted to negotiate with management to require employees to pay dues or to join. Consequently, when compared with the public sector, private sector unions are not in an on-going battle with economic security.

Integration, Coordination, and Reciprocal Relationships

As Follett noted, it is not enough for a conflict resolution system to be free of the zero-sum or adversarial techniques described. There must also be coordination between the parties, which includes the requirement that the parties have direct contact when addressing problems.

The CSRA falls short of this in several ways. As discussed above, when OPM goes through the process of issuing personnel rules and regulations, it is not required to have any direct contact with the employees or their unions. It can simply issue rules unilaterally after a brief notice and comment period.[2] Beyond this, there is nothing in the CSRA that encourages individual agencies and unions to meet at the time the problem arises and before either side starts considering the solutions it would prefer. In matters where the union is prohibited from negotiating over the substance of the issue (for example whether the standard for a typist should be 60 or 90 words a minute), the law does not require that management approach the union about a problem or pending decision until the decision is made. Management is only required to do so before the decision is implemented, but that is hardly early enough to stop management from having developed a predisposition on the issue, or the union from resenting the fact that the issue has developed this far without its involvement. The result is a hole from which both parties must extricate themselves before they can begin to make progress integrating basic interests.

On those issues the union is free to negotiate, it must be approached by management in advance of implementation, and management can only present its proposed solution, it cannot impose a final decision. For example, unions can generally negotiate over floor plans in an office. Under the law, if management wants to change a plan, management must develop an alternative one and propose it to the union. The union can then negotiate over the substance of the plan. This interaction occurs earlier than it does in other situations, but it is still long after the problem has arisen, and management has often developed a firm idea of the solution it prefers.

The heart of the coordination or integration process is the requirement that the parties be able to reciprocally relate all the interests in the situation. The process not only involves certain rules of how to treat one another, but more important, it focuses the discussion on the basic interests of the parties rather than bargaining proposals. Proposals generally are nothing more than preferred solutions placed on the table before there has even been a detailed, joint discussion of the issues.

Bargaining under the CSRA depends upon the use of proposals and counter proposals. Indeed, if one party tried to invoke the right to negotiate without presenting proposals to the other party, the invoking party would probably lose the legal right to bargain (U.S. Customs Service and NTEU, 1987). As a result, the law actually makes it difficult for the parties to place all their cards or interests on the table. The union is not required to think in term of interests before the proposals are submitted, and management is often not obligated to tell the union why it is proposing certain changes.

When the union is not permitted to bargain on the substance of an issue, it is generally permitted to bargain over the adverse impact or implementing procedures of the unilateral management decision. This situation creates another obstacle to the honest presentation of interests. For example, management can unilaterally decide to reassign a position (for example, Accountant, GS-11), from one office to another, but the union can bargain over which employee in the position must go, how soon, what moving expenses he will be given, and how soon he can move back to the original office if a vacancy occurs. As a result, impact and procedural proposals are often put on the table when in reality the union is trying to influence or reverse the nonnegotiable, unilateral management decision. This hardly makes for a candid discussion and all too often amounts to nothing more than the union and employees exacting retribution while the underlying problem remains unresolved.

Beyond whether it is possible to place all the interests on the table at the start of bargaining, if the dispute goes to impasse, it is traditional that a party had better have several things it is willing to give away as part of a compromise to protect more essential matters. Federal sector bargaining is a trade-off process, not a search for the facts, interests, and law of the situation, as Follett envisioned it could be.

The law does permit the parties to subdivide and analyze their initial demand as part of a search for their real interests. However, there is nothing that encourages this strategy as a way of learning more about one another or of discovering possible areas of agreement. Indeed, the strategy runs counter to the bargaining habits that are dominant in U.S. culture, habits developed in another time and in the private sector, when agreements came from power rather than reason. More important, as the parties proceed through the impasse process, mediators and arbitrators traditionally try to get the parties to combine or package proposals as a way of building a compromise. If the parties do not follow Follett's advice on their own, they will get no help from the system.

As for the joint pursuit of facts, about all the statute provides on the question of information is that management has to give the union the "reasonable and necessary" information the union needs to fulfill its obligation to represent employees (Title 5, U.S. Code Section 7114). Case law under the statute holds that management is free to survey employees and conduct other studies without the union's involvement (IRS and NTEU, 1988, p. 832). But the statute fails to encourage joint fact gathering. The administrators of the CSRA had a chance to set up joint fact-finding but passed over the opportunity.

"Evoking" or brainstorming has no formal role in the statute. The law simply says that the parties must deal in "good faith." This is nothing more than a purposely vague concept around which the courts have been expected to develop a tradition. That tradition does not require either party to engage in brainstorming solutions and, indeed, it specifically permits a party to refuse to change from its original position if it so wishes. The intent is that each party will put on the table its idea of the "one best way" to solve a dispute and, through the clash of arguments, evidence, and power, one solution or compromise will emerge. When parties work this way, they sometimes can enrich one another and evoke ideas they would not have found alone, but it is neither a required nor valued part of the legal tradition.

Returning to the final aspect of coordination, that is, continuous interaction, the law requires that the parties deal with each other as long as the union is the certified representative. However, the legal tradition also requires that when the parties negotiate an agreement over a specific issue or working condition, they commit themselves to follow the provisions of the agreement for a specific length of time. This is commonly known as the term of the agreement. Consequently, under this statute it is unusual for the parties to be continuously involved over an issue. More commonly, they deal with it at specific time periods, generally two to three years apart.

THEORY INFORMS PRACTICE

Table 7.2 summarizes the more troublesome obstacles to integration that are found in Title VII. Using Follett's theory to analyze Title VII of the CSRA illustrates how the law inhibits the ability of the parties to integrate their interests as a way of solving conflicts. Public unions and management are virtually required to use domination, compromise, and other zero sum power techniques, while the CSRA systematically blocks any incentive to use interest integration.

Table 7.2
How the Civil Service Reform Act Interferes with Interest Integration

1. Prohibiting parties from discussing certain topics in an effort to gain a mutually beneficial resolution
2. Reliance on the balance of power and compromise as the preferred methods of resolving conflicts
3. Use of legal techniques to settle disputes, e.g. third party adversarial fact-finding and decision-making, appeals outside the Executive Branch, the valuing of case law, etc.
4. Use of the private sector tradition to shape federal sector labor law

Whether this is due to relying on a fifty-year-old private sector model or even to the U.S. constitutional ethos that pluralistic interests should be allowed to clash as the preferred method of progress is of tangential importance here. Of far more importance is to acknowledge that the CSRA provides a false sense of control to government officials. The statutory system that authorizes the hierarchy to force its will on the organization is of little long-term value if the individuals in an organization are able to defeat, stalemate, or chip away at agreements in the natural desire to meet their own interests.

Some readers may believe that Follett's idea could never work in U.S. public organizations, either because of structural barriers or because of human nature. But as I will next attempt to show, Follett's theories do work.

EXTRALEGAL EXPERIMENTS WITH LABOR-MANAGEMENT COOPERATION

In the early 1980s the U.S. Internal Revenue Service and the National Treasury Employees Union (NTEU), which represented IRS employees, found themselves heavily engaged in the combat techniques encouraged by the CSRA. The most recent labor agreement had taken nearly two years to negotiate, there were almost 1,000 grievances, complaints, or charges filed against management by the union, and NTEU increasingly was turning to parties outside the union-management relationship for help (for example, to Congress and the press). It was a model CSRA clash.

For a variety of reasons, including the costs of the conflict to each party, and the "encouragement" of an administrative law judge, both parties decided that for certain issues they would experiment with abandoning their legal rights and processes under the CSRA in favor of more appropriate problem resolution techniques. They chose to use an "interest-bargaining" process, which is the term Fisher and Ury (1981) use for what Follett called integration or coordination. Reviewing the results of these experiments will provide an opportunity to show how Follett's theory works in practice, and to identify the ways in which both the CSRA and Follett's idea could be improved.

The Incentive Pay Experiment

The Internal Revenue Service had a problem in the early 1980s with the productivity of its 10,000 data transcribers. IRS studies show that the service was substantially less efficient than were private sector transcribers. The union, on the other hand, was troubled by the low pay of transcribers, and it argued that pay explained the lack of performance. Because the concerns of union and management were not mutually exclusive, there was an obvious potential for a negotiated settlement or adjustment. However, if the parties tried to create one under the rules of the CSRA, they would have been prohibited by law from jointly determining the production standards or the payouts to employees, the core of any resolution strategy. In short, interest integration would have failed under the rules of CSRA.

Realizing this, the parties decided to experiment lest neither side's problem be resolved. Management agreed to let the union jointly determine all policy questions irrespective of the CSRA. In return, the union agreed to ignore labor's traditional disdain for piece-rate incentive systems, and, by so doing, they avoided taking a position early in the interaction. Beyond this, the parties agreed to use procedures very different from traditional position bargaining to enhance the possibility of agreement.

First, the union and management representatives were higher level officials than were traditionally used in bargaining. They also hired a facilitator for their discussions, a practice totally new to the parties. The facilitator was an organizational psychologist from the University of Michigan whose role was to keep the parties focused on the process. He trained the parties in an interest-bargaining approach, helped them set an agenda, and, most important, when a dispute arose, he brought the parties back to the process rather than let them resort to traditional emotional clashes that destroy trust. He kept the disputes technical rather than personal and power oriented.

Second, the discussions between the parties were based on interests rather than on bargaining proposals. The decision on how much of the savings from a piece-rate incentive system should go to employees illustrates this point. Instead of starting with proposals from both sides as to what percentage the employees should receive, the parties first discussed the interests involved in the problem. The employees needed to believe the split was fair. The employer needed a split that enabled the program to produce a savings for the organization. The union needed to be able to defend politically the money split to outside organizations. The process of understanding interests and separating them into their constituent parts also helped the participants to see that some of the matters they originally thought were interests were not essential to the final resolution.

Once the interests were clarified, the parties brainstormed possible solutions, calling forth or "evoking" one another's ideas. This process helped them to realize that several solutions were feasible, and that it was not a matter of finding the one best way to do something. The parties used the list of interests they had developed as criteria to select a solution with which they could experiment.[3]

A third critical aspect of the negotiation process was the decision to use consensus to settle questions. In the past the parties generally decided issues by having each side vote for a position it could support against the other side. The parties now recognized, however, that each of the ten or more participants in the discussion had some unique interests, and that all these should be met before a solution was chosen. As a result, the "team position" concept was abandoned in favor of unanimous agreement. It was slower, but it worked.

In addition to changing the negotiating technique, the parties also agreed to implement the solutions they reached on an experimental basis. In this way, they could learn from jointly evaluating the solutions' results and discover any new interests that may not have been obvious in the opening round of discussions. Either side was free to reopen discussions at any time the solutions created substantial problems.

Perhaps most significant, the participants recognized that despite the high level of expertise on the national negotiation teams, they did not have the knowledge or even a sufficient appreciation of the interests of the local employees and managers. So they left several issues to be resolved at the local level. This turned out to be critical because as the local joint committees came up with solutions to the issues in their domain, they also came to accept the incentive system as their own creation.

Quality Improvement Processes at the Internal Revenue Service

The 1985 tax-filing season was a near disastrous one for the IRS (Barrett, 1985). The agency was unable to process returns within the legal deadlines; it made repeated mistakes; and it was criticized almost daily in the national press. The first response of IRS was to make technical corrections to existing systems, a strategy that failed to remedy the problems.

The union argued vehemently against technical fixes imposed by the IRS national office on all local offices, and it urged management to increase staffing and to rely on the wisdom of local employees. When it appeared that the efforts to improve the process had stalled in a CSRA impasse, the parties agreed to try the interest bargaining approach once again. Otherwise, they would have been able to stalemate each other until public anger rose to such a level that both parties suffered.

The highest-ranking officials of both parties came to the table, that is; the National President of the union and the Deputy Commissioner of the IRS. Management offered to let the union jointly determine all issues that would be discussed, in return for which the union agreed not to exclude discussions about the quality improvement program in which IRS had already trained its managers. The parties agreed to use a facilitator and to work with interests rather than proposals.

The national officials also agreed to permit local joint committees to decide a substantial number of local issues. The local representatives of labor and management in the nearly one hundred local IRS offices were given a national charter outlining some broad principles and procedures, and they were instructed to fill in the gaps by tending to their own peculiar interests, again using the interest bargaining and consensus process.

A National Quality Improvement Process Council was established to handle any emerging national interests that were discovered in local IRS jurisdictions. Finally, they decided that all communications with employees and managers would be joint, in order to express to the field that this was not simply two sides working together but rather one unified body. The parties even created their own letterhead to advance this message symbolically.

EXTENDING FOLLETT'S THEORY

Both the Incentive Pay and Quality processes continue in operation today, confirming the utility of Follett's model, while also illustrating the futility of the CSRA. However, these experiments outside the legal structure of CSRA also draw attention to the usefulness of certain strategies that Follett did not address.

First, the parties in the two cases outlined here started the move to interest integration in very small steps. It is very doubtful they could have transformed their entire relationship overnight to this model even if they had wanted to. Follett did not stress the importance of starting with very small experiments to implement this change. Moreover, as can be seen from both of these situations, it helped that the parties were faced with a problem that could not be solved using traditional means of resolving conflicts. Intractable problems may be a good indicator that the situation calls for integration techniques.

Second, Follett made no mention of facilitators, yet these proved invaluable to the IRS-NTEU parties by helping to identify and analyze problems, to maintain accurate and open communications, and to motivate the parties to stay with the process. It is unlikely that the parties could have avoided letting disputes become personal, emotional power battles if facilitators had not been present to encourage the parties to use Follett's reciprocal relating process to solve disputes. In a sense, the two principal parties need someone in the room with them to represent and advocate the process as opposed to the substantive interests.

Third, even though Follett stressed the importance of identifying all the interests in a situation, she failed to emphasize the value of recognizing that, when a macro-level system is being structured, micro-level supplemental processes should also be established. These will permit local issues and interests to be dealt with at the appropriate level. It would be an error for national parties to assume they are capable of representing all the interests of any complex system simply because of their position in the hierarchy.

Fourth, although Follett spoke of the need to treat the union as an integral part of management, not just an adjunct, she could have stressed more the need to ensure the security of the union. Both experiments described here granted the union more security through indirect means, such as joint communications with and training of employees. They made the union visible to employees and probably enhanced its ability to get members—its economic lifeblood.

Finally, I would recommend that more attention be given to using consensus decision making where each party is represented by more than one person. It seems contradictory to require that the needs of two sides be integrated, but not that the needs of all members of each side by similarly treated. In my experience, consensus reduces the risk each person has in openly discussing needs because each person could in essence veto any solution that failed to meet those needs.

CLOSING COMMENTS

Follett held that a democratic government or organization is primarily responsible for fruitfully relating the various interests in a society into a unified co-functioning order (Metcalf & Urwick, 1940, p. 3). Control is not imposed by law or by hierarchy but arises from within, based on a shared view of the facts of a situation (Metcalf & Urwick, 1940, p. 28). If this vision is ever to prevail in federal sector labor relations, the Federal Labor Relations Authority (FLRA), the agency charged with administering Title VII, is going to have to reframe its responsibilities significantly. At present, it is oriented to legal rights. It settle disputes by producing and applying case law. At the request of either party, it will interject itself between the parties and impose a solution that is designed to settle the case at issue, not to improve the relationship or accommodate developing interests.

To fulfill Follett's vision, FLRA will have to train its staff in interest-bargaining techniques. It will have to encourage local supplemental bargaining and discourage unilateral fact-finding. It will have to delay as long as possible interjecting its legally oriented process in a dispute by encouraging and rewarding interest-bargaining processes. It will have to lobby Congress to change the law so that neither OPM nor the statute can stop the parties from directly discussing matters. Finally, it will have to redefine the legal concept of ''good faith'' bargaining to reflect the desire to integrate rather than dominate interests. Table 7.3 summarizes the more important changes that will have to be made in CSRA and the FLRA to promote the use of integrated solutions.

Beyond federal sector labor relations, Follett's ideas enable public administrators in virtually any area of government or organization to analyze the way in which conflicts and differences are managed. Follett's theories suggest alternatives

Table 7.3
Changing CSRA And FLRA to Promote the Use of Interest Integration

---

1. Remove or minimize the opportunities for parties to dominate or stalemate one another in a dispute, e.g. remove the limitations on the topics that can be negotiated.

2. Promote interest integration techniques to compete with compromise strategies. Act more like facilitators than case handlers.

3. Offer parties training and assistance in the techniques of interest integration.

4. Require the use of interest integration techniques in a dispute before other methods are relied upon.

5. Provide opportunities for the union to achieve economic security so that issue does not obscure the discussion of all others.

---

to the commonly used strategies of domination, stalemate, and compromise. Follett saw what many people still do not realize: conflict can be an asset and energy source to public administrators.

NOTES

1. Much of Follett's work and commentary about its meaning and utility can be found in edited collections of her writings (Metcalf & Urwick, 1940, and Fox & Urwick, 1973), and in other sources (Parker, 1984; Stever, 1986; Wood, 1926; & Wolf, 1988).

2. OPM is required to publish notice of some proposed rules in the *Federal Register* and to review the written comments.

3. Ultimately the parties created an incentive pay system through which employees were given one-half the savings they produced by entering data over a certain numerical standard that the employees helped to set locally.

PART III

STRUCTURE AND PUBLIC ORGANIZATIONS

Organizations have a variety of structures. They create structures around communications, power, rewards, problem solving, decision making, social relationships, and other activities. Many structures are the artifact of routine behaviors. Other structures are designed to prescribe behaviors. The four chapters in part III describe what can happen when one looks at existing structures in a nonroutine way.

Arthur Ciarkowski regulates medical devices for the Food and Drug Administration. In chapter 8 he describes how an organization's formal structure can limit its ability to respond to a turbulent environment. The textbook solution to this problem is to change the organization's structure. Ciarkowski's solution was to use multiple structures. He writes about the value of conceptualizing organizations as "chaotic aggregates."

Ciarkowski tells how he and his staff informally developed a computer bulletin board to remedy an information problem. The board was used initially to facilitate communication among the FDA, medical device manufacturers, and researchers involved in the development of the artificial heart. Eventually the bulletin board was used for other issues. The board created a new communication structure, or web, that linked people inside FDA with other experts inside and outside the organization. Instead of replacing the existing structure, the web allowed the formal hierarchical structure to cope more effectively with the discontinuities of environmental change.

Ciarkowski is Chief of the FDA's Prosthetic and Monitoring Devices Branch. He was a chemist and a biomedical engineer before joining FDA, where he has been employed for ten years. He is a public administrator doctoral candidate at the University of Southern California.

Paul Waldo has been a public administrator for almost thirty years in the U.S. Department of Defense. His experiences in project management, resource management, and strategic planning drew his attention to the structure of learning in organizations.

He begins chapter 9 by arguing that the philosophical underpinnings of most organizational theories do not adequately capture what organizations should be concerned with. For Waldo, learning should be the means and the end of organizations.

To support his position, Waldo reviews major learning theories, and constructs a model that links individual and organizational learning. He presents seven propositions that follow from his model. To show how the model can be used, he interprets the 1962 Cuban missile crisis through the analytical lens of the Learning Model of Organizations. Waldo concludes that the central value of the group advising John Kennedy was that it amplified the president's individual learning.

The chapter shows how organization can be conceived not as structures to facilitate production but as structures to encourage learning. For the author, production will be a beneficial and inevitable side effect of the learning organization. Waldo is presently completing his public administration doctorate.

In chapter 10, Judith Lombard describes how archetypes, a concept originated by Carl Jung, reflect an organization's psychological structure. Archetypes are represented by organizational stories, symbols, and rituals. While they are the products of individuals, their psychological power is projected onto and experienced by the collectivity, that is, by the entire organization.

Lombard uses archetypes to analyze the more than one hundred-year history of Saint Elizabeths Hospital, an internationally known mental health facility in Washington, D.C. The author describes the sometimes positive and sometimes demonic tension between feminine and masculine archetypes that have appeared in stories and symbols concerning the hospital's origin, purpose, and leadership. She concludes the chapter with ideas about how administrators can use her analytical framework to understand the psychological structure of their organizations.

Lombard received her D.P.A. from the University of Southern California in 1988. She is currently an employee development specialist for the U.S. Department of Agriculture. For twenty years she was a mental health specialist at Saint Elizabeths Hospital, U.S. Department of Health and Human Services.

Frank Nice is a captain in the U.S. Public Health Service. In chapter 11, he identifies three structural dimensions of power. First-dimension power is visible power. Second-dimension power is frequently below the surface. Third-dimension power is latent, rarely discussed, and according to Nice, the key to managing organizational power dynamics.

The chapter starts with a brief summary of the meaning and function of power. Nice then describes the matrix that structures each dimension of power and shows how the dimension can be used to analyze organizational power. The author illustrates his presentation by discussing how awareness of the three dimensions helped an administrator change the power structure in an organization. The chapter concludes with eight ideas administrators can use to increase their ability to manage organizational power.

Frank Nice has been a public administrator for sixteen years. Since 1981 he has been a branch and program administrator in the National Institutes of Health, Neurology Institute. He is also the Chief Pharmacist administrator for the National Boy Scouts of America Jamborees. He is a doctoral candidate in public administration at the University of Southern California.

8

Influencing Structure:
From Hierarchy to Chaos

Arthur A. Ciarkowski

When spider webs unite,
They can tie up a lion.

—Ethiopian Proverb

Effective administrators cannot depend for information solely on the organization's formal communication structure. They need to create their own communication web to other people in the organization, and to people outside the organization. This web allows administrators to cope with a rapidly changing environment and to reduce the discontinuities among levels of the organization that inhibit effective communication, learning, and action. This chapter describes how a communication web was created in a public organization. At a more theoretical level, the chapter discusses the limitations of holding a unitary view of organizational structure.

A PUBLIC ADMINISTRATOR'S JOURNEY

When I first joined the Food and Drug Administration, I took a trip from Washington, D.C., to Chicago that taught me a practical lesson about communication structures in organizations. My secretary made my arrangements for the Chicago meeting, using the government travel agent. The trip required that I meet a technician at a hotel near O'Hare Airport and then go to a nearby hospital to observe a clinical trial of a new medical device. Rather than sending me to O'Hare, the government travel agent put me on a flight to Chicago's Midway airport, followed by a shuttle to downtown and a second shuttle to the hotel. Although I arrived in Chicago on the right date at the right time, the unnecessary travel across town made me late for my rendezvous and the medical procedure at the hospital. The trip may have been the lowest cost, thus satisfying the travel agent's objective, but it did not fulfill my needs.

After this incident, I closely examined the travel regulations and asked other experienced government travelers about the options available for travel. I learned that I had greater flexibility in making arrangements than I was told by the government travel agent. Depending on a single source of information received through formal communication lines limited the information I needed and led to an undesirable outcome.

The story illustrates a larger, more significant point. It is important to establish links to other people throughout the organization and to people in the external environment. One can still use formal communication channels, but other sources are needed to assure that the information received is not distorted and that the available options for action have not been limited.

In the not too distant past of bureaucratic theory, it would have been heresy to argue the value of redundant structures. But the rate of change facing contemporary public administrators requires a reexamination of the utility of many taken-for-granted beliefs about organization structures. My focus in this chapter, as suggested by the story of my trip to Chicago, is the structure of organizational communication systems.

INFORMATION ANXIETY AND THE RATE OF CHANGE

Men and women have lived with change since creation. We see the sun rise and set; we experience the change of the seasons; we hear the crash of a falling branch; and we feel the ripples that our hand creates when put into a stream of flowing water. These changes are cyclical and predictable. We anticipate the change and respond, or we can predict what will occur.

When change occurs suddenly, we become perplexed and grasp for ways to cope. Given a new set of circumstances, we have a tendency to respond to the unusual with old behaviors that may be inappropriate. When a goldfish that has lived in a small fishbowl is released into a pond it continues to swim in small circles. For people, responding appropriately to change can be difficult, particularly when the change is rapid and when organizational structures act as barriers, rather than aides, to communication and action.

I have found that it is helpful to think of change occurring in three dimensions: change that has occurred (past), change that is occurring (present), and change that is going to occur (future). We adapt and adjust to change that has passed. For change that is taking place in the present, we have the opportunity to initiate action and influence events, to shape the change that will affect us, our organization, and our environment. For future change we can anticipate and plan for what will occur.

To achieve a comfortable balance in dealing with change we need to reflect on how we allocate our time in dealing with past, present, and future change. We are operating reactively if we spend most of our time adapting and adjusting, little time initiating and influencing change, and less time planning and anticipating future change. If we are preoccupied with the past, we fix on accomplishments.

We are surprised and disappointed by anything new, and we develop a pessimistic attitude toward life (Gardner, 1981).

Change, especially in my organization's areas of responsibility, is a function of social and technological development (Bezold, 1983; Dator 1981). In the health field, the demographic shift in the population, and the change in attitudes toward medical procedures, such as organ transplants, are social developments that are having an impact on the technologies of medical devices. The complexity of the technology also affects the social process of how innovation occurs. A medical device is no longer just electronics, tubing, or mechanisms, but a composite of tissue, fabric, organic sensors, computer software, electronic controls, pneumatics, and mechanical instrumentation. The age of the single inventory or the small group of engineers who develop innovative medical technology is fading rapidly into the past. New technology requires a multidisciplinary approach to development. The combination of demographic changes, new technologies, and the fast pace of development is creating a revolution in medical device technology. To cite a few examples:

Information Processing: Most medical devices today include digital circuitry with a capacity to process information, such as thermometers, respirators, dialyzers, and cardiac monitors. More sophisticated devices such as diagnostic ultrasound are essentially small computers that can instantaneously change acoustic power levels, scanning rates, and beam width while displaying the information in color, performing calculations, and comparing patient performance parameters to an internal database collected from thousands of other patients.

Materials Technology: Although new mixtures of organic (carbon-carbon molecules) polymers are still being formulated, nonorganic polymers containing phosphorous-nitrogen structures are being developed. These materials offer a range of characteristics unattainable by organic polymers, and they have the prospect of greater compatibility when implanted in the body. Other materials such as ceramics, fabrics, and metals with a memory are used in medical devices today.

Tissue Harvesting: The improved understanding of the immunologic system is revolutionizing the use of human and animal tissues. Hearts, livers, and kidneys are transplanted routinely, and surgeons are investigating a range of products such as blood vessels, muscles, nerves, tendons, and bones for use in body replacement. Linking human tissue with synthetic materials, such as using pig tissue to make heart valves, is in development. Investigators are already developing techniques to coat the inside of replacement vascular grafts and the artificial heart with human cells and retrovirus to make the surface more compatible with a patient's blood.

Biology: The revolution in biology has created the possibility of putting biologic sensors on the tip of a microprocessor. This union is producing instantaneous feedback on a patient's physiologic condition. Probes to monitor the level of insulin and sugar in diabetics and to control the rate of infusion of genetically engineered insulin are available.

These examples illustrate that health, like many other fields in government's purview, is too turbulent and complex for any individual or group to master completely. To deal effectively with the information requirements created by the multiplicity of social and technical forces, an organization must recognize its interdependence with its environment and create channels for effective communication inside and outside its boundaries.

LOCKED IN AN OPEN ROOM

A public administrator, like any decision maker, seeks as much relevant information as possible before making a decision. All too often, however, decisions must be made with imperfect information, and at times, with precious little information at all. If the available information is limited to what you and your organizational colleagues know, decisions can be flawed.

Sometimes the information you would like to have simply does not exist. At other times, the discontinuities in an organization's communication structure and the constraints on an individual's capacity to collect and understand information inhibit the flow of information. If the doors to your room are locked, you can understand that there are physical barriers to obtaining the information that you need. A more insidious situation is one where you are locked in your room, but the doors are wide open.

Being locked in a room with open doors may seem peculiar and contradictory. This situation, however, is what happens everyday in public and private organizations. It occurs, in part, because we let it happen. The number of hours in a working day are often inadequate to do what we feel needs to be done. We pour over our work, get wrapped up in the process, and forget what is happening outside our door. We do not go out and nobody comes in, though the door is open. We may not even realize that we are locked in since we have not tried to venture out. The unfortunate part is that everyone on the other side of the door is doing the same thing.

ORGANIZATIONAL DISCONTINUITIES

An organizational chart describes certain relationships among individuals (Figure 8.1). The chart is useful for describing the general responsibilities of different parts of an organization, the persons in authority, the positions available for the organization to achieve its goals, and the flow of communication in the organization. Most of us, however, are aware of the chart's limits in describing what really goes on in the organization.

For example, it is a common experience that communications are not restricted to lines depicted in the organizational chart. It is also not unusual for us to feel that other parts of the organization do not know what we are doing or are engaged in activities that seem counterproductive to our own. We often do not depend on formal lines of communication to learn what the rest of the organization is doing, or what is happening in the external environment.

Figure 8.1
The Organizational Chart

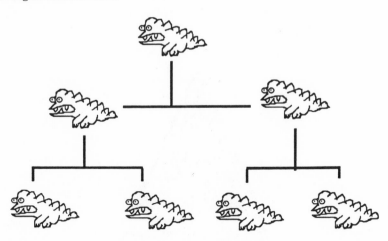

On the other hand, most people also communicate with their superiors or subordinates in a manner described by the organizational chart. Information is received and returned regularly, and it may be voluminous at times. The information, however, may also be irrelevant to the tasks at hand.

What can be even more frustrating is to send a message through the communication channels and then to hear your message distorted. It is as if you had spoken into an electronic voice scrambler used to hide the identity of a drug informer. The message sent is no longer recognizable as one's own, nor does it accurately express the ideas in the original message. It sometimes seems as if someone took the organizational chart and made a tear at selected points of the paper. The communication that one would expect does not happen readily, and the communication that does arrive has made its way across a system pervaded with discontinuity (Figure 8.2).

Talcott Parsons was one of the first theorists to describe the phenomenon of breaks between levels in an organization (1960). He identified three broad levels of responsibility in an organization: the technical system, the management system, and the institutional system. The technical system is responsible for doing the basic or core work in the organization, such as testing products or delivering services. The management system is responsible for mediating between the technical component and the organization's environment. Parsons believed that "qualitative" breaks or discontinuities occurred in organizations between the technical and management levels and between the management and institutional levels. Today, these breaks may have a particularly adverse impact on organizational performance. For example, when technical issues drive the organization, as happens in research and demonstration organizations, or science-based

Figure 8.2
Organizational Discontinuity

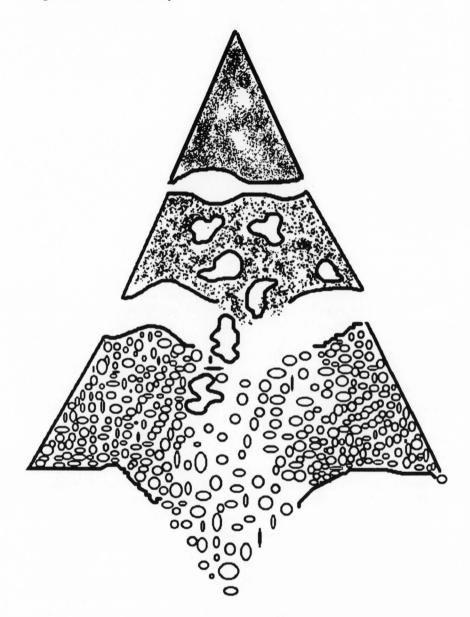

agencies, management may not have the technical expertise to know how to mediate effectively between the technical core and the environment.

ALTERNATIVE CONCEPTS OF ORGANIZATION STRUCTURE

The open-system model described by Katz and Kahn (1978) and the sometimes open and sometimes closed system described by J. D. Thompson (1976) consider an organization's interaction with its environment. An organization, when seen as an open system, is indeterminate and faced with the uncertainty created by environmental interdependence. Simultaneously, however, the core system of the organization is subject to criteria of rationality and hence needs determinateness and certainty. Thompson argues that to deal with these complex situations, an organization must develop processes for searching and learning, as well as for deciding.

Meltsner and Bellavita (1983) provide another open model that they describe as a policy organization. The policy organization is a conceptual tool to aide in understanding how policy is implemented. The policy organization looks beyond the boundaries of any single organization to include all the actors involved in a particular policy. Although the policy organization is hypothetical, it provides a framework in which a manager can look at the specific design elements of an organization and institute changes to improve policy implementation. The basic tenets of this construct are:

- a policy organization is not a formal organization but a fluid interorganizational network that is open to its environment
- an organization's *structure* and *features* determine its *capacity* to process information
- the policy organization has links to its environment

The structure and features are a function of *design elements* that are under the control of the manager. Hence, by changing the design elements, the manager can modify the organization and its ability to process information. The design elements include goals, resources, members, tasks, environment, decision making, structure, and communications.

One limitation that I find with the policy organization model and other open model systems is the belief that organizations can be described with a single structure. According to Clark (1985), our assumptions about a unitary structure in organizations are based on a problematic adherence to Max Weber's concepts of ideal structure. Schwartz and Ogilvy (1979) believe that there has been a shift in the profile of organizations. As boundaries shift from the clear and simple to the ambiguous and complex, it is more appropriate to have heterarchical (mixed) structures than hierarchical ones (Figure 8.3). The relationships between the members of an organization no longer fit the image of a mechanical system but

Figure 8.3
The Heterarchy

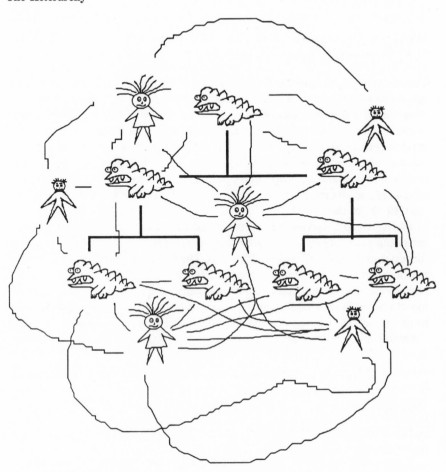

can be more easily likened to a holographic picture whose elements are all holistically interrelated. The sequence of events linked to achieving goals are no longer linearly causal but have multiple and mutual causes. The change process can no longer be viewed as a rational movement in an assembly line but must instead be seen as a dynamic process of morphogenesis (that is, the creation of new forms).

Schwartz and Ogilvy free us from a unitary view of structure and allow us to consider the idea that an organization can have multiple structures, with some elements arranged in hierarchical fashion and others not. One can envision a continuum of heterarchical structures, ranging from the more to the less rigidly organized: for example, from hierarchies to matrices to networks, to fuzzy groupings and chaotic aggregates.

FROM HIERARCHY TO CHAOS

It may seem strange to describe organizations as "chaotic aggregates," since individuals appear to use organization to reduce, not encourage, chaos and complexity. We arrange the creatures of the world into classes, genera, and species to allow us to comprehend and study the variations that exist. We subject to classification most complex phenomena, including our organizations. In the classification process, however, we lose sight of the diversity that exists in nature and confuse rigidity with rigor. We work vigorously with a classification system even though many parts don't fit the slots. The social world is fuzzy and difficult to put into categories. It is difficult to define precisely and objectively such fuzzy categories as fat men, small ladies, the best leaders, or successful organizations. Attempting to derive a single image of an organization's structure encounters similar problems. It is my belief that restricting our view of organizations to unitary structures inhibits the creativity of the organization and its members.

Rollo May (1980) wrote of those who are involved in the creative process as people who love to immerse themselves in chaos, to experience the fuzziness that exists around them, and then to express it in a simple form, just as God created form out of chaos. The genesis of new ideas seems associated with chaos and reaching into the depths of one's unconscious. Linus Pauling, a recipient of the Nobel Prize in chemistry, has said that to have a good idea you need to have lots of ideas. For an organization to have lots of ideas, channels have to be created to let the ideas in and let them be expressed.

Mueller (1986) maintains that organizational networks have the potential to help develop creative ideas. He notes that through networks we can foster the innovative side of organizations and allow people to express their humanity and creativity. Instead of interacting with people based on their position in an hierarchical organization, we can interact with them as colleagues and use the relationships to hear ourselves think, to share dreams and stories, to empathize with problems, and to share in successes. Each of us can weave a human network and fish ideas from the sea of chaos. The challenge is to develop an interface between, for instance, a hierarchy, a network, and other structures, and to find a functional and dynamic balance between them.

Like a work of art that has only a single subject with no variety or balance, an organization that is designed and acts in the ideal Weberian sense can be boring and nonfunctional. Unity of structure will allow an organization to succeed if there are no changes in the environment. If changes occur, the breaks in the successive levels of the organization described by Parsons will become insurmountable. As a result, the organization will no longer be able to serve its environment and will cease to exist.

Because of these factors and the rapid change occurring in our environment, I would argue, along with Mueller, that the Weberian image of bureaucracy is already obsolete in our information society. Formally, as evidenced by organizational charts, most organizations recognize the existence of only a single structure.

Operationally, most organizations already have multiple structures. These structures provide the variety that is needed to counteract the deficiencies and limitations of a unitary structure.

CREATING AN ALTERNATIVE STRUCTURE

By using the design elements described by the policy organization model, a manager can think about how change in an element can impact the flow of information and the organization's ability to learn and act. A manager may not have the ability to change all the design elements. But, as I will describe, small changes in one element may have a significant impact on the effectiveness of an organization.

An organization can increase its capacity to process information by expanding its informal membership. The seemingly benign introduction of technological devices such as electronic mail systems and electronic bulletin boards can expand an organization's informal membership by including into the communication system experts who are not formally part of the organization. Electronic bulletin boards can also facilitate communication, and provide managers with information for decision making that they would not normally have access to. In exchange for their participation, external contributors have the opportunity to influence the organization's policies through the information they provide.

A few years ago, my staff and I began working on a document that outlined the information that would be needed to evaluate the safety and effectiveness of an artificial heart. We included requirements for information that described the design and fabrication of the device, specifications for laboratory tests, guidance for conducting animal experiments, endpoints for human clinical trials, suggestions for explant retrieval analyses, and an outline for the statistical analysis of data. During the development of the document, I became aware that my staff and I could not provide all the technical details that would need to be included, nor could other experts within the organization. The scope of technical information covered so many topics on the front of scientific and medical development that no single person or group could address each authoritatively.

By pooling information from individuals within the organization and consulting experts on the outside, we produced a preliminary draft of this document. Based on my previous experience, I anticipated that there would be some disagreement about the contents of the document. I expected that manufacturers and researchers would interpret the process we used to prepare the document to mean that the FDA was establishing nonnegotiable criteria for the development of new medical devices.

The open-system models of organizations, such as the policy organization model, suggest that by expanding an organization's membership the organization alters its boundaries and its relationship to the environment. By establishing links into its environment, an organization has the capability to reduce conflict with sources outside the organization.

The electronic bulletin board has been a tool familiar to computer users and academic researchers. With a computer and telephone modem, an individual can access a bulletin board to read messages left by others, respond to messages, download or upload information (that is, transfer information from or to the host computer), or leave a message for others to read. If a message is left, the bulletin board can be accessed a day or a month later to see if anyone has responded. An electronic bulletin board also has the advantage of being independent of time, in the sense that access to another person's thoughts are not dependent on the need to coordinate schedules.

Our office established an electronic bulletin board, and the artificial heart guidance document was posted, along with a message about the purpose of the document and a request for comments and suggestions.

Before using the electronic bulletin board, medical device manufacturers and researchers involved in the development of the artificial heart that I talked with said that they were unaware of the requirements FDA expected them to meet. They also did not know, in general, how they could effectively communicate their ideas to the agency about policies that agency personnel were drafting. Using the bulletin board to solicit their assistance in developing the guidance document helped change their views of the agency and its procedures. As a result of their experience with the bulletin board, these same people felt that they could contribute and participate in the development of policies that incorporated their concerns.

With this positive response, I put other guidance documents that were in different stages of development on the electronic bulletin board. I contacted other individuals in the agency to tell them about the board, and many of them contributed their own guidance documents.

Once manufacturers began to learn about the electronic bulletin board, they began to contribute too. In one case, external contributors helped the agency improve its internal review process. A group involved in medical ultrasound devices used the bulletin board to establish a consensus among manufacturers on the format to be used for submitting information the agency needed to evaluate new devices. This format reduced the variability in applications submitted to the FDA and aided agency staff in reviewing these applications.

As the electronic bulletin board grew, it began to be a repository for guidance documents developed by the agency. As a result, the time to maintain the hardware and its contents soon expanded beyond the available time of the few individuals who organized it.

In the 1988 budget cycle, I proposed that the agency provide support for this project. The proposal was accepted, and personnel from the agency's computer staff became responsible for operation and maintenance. Personnel from the Division of Small Manufacturers within the agency became responsible for letting outside groups know of its availability.

Figure 8.4
Linking the Hierarchy and the Web

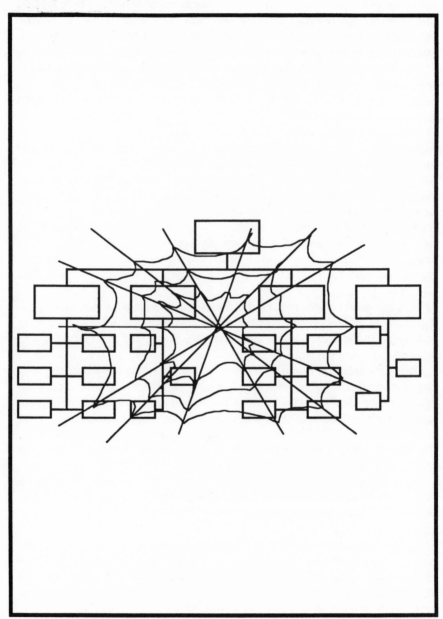

CONCLUSION

Social and technological changes in an organization's environment exaggerate the discontinuities that occur among the technical, administrative, and institutional levels. To contend with these discontinuities, organizations need to recognize and encourage the development of multiple structures. The spider web network of communication described in this chapter is one example of the form and function of alternative structures (Figure 8.4).

An electronic bulletin board was used to establish a new communication channel between the organization and its environment. By using the bulletin board and personal contacts, an individual can be linked to others within and without the organization in a way not envisioned by the organizational chart.

Although the primary structure of the agency was not visibly changed, the hierarchy now behaves differently than in the past. From the perspective of people working in the organization, the communication structure is more like a spider web than a hierarchy. This information network makes the operation of our knowledge-based organization more ''flat'' than the organizational chart would lead one to believe.

Managers need to realize that the driving forces of change are shifting the bases of organizational influence (Raven & Kruglanski, 1976). To make effective use of this awareness, managers need to develop new concepts of organizational design that are congruent with the reality of today's organizations (Lawler, 1986). The web of interrelationships described here expanded the communication capacity of the organization and allowed the hierarchy to cope creatively with the discontinuities that change creates.

Fritjof Capra (1982) points out that we live in a globally interconnected world in which biological, psychological, social, and environmental phenomena are all interdependent. Just as Newton's concepts no longer adequately describe these interactions, the concepts of Weber are no longer adequate to represent the interconnectedness of today's organizations. Through the use of a web, we provide ourselves with a link and a key to break out of the isolation of our office.

9

A Learning Model of Organization

Paul W. Waldo, Jr.

Most organization theories are based on philosophies that assume organizations are goal-driven, concrete realities whose ultimate objective is to provide products and services. Human beings are seen as the means to achieve organizational objectives. It is problematic whether organizations can function effectively in accomplishing the goals for which they were constructed and, simultaneously, provide an environment for organizational members that is supportive of personal satisfaction and development. Effective organizational operation and charitable human means seem to conflict at every juncture. Yet, because organization is undertaken to advance humankind, should not its ultimate goal be human action?

"Humanistic" approaches to management, such as Theory Y, human resource management, and quality of work life have sought to discover humane ways of achieving organizational goals. But they retain the goal of production as the bottom line. The public sector is not immune from the productivity criterion. Public organizations too are driven by the demand that services be delivered effectively to clients. Indeed, the emphasis on production *appears* appropriate, for the notion of an organization whose fundamental concerns is not productivity is tainted by a sense of perversion.

This chapter reexamines the issue raised here by postulating a model of organization in which the end and the means are human oriented. Theories that underlie how the concept of organization is understood can affect the way people perform tasks, how they interact with one another, and what they consider to be successful outcomes. The Learning Model of Organization, described in the chapter, posits that the fundamental task and pleasure of humans is learning. In an organization premised on a learning model, the focus of activity is on individual learning experiences, and on the way people organize to enhance their ability to learn. The model is grounded in a definition of learning that includes both the acquisition of knowledge and the manner in which knowledge is processed. To illustrate the model's utility, it is used as a framework for a reinterpretation of President Kennedy's Cuban missile crisis advisory group.

BASIS OF THE LEARNING MODEL

The Learning Model of Organization has emerged from my experiences as a member of a corporate-level staff for a large national government agency. Partly because of the perspective such a job enjoys and partly because of explorations in the organizational literature, I have observed ten features of organizational life that were not evident earlier in my career (Table 9.1).

There is no single body of organization theory that explains these observations, although at least one empirical study has described many of them (McCall, Lombardo, & Morrison, 1988). There are, however, disparate segments of the theoretic literature that together address these organizational phenomena. For me, the subject of human learning processes, interpersonal relationships, and organizational action are a base from which the ideas of interpersonal learning and the organizing of learning experiences can easily be derived.

Table 9.1
Ten Lessons from a Career in Government Organizations

- Most of what is required on the job can be learned only by doing the job.
- Much of what is learned is based on experiences gained by recognizing past mistakes.
- Individuals who are given challenging work attack their jobs with determination and excitement.
- Individuals are concerned about their continued progress in meeting successively greater job challenges and seek growth in the assignments they consider.
- People who serve primarily as catalysts or facilitators of ideas or action make significant contributions to organizational successes.
- Some people are involved in a continuing search for their roles in the organization, finding that their orientations to tasks change frequently.
- Effective leaders not only teach their people but expect to learn from them as well.
- As one progresses into broader management responsibilities, the job becomes more concerned with understanding other people, their motives, and their plans.
- The assignment of a task often follows a process of a superior and a subordinate jointly searching for and discovering what needs to be done.
- Definitions of organizational mission, and even of day-to-day tasks, are confused, ambiguous, and changing. Each person has a different perception of organizational goals.

LEARNING AS A FUNDAMENTAL ADAPTIVE MECHANISM

Life is change, a constant interaction with the environment. To adapt, individuals develop personal theories to describe, explain, predict, and use the lessons of prior experiences in planned future acts.

Learning permits positive change and adaptation. Humans grow and develop through their continuing responses to the tensions between existing and desired states. By successfully confronting obstacles, individuals develop the capacity for new accomplishments. Fred Friedlander (1984) attributes human adaptive needs to changes in the environment or to changing internal states. He argues that continual learning is needed to cope with the uncertainty, ambiguity, and unpredictability encountered in life. To Chris Argyris, learning is a process of discovering a problem, inventing a solution, and evaluating the outcome (Argyris, 1982). David Kolb (1984) emphasizes the importance of the transaction between the individual and the environment in the learning process; he conceives learning as an adaptive process. In this sense, learning is an adaptive process that people pursue throughout their lives. Kolb views humans as unique in their ability to adapt to environmental stresses and to modify and refine the environment by constructing social institutions that create new opportunities for further learning experiences.

THE PROCESS OF LEARNING

Early research in learning emphasized *what* people learn rather than *how* they learn. Cognitive theories studied the acquisition, manipulation, and recall of abstract symbols. Behavioral theories treated knowledge as an accumulated reservoir of information or habits representing responses to specific stimuli. Neither regarded the role of experience in the learning process.

In the writings of David Kolb, Donald Schön, and Chris Argyris, learning is viewed as an intrapersonal process that links an individual's internal activities with the environment. Karl Weick's ideas about organizations, discussed below, make a similar point. Learning is grounded in experience. It is a process in which exchange between the individual and the world around him or her are critical to survival and growth. Figure 9.1 portrays learning as a circular activity. An individual learns through sequential stages of perception, reflection, generalization and action. Figure 9.1 also illustrates how different authors, using different terms, have similar understandings about the learning process.

Kolb's Experiential Learning Process Model

Kolb (1984) sees learning as the ultimate adaptive process, one that creates knowledge. Kolb's efforts have focused on individual experiential learning, an intrapersonal process "whereby knowledge is created through the transformation of experience" (p. 38). Knowledge is generated through the interplay of two independent orientations: (1) *prehension*, the acquisition of experience, and (2) *transformation*, the process by which experience is converted into knowledge.

Figure 9.1
The Intrapersonal Learning Process with a Comparison of the Processes Developed by Kolb, Weick,
and Argyris

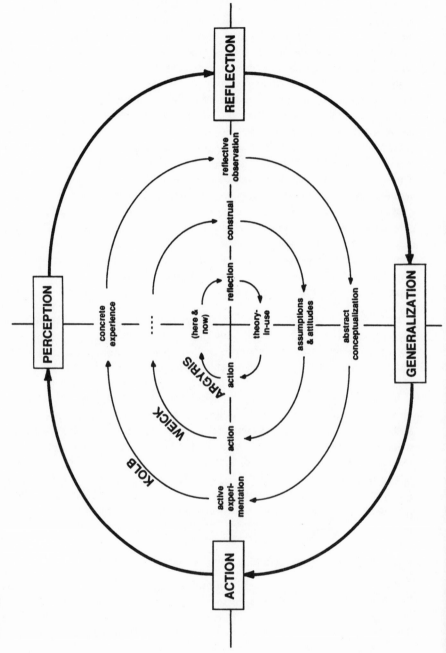

Prehension has to do with the way we grasp experience, and it may be either an abstract or a concrete activity. Through *apprehension*, we directly encounter what is before us in a concrete way, openly gathering data from our experience, without reflection or confirmation. We simply "apprehend." Through *comprehension*, we generalize and organize experiences by sequencing them and attaching symbols to them. In so doing, we acquire experience more abstractly, distorting what we have previously apprehended, deleting some information and emphasizing other. But comprehension allows us to structure the world of apprehended sense data so that it can be conceptually manipulated.

The second aspect of Kolb's learning process is transformation, processing experience into knowledge in a subjective or objective way. Through *intention*, we subjectively reflect on what we have apprehended, imaginatively reinforcing concrete experiences with additional perspectives that give meaning to what we know. Through *extension*, we objectively use what has been comprehended by being actively involved in the environment.

All four of Kolb's orientations—apprehension, comprehension, intention, and extension—are equally important and necessary ingredients of the learning process. They interact in a process that Kolb calls experiential learning, a cyclical phenomenon that continuously traverses four stages (see Figure 9.1). In the first stage, *concrete experience*, one experiences data about the world directly through apprehension. Next, in *reflective observation*, intention is used to attach meaning to the data. In stage three, *abstract conceptualization*, comprehension is used to construct generalizations and conclusions about the experiential data. Finally, in the *active experimentation* stage, the products of stage three are transformed, through comprehension, into new behaviors and new experiences, thus beginning the next iteration of the learning cycle.

Schön's Reflection in Action

Donald Schön (1983) describes a process similar to Kolb's that he calls *reflection-in-action*. It involves approaching new situations by viewing them as analogues to familiar situations and reframing them based on past experiences. Schön's work has been stimulated by the differences he perceived between knowledge dispensed in the academic setting and knowledge that practitioners use with competence and artistry.

Schön's quest has been to explore the process by which practitioners decide how to act. He notes that "practitioners themselves often reveal a capacity for reflection on their intuitive knowing in the midst of action and sometimes use this capacity to cope with the unique, uncertain, and conflicted situations of practice" (p. viii). He claims that reflection and action are complementary activities, and reflection-in-action is a continuous process of "reflective conversations" between hypothesis testing and problem solving, in which hypotheses are re-formed and problems are reframed.

Reflection-in-action begins with questions about the assumptions that underlie what is happening or what is desired. Answers to these questions lead to new interpretations that form a working hypothesis about what to do. The hypothesis is tested in action, and, to the extent the experiment leads to new understandings, new questions are asked. Repeating this process guides the practitioner through a continually increasing awareness of what he or she is doing, of the mistakes committed during action, and of the adjustments that need to be made to reduce mistakes.

Argyris's Learning Process

Chris Argyris's work is concerned with communication between people, and how they gain understanding about themselves and others through learning processes. His model of individual learning focuses on a process of self discovery, in which underlying attitudes, values, and theories of action are questioned and changed when needed.

Argyris distinguishes between *theories espoused* and *theories-in-use* (Argyris, 1982). Espoused theories are derived by asking people to articulate the reasons underlying action. According to Argyris, although many people believe that these theories reflect their attitudes and behaviors, important actions are rarely associated with espoused theories. True attitudes and values are revealed in action, and they may differ considerably from that which would follow from action based on espoused theories. Understanding one's theories-in-use, thus, becomes the key to the adaptive learning process.

To Argyris, learning is a circular, repeating process in which action is based on the cognitive system of complex propositions that defines a theory-in-use. In this process, an individual performs an act, reflects on the action, through the reflection discovers the theory-in-use, and then experiments with new theories, thereby leading to new behaviors for further reflection. As people become aware of how they traverse this process, they increase their self-understanding.

There is more to be said about the relationship between these models and the thesis of this chapter. It is necessary first, however, to discuss interpersonal processes as a link between individual and organizational learning.

INTERPERSONAL PROCESSES

In an organization where individuals must work together to accomplish goals that will benefit the greater whole, interaction among individual members is required. Nisbet & Perrin (1977) observe that human beings are joined in "social molecules" from the moment of their conception. We see individuals in the context of their roles, statuses, and socially derived behaviors. However, each individual, grounded in a different past, has needs and perspectives that differ from those of every other individual. Social bonds among people are not adequate to ensure effective coordination of organizational endeavors. Each person assigns unique meanings to relationships and events and has a unique understanding of the larger whole. It is through interpersonal processes that individuals understand one another and develop the capacity to coordinate their efforts.

While many people have written about this topic, Karl Weick (1979) has developed a model of interpersonal exchange that leads directly to interpersonal learning. He posits that personal interaction is the essential feature of organizational life, and that organizational phenomena are most usefully thought of as relationships that are assembled in a systematic fashion. He argues that the noun "organization" is a myth, that reality is better captured by the verb "organizing." For Weick, an organization as a materially real object does not exist, so descriptions of what goes on in organizations must center on the processes involved in relationships, and not on such artifacts as organizational structures. Preferring to conceptualize in terms of processes rather than structures, Weick treats interpersonal relationships the way Kolb, Argyris, and Schön treat learning.

Weick's basic unit of organizational analysis is the process of interlocked behaviors in an interpersonal relationship. From this perspective, relationships can be linked like subassemblies to form larger networks of communication and influence. Weick calls his elemental organizational unit a *double interact*, which proceeds as follows: Person acts, Other responds; Person readjusts on the basis of the Other's response, and so on. The relationship is viewed as a process; events are noticed, actions are taken, their consequences are construed, and the construals are stored and used in subsequent cycles. Figure 9.2 illustrates this process.

Instead of viewing attitudes as antecedents of behaviors, or vice versa, the model views both as a part of a larger process. In the same sense that Argyris suggests comparing espoused theories with theories-in-use, Weick embraces any discrepancy between attitudes and actions as opportune, for the individual may then compare the two to discover more about reality. Attitudes and behaviors, and the relationships between them, will change as each person learns more about the other and the other's assumptions.

ANALYZING THE LEARNING MODELS

I have examined models of intrapersonal learning and interpersonal relationships from several viewpoints and have noticed some remarkable intersections, summarized in Table 9.2.

Weick explores learning at an interpersonal level, but his analysis implies an intrapersonal process as well. Kolb attends to the intrapersonal process, while Argyris probes both levels. Figure 9.1, presented earlier, compares the terminology the authors use to describe the learning process. Together, the three authors describe a cycle of learning.

Stage 1 in the cycle is perception. For ease of analysis, Kolb chooses "concrete experience" to be the first stage in a process that repeats without beginning or end. Argyris emphasizes "here and now" data.

Figure 9.2
Karl Weick's Model of Interpersonal Exchange, Featuring the "Double Interact"

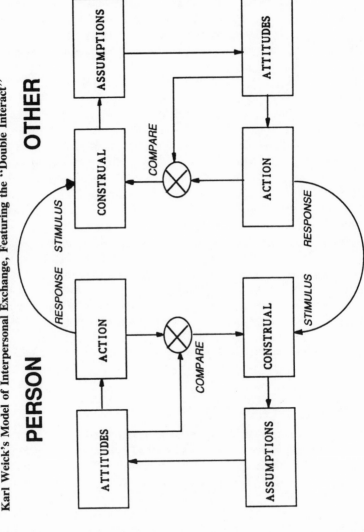

Table 9.2
A Comparison of Concepts of Intrapersonal and Interpersonal Processes

	WEICK	ARGYRIS	KOLB
PERSPECTIVE	Organizational structure theory	Social and organizational inquiry	Adult development
LEVEL OF ANALYSIS	Interpersonal	Interpersonal Intra-personal	Intra-personal
INDIVIDUAL CYCLICAL PROCESS	Implied	Yes	Yes
INTERPERSONAL CYCLICAL PROCESS	Yes	Implied	No

Stage 2 is reflection. After perceptions, one reflectively looks inward to contemplate and find meaning in the data. This part of the model is identified by all the authors discussed above, although Weick uses the term "construal."

Stage 3 is generalization, the resultant product of deriving meaning from experience. Kolb calls this stage abstract conceptualization. Argyris's term theory-in-use carries the connotation of a general principle that guides action. For Weick, the generalization takes place within a specific environment: the relationship with the other person.

Stage 4 is action. All the authors reviewed agree on the meaning of action, or active experimentation. It is a proactive venture, a testing of the environment. Action lies at the junction of both the intrapersonal and the interpersonal learning processes, and it is essential to both.

THE LEARNING MODEL OF ORGANIZATION

The intrapersonal learning models previously examined can be combined to form a model of the interpersonal learning process. It is depicted in Figure 9.3. The figure overlays Weick's interpersonal exchange model on the intrapersonal processes described by Kolb and Argyris and suggests the interdependence of

Figure 9.3
The Interpersonal Learning Process, in which Two Individuals Synchronize Their Intrapersonal Learning Processes

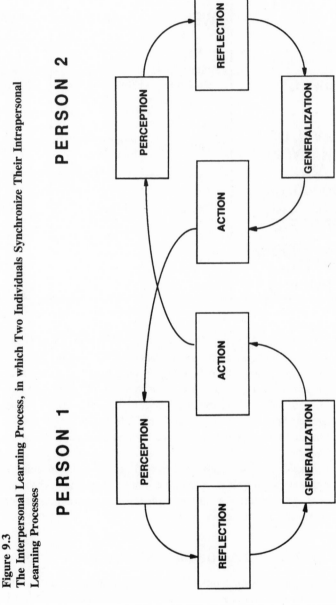

PERSON 1

PERSON 2

intra- and interpersonal learning. In an exchange between two people, one of them perceives the acts of the other, reflects and construes meaning, generalizes that meaning within the framework of past experiences, and acts accordingly. The act is perceived by the other, and the process continues. They learn together, in synchronism, each reinforcing the learning experience of the other.

When individual and interpersonal learning takes place in the context of an organization, the interpersonal learning model also describes the Learning Model of Organization. Further, it suggests seven normative propositions that form the preliminary outline of a theory of the ''learning organization.''

1. *Learning is humanity's fundamental adaptive mechanism to cope with change.* By successfully responding to the challenge and stress of change, individuals adapt to the environment, experience personal development and growth, and, through concerted efforts with other people, adjust their environment to enhance their capacity for further development.

In an organization based on learning, events that might otherwise be construed as problems are perceived as opportunities. Stress is viewed as a challenge. Difficulties are not seen as pain that must be endured but as occasions to broaden capacities and to grow. Individuals are anxious to assume new and challenging tasks, and they will accept the ambiguities of risk. Change is the stimulus needed to provoke further growth. It is not a threat but an opportunity for new experiences from which flow new learning.

2. *Learning is a circular process in which the components are of equal importance.* Both modes of learning I have discussed—intrapersonal and interpersonal—alternate between the abstract and the concrete, between the objective and the subjective. No single pole in the process predominates. Mistakes provide important feedback and are a necessary part of learning. Making mistakes is seen as neither wrong nor the result of incompetence but rather as opportunities for directing and focusing change, and for securing improvement. Schön's reflection-in-action illustrates this point. By alternating periods of experimentation and reflection, the practitioner is guided through a continuing increased awareness of action, of errors made during action, and of the adjustments that need to be made to decrease error.

3. *Interpersonal learning results from a confluence of individual learning processes and expands the capability of each individual to learn.* Intrapersonal learning influences interpersonal action, and the interaction is in turn incorporated into the learning process of the individual. Interpersonal learning occurs when two people synchronize their individual learning processes. As a dyad, their learning is greater than the sum of what they could learn individually. When two or more people orient their learning styles to one another, interpersonal learning becomes synergistic, and effective organization emerges.

4. *The central purpose of organizing is to increase the capacity of each individual to learn.* Action is not the sole purpose of organization. Action alone lacks meaning or value to the individuals who make up the learning organization. It is more usefully seen as a part of the learning process that includes perception, reflection, and generalization.

5. *Organizational behavior can be understood by examining the relationship between individual and interpersonal learning processes.* The Learning Model of Organization uses learning as the basic unit of organizational analysis. It assumes that people organize most effectively when individuals realize that interpersonal learning enhances intrapersonal learning.

6. *Organizational goals are the product of interpersonal learning processes.* Goals emerge from the intersection of the various subjective ambitions, motives, and expectations of each member. Those goals that have meaning to the individuals in the organization and that are perceived as helpful to learning will be supported. Externally imposed goals that do not contribute to learning will tend to be ignored.

7. *Learning is the means and end of organization, for it is through organization that members' learning processes are amplified.* An organization is the result of organizing, not people and tasks, but learning processes that can be simultaneously comprehended and grouped into progressively larger clusters. Organization is a means of accomplishing tasks that serve individuals by integrating their efforts and ideas in the service of learning.

THE CUBAN MISSILE CRISIS AS SEEN THROUGH THE LEARNING MODEL

The Learning Model of Organization provides a framework that can yield a new perspective of organization. The model permits an organizational analyst to understand in novel ways how tasks are performed, how people interact, and the reasons for acting. To show how the model can be used, I will apply it to the Cuban missile crisis of 1962, during which a group known as the ExComm (Executive Committee of the National Security Council) was organized to help decide how the government should react to the crisis.

The crisis began on the morning of October 16, 1962, when President John F. Kennedy was informed that the Soviet Union had been installing missiles in Cuban bases. The missiles had the offensive capability of launching nuclear warheads to much of the United States. Kennedy quickly assembled a group of advisors, known as the ExComm. For thirteen days, ExComm deliberated over what course of action to follow during the crisis. The ensuing events—a naval quarantine on Cuba, Soviet submarines in the Caribbean area forced to surface, an informal ultimatum issued to the Soviet Union about an air strike on the Cuban bases, Nikita Khrushchev's announcement that the missiles would be removed, and their actual removal—describe the actions that took place as the crisis unfolded and was resolved.

But actions define only part of an event. The processes that led to those actions must also be examined to understand fully why the events occurred. However, explanation of any activity in which humans are involved is necessarily influenced by the model that one uses to represent the events to be explained. The best known demonstration in public administration of this methodological truth is Graham Allison's analysis of the missile crisis (1971). Allison presents three explanations of the crisis in which events were conceptualized alternatively as the output of (1) rational deliberation, (2) organizational operating routines, and (3) political bargaining. The Learning Model of Organization provides a different view of the crisis. As I will illustrate in the remainder of this chapter, the Learning Model allows one to see the resolution of the crisis as the output of people engaging in interpersonal learning.

The crisis was intense and personally significant to the ExComm members, as evidenced by its prominence in the biographies and memoirs of the participants (for example, Sorensen, 1965; Kennedy, 1969; Bundy, 1989). Barriers to expression and communication were lowered because of the immediacy of the events; thoughts, doubts, and emotions were shared openly. Consequently, the individual learning processes were more accessible to one another, and the interpersonal learning processes were unusually intense, swift, and comprehensive.

The Cycle of Learning

The President, upon being informed of the missile buildup, needed to learn. He had to eliminate ambiguity and minimize the chances of error. Though the objective seemed clear—get the missiles out of Cuba—the facts were uncertain. Kennedy's first inclination was to respond, to act without reflection (Kennedy, 1969, p. 31). But prudence dictated the need to embrace the learning process. The President needed to understand the implications of alternative and interim actions; so, in the terms of the Learning Model, he delegated much of the learning process to the ExComm. That group's tasks were to identify the concrete facts of the situation (that is, "concrete experience"), think about and understand the meaning of those facts ("reflective observation"), generalize from the relationships among the various pieces of information theories about Soviet intentions and strategies ("abstract conceptualization"), and then propose the actions the President should take ("active experimentation"). The complexity and importance of the events required that the ExComm had to cycle often through the learning process.

Organizing the ExComm

President Kennedy had learned from the Bay of Pigs invasion the importance of getting accurate information and competent advice (Janis, 1982). While none of the people who have written about the missile crisis argue that the ExComm's goal was to help the President learn, that goal is strongly implied by the actions Kennedy took with the group and by the group process norms established by Robert Kennedy, a member of the ExComm.

The structural relationship between the ExComm and the President promoted openness, candor, creativity, and individual expression. The President did not attend all the meetings of the ExComm. He did not want his presence to inhibit the free flow of communication and probing among its members. The President wanted a group that would be creative and critical, one that would not shy away from conflict. The group environment he wanted could not emerge in his presence, he believed, because the group would defer to his judgments, whether direct or implied, and might fear making errors that would inhibit learning. Robert Kennedy recalled that "there was danger that, by indicating his own views or learnings, [the President] would cause the others just to fall in line. I felt the process of discussion, of truly hammering out the alternatives, was essential" (Abel, 1966, p. 60).

The group responded to the ambiguity of their task by employing an informal, open-ended process with no agenda. Dean Acheson described the group as "rather formless and confused" (Abel, 1966, p. 57). Although Dean Rusk was the senior cabinet official, he refused to exercise the chairman's function. Robert Kennedy emerged as the leader. He promoted candor by ignoring rank. He wrote that "we all spoke as equals" (Kennedy, 1969, p. 46).

Robert Kennedy (1969) believed that fact and opinion were best judged by purposeful conflict and debate (pp. 111 ff.) and by "skeptical probing and questioning" (p. 120). He was careful not to espouse any position. He choose instead to play the advocate so that various positions could be developed, examined, and extended. The ExComm members considered the probings not as attacks on their personalities but as tests of their ideas. The metaphor that underlay the ExComm's interactions was "Ideas Are Experiments," rather than "Ideas Are Possessions." By assuming a dialectical orientation to the ideas the individuals in the ExComm developed, Robert Kennedy ensured that interpersonal learning was enhanced.

Interpersonal Learning in the ExComm

From the beginning of their deliberations, the ExComm members were divided between two factions, usually described as hawks and doves. Although most of the members changed their positions one or more times during the crisis (Abel, 1966, p. 57), the two factions existed in dialectic tension throughout. Blight and Welch (1989) comment that "The hawks' Cuban missile crisis was relatively understandable, predictable, controllable, and safe. The doves', on the other hand, was inexplicable, unpredictable, uncontrollable and, above all, dangerous" (p. 201).

The hawks favored an immediate air strike to destroy the missiles. They preferred to forego the continual debates about alternative strategies or the morality of an air strike, and to proceed with plans for implementing action. The doves were inclined to consider carefully the possible consequences of proposed actions and the meaning that the Soviet Union might attribute to them. Secretary of the Treasury Douglas Dillon, a hawk during the crisis, believed that the doves' inexperience of military matters was responsible for their fear of nuclear engagement (Blight and Welch, 1989, pp. 153 ff.). As he characterized the difference between the two factions, "one side . . . wanted to do something forceful and decisive about the situation, while the other wanted to put off making a decision" (p. 162).

The Learning Model of Organization suggests another way to characterize the differences between the factions. The hawks were oriented toward what the model would term concrete experience and active experimentation. The doves were oriented to reflective observation and abstract conceptualization. These opposed and complementary elements of the learning process enabled the members of the ExComm to explore the issues thoroughly.

The critical probing and candor in the group enabled the President to learn vicariously. When oral reports of the ExComm's activities were delivered to him, the President could "study the men as they spoke and absorb the intangible factors which might help to refine his thinking" (Weintal & Bartlett, 1967, p. 65). The periodic reports helped John Kennedy synchronize his individual learning process with the ExComm's interpersonal learning For example, when the group formally presented him with the blockade recommendation on October 18, he "raised probing questions" (Abel, 1966, p. 54) that caused the ExComm to doubt its own recommendations. The President sent them back for further deliberations (Kennedy, 1969, p. 43). John Kennedy had detected some remaining uncertainty and capitalized on it to force the group to engage in further reflection, thereby continuing the learning process.

Outcomes of the Crisis as Seen through the Learning Model

What result did the ExComm achieve? Of what value was it? Was it the group's recommendations that led to the removal of the missiles from Cuba? The Learning Model of Organization suggests not. It is obvious that the recommendations were in part responsible for resolving the crisis, but in my view the part played was a comparably small one.

The ExComm's recommendation of October 18 to initiate a blockade was met by John Kennedy with intense probing, and it was finally rebuffed. On October 27, there was nearly unanimous accord in ExComm for military action in response to the downing of a U2 reconnaissance plane (Kennedy, 1969, p. 98). John Kennedy's final response to the missile crisis was not the product of the ExComm. It was the President himself, with Secretary Rusk, who improvised the ultimatum that Robert Kennedy presented to Soviet Ambassador Anatoly Dobrynin, which was followed the next day by Khrushchev's announcement that he was withdrawing the missiles (Kennedy, 1969, p. 106).

The central value of the ExComm was that it amplified the President's individual learning. The interpersonal learning that took place in the ExComm enabled the President to become aware of the facts, to reflect on their meaning, to use the information to generate theories of action, and then to decide how the United States should act in response to the presence of missiles in Cuba.

The primary result of the ExComm was the service that it provided to its members, to the President, to the United States, and, given the stakes, to the world. The significant outcome of the ExComm was the validation of a process in which individual learning processes flowed together, and in which the group perceived, reflected, generalized and acted—again and again.

CONCLUSIONS

The model of organization presented in this chapter is idealist in the sense that it described the way people could conceptualize their organizational interactions. People who work in an organization based on the Learning Model would view each day as another occasion to learn. Events provide opportunities to observe, to reflect upon observations, to construct hypotheses and theories about how to act, leading, ultimately, to thoughtful action.

The Learning Model of Organization is not a prescription for immediate change in existing organizations. The philosophy imbedded in this model will not be workable without radical changes in traditional attitudes and assumptions about organization. Adopting the concept of the Learning Organization requires surrendering the "time-proven" concept that was planted with the seeds of the industrial revolution, that production is a necessary and sufficient condition for achieving the good life. A learning organization must reverse those means and ends, returning to the far older concept that the end of organization is to serve its members and society. It is my view that when that change is made, we will discover that learning and human growth are both the means and the ends of organization. Production is a beneficial and inevitable side effect.

10

Archetypes in Organization

Judith M. Lombard

We live in a world of symbols. These symbols are an expression of the dynamic nature of the human psyche, projected as archetypes in a never-ending collage of forms and images onto the external world. Archetype is a term used by psychiatrist Carl Jung to describe recurring themes found in the stories and dreams of individuals throughout the world. Organizational stories, myths, symbols, and rituals are manifestations of archetypes. They represent unconscious themes and images that evoke and constrain human energy and action in organizations. An awareness of archetypes can provide insight into organizational behavior, and it can expand our organizational consciousness.

Human beings are symbol makers, storytellers, and mythmakers. From my experience in organizations and my background in mental health, I believe we must pay attention to organizational symbolism to understand what is occurring below the surface, out of the conscious awareness of the participants. Moreover, I contend that organizational stories and symbols serve the same function in organizations that myths and symbols do for individuals and society.

Individuals tell stories about their creation, about heroic deeds, about transformation and death to explain their existence and to provide guidelines for living a meaningful life. Many stories become the legends that give character to a society. So it is with organizations within society. In organizations, people tell stories about founding, development, and decline; stories of organizational heroes and enemies; and stories about battles, defeats, and victories. Organizations have physical presentations of these themes in statues, pictures, and architecture, and they have recurring practices or rituals that enact the stories.

The method of analyzing organizations presented here is informed by the work of Jung, Joseph Campbell, and my twenty years of experience as a therapist in the mental health field. The chapter begins with a discussion of new directions in organizational theory, and a description of the theories of Jung and Campbell about mythology and symbolisms. Next I describe how I used the concept of archetypes to analyze the evolution of a specific organization. The main story line of the analysis is the tension between feminine and masculine archetypes—archetypes that have a dual nature, positive and demonic. The subplots in the analysis concern the stories and symbols of organizational founding and purpose, wise fathers, and demon parents. The chapter concludes with some ideas on how one may begin to look for archetypes in one's own organization and how this method of inquiry can be used by administrators and theorists.

THE SUBJECTIVE SIDE OF ORGANIZATIONS

During the past decade, organizational theory and research have moved from their traditional, functional, prescriptive, "how-to-manage" orientation toward a greater sensitivity to descriptive, interpretative, psychological causes of behavior in organizations. The meaning of organizational stories and rituals is an aspect of organizational theory that reflects this change. The traditional approach to organizational culture, for example, is objective and functional. It suggests that managers can change the behavior of individuals by changing the stories and rituals that provide symbolic content to organizational life (Schein, 1985; Harrison, 1984; Stephens & Eisen, 1984; Wilkins, 1983; Deal & Kennedy, 1982; and Pondy, 1983).

Myths have been explored and described as the basis for organizational belief systems (Ferris, Fedor, Chachere & Pondy, 1989; Pondy, 1983; and Boje, Fedor, & Rowland, 1982). According to this argument, individuals use the myths portrayed in organizational stories to invest meaning and validity in their work place activities (Ferris et al., 1989, p. 86). By attending to symbolism, managers can introduce new symbols and thus change organizational myths for goal-oriented, utilitarian purposes.

A more subjective, interpretive approach to organizational symbolism is based on Freudian psychoanalytic theory and Jungian analytic theory. Both Freudian and Jungian theorists look at organizational stories, forms, and rituals as projections of unconscious material from individual participants in the organization.

Theorists using psychoanalytic theory typically diagnose organizational dysfunction using Freudian concepts. For example, Diamond (1988) suggests that people project significant early childhood experiences and relationships onto situations and persons in the present, including those in organizations. In this regard, Diamond describes organizational identity as repetitive patterns of individual behavior and interpersonal relationships that are unconscious and often dysfunctional. Hirschhorn (1988) describes models of social defense expressed in "collective fantasies and delusions" employed unconsciously, yet collectively, by groups of individuals to escape the primary anxiety of psychologically dangerous situations in organizations. Schaef and Fassell (1988) suggest that organizations can foster addiction, and Kets deVries and Miller (1984) suggest that dysfunctional organizations display neurotic styles—paranoid, compulsive, dramatic (hysterics), depressive, and schizoid—that are derived from the inner, psychic world of the people in the organization. These conditions are revealed by stories, behaviors, and rituals.

Jungian-based analytical theorists look not for evidence of dysfunction but for how organizations either alienate people or release their potential. Owen (1984, 1987) suggests that organizational stories or myths capture, represent, and manifest organizational Spirit in experiential terms. Owen uses the term *mythos* to describe the ongoing process through which Spirit is imaged. Mythos is the story arising from the life experience of any group, through which they come to experience their past, present, and potential (p. 16). It serves as a record of transformation (history), an agent of transformation, and as transformation itself. In a similar vein, Mahler (1988) studied stories in the Agency for International Development. Using Jungian theory, she described organizational stories that parallel classic, archetypal hero myths and depicted the organizational quest for meaning.

When Mitroff (1983) wrote *Stakeholders of the Organizational Mind*, he concluded that the Jungian concept of archetype was a kind of psychological stakeholder that influences organizational behavior. Although Mitroff suggested that archetypes exert a considerable hold on individuals, groups, organizations, and societies, he felt that archetypes have been almost totally ignored by most organizational theorists. The present chapter attempts to help fill that gap in organizational theory.

JUNG AND CAMPBELL: ARCHETYPE AND MYTH

Carl Jung, the psychiatrist whose theories of human personality inform the Meyers-Briggs Personality Type Indicator (Briggs-Meyers, 1976; Keirsey & Bates, 1978; Kroegar & Thusesen, 1987), became greatly interested in myths while working with hundreds of patients. He found recurring themes and images in his patients' fantasies and dreams. In studying world mythology, Jung found common threads between the symbols in patients' fantasies and dreams and the symbols in mythology. Jung concluded that individuals project aspect of their unconscious onto the environment and then deal with these symbolic projections as if they represented objective reality. Jung identified and described the psychological significance of many archetypes and archetypal events, including the mother archetype (1956; 1968a; 1968b), the child archetype (1968c), masculine archetypes (1956, 1958, 1968a), the Self archetype (1968c, 1968d), the hero archetype (1956), and the archetypes of birth and transformation (1956, 1968d). Kerenyi and Jung (1963) described the importance of birth or founding stories for people and cultures. Odajynk (1976) described the God archetype and how it triggers the child archetype, and the implications for leadership.

An example of the use of archetypes to predict group behavior is Jung's account of Wotan (1970). From this German patients' dreams, Jung identified an archetype that was emerging in the collective German unconscious. According to Jung, the cultural and economic strain of World War I caused a collective regression in the German people and evoked Wotan, a primitive Germanic god; this dark power invoked the myth of a Master Race, complete with a set of demonic enemies to be destroyed. As the Nazi movement grew to power in Germany, Jung watched the myth he had seen in dreams acted out on the national scene. For Jung, as long as people are unaware of the unconscious forces within themselves, they are powerless to deal with them.

Many books and articles have been written about how archetypes influence and inform individual and group behavior (Neumann, 1964; Perera, 1981; Whitmont, 1982; Bolen, 1984, 1987; Ulanov & Ulanov, 1986; Bernstein, 1987; Wehr, 1988). Joseph Campbell wrote several books on the influence of myths on the behavior of individuals, including *The Hero with a Thousand Faces* (1949) and *Myths to Live By* (1972). In these, he depicted various manifestations of the universal hero archetype and prevailing societal myths that inform the actions of Western societies today.

Campbell believed that myths are metaphorical revelations of fundamental, universal truths about human behavior and recurring life experiences, such as birth, maturation, love, and death. The source of myth is the human unconscious and the language is the metaphorical symbol. Symbols in dreams and myths are essentially the same, according to Campbell. He contended that recurring patterns of human behavior (rituals) are the means by which we enact our myths. Campbell wrote that " . . . both myth and dream are symbolic in the same general way of the dynamics of the psyche. But in the dream the forms are quirked by the peculiar troubles of the dreamer, whereas in myth the problems and solutions shown are directly valid for all mankind'' (1949, p. 19).

MY SEARCH FOR ORGANIZATIONAL ARCHETYPES

In 1986 I became intrigued with whether archetypes could be identified in an organization and, if so, what their presence might mean. I turned my attention to my organization, Saint Elizabeths Hospital, a public psychiatric hospital in Washington, D.C. The social behavior of patients in this institution was studied and analyzed by I. Goffman in *Asylum: The Social Situation of Mental Patients and Other Inmates* (1961). The hospital was built in 1852 by the federal government and it remained a federal facility until October 1987, when it was transferred from federal jurisdiction to the District of Columbia government.

My search for archetypes had four objectives. First, I was interested in whether I could identify recurring stories, themes, and symbols in the institution's history. If so, could I then identify the archetypal content in these stories and symbols? Next, could I determine if or how the archetypes inspired or constrained organizational behavior over time? Finally, had the stories changed or been revised over time and what did that mean for the organization?

I was aware from the onset that I was in a very subjective area of inquiry, and that I had to guard against projecting my own unconscious material as much as possible. To find recurring symbolism, I used the case study method and an historical comparative analysis approach to uncover recurring organizational stories, themes, and images. I searched through 135 years of official government documents— histories, autobiographies, annual reports, minutes of meetings and records of hearings in the U.S. Archives, newspaper articles, employee orientation materials, old photos, and maps. My objective was to record the words and descriptions used to depict the organization's founding, its special people, and its important events.

With little difficulty, I found many recurring stories about the founding of the institution: its special purpose and mission; the uniqueness of its name, Saint Elizabeths; its heroes and its enemies; and its good fathers and demon parents. I also found recurring references to the hospital's physical environment that seemed to relate to the healing purpose of the institution. Further, I found that the stories changed over time as did the attention paid to the physical environment.

To accomplish the second objective, identifying the archetypal content of the stories and symbols, I relied heavily on Jung's works on archetypes and symbolism (1956, 1958, 1964, 1968a, 1968b, 1968c, 1968d, and 1968e). To uncover the meaning of archetypes manifested in the recurring stories, I looked for discussions of that aspect of human nature in Jung's works. I searched the citations by Jung and Campbell of myths that dealt with the same phenomena or that contained the same elements as did the stories from the hospital. For additional insight, I reread Greek, Roman, and German mythology, looking for patterns in the classic myths that matched the story I had found (Graves, 1966; Hamilton, 1969). When I discovered that certain physical objects, such as trees, seemed significantly portrayed, I consulted Jung's work on the symbols of transformation (1956, 1958, 1968c) and encyclopedias on symbolism (Jobes, 1961; Olderr, 1989) to learn what special meaning people have historically attributed to such objects.

What I found in the recurring stories was the manifestation of feminine and masculine archetypes in the hospital's creation and development. There were stories about a heroic founding mother, a feminine goddess of healing, masculine ideals, good fathers, a demon mother, and a demon father.

The third objective, determining if or how the archetypes influenced organizational behavior, was the most difficult task. It required comparing and interpreting historical and contemporary behavior through the lens of the archetypal representations. However, I uncovered what I believe was a constructive tension that existed for nearly one hundred years between masculine and feminine archetypes. I found that these archetypes did permeate organizational belief systems and activities. I also discovered new stories and changes in the old stories. From the stories, it appears that the masculine-feminine balance became disturbed about thirty years ago. Negative, rather than positive, aspects of these archetypes were evoked and represented. Persons in the organization became enmeshed in severe archetypal conflict and they regressed toward infantile behavior.

After concluding the year-and-a-half-long study, I became increasingly convinced that useful organizational change at the institution was not possible until or unless the persons working there became aware of the myths they were caught in and were acting out.

THE CENTRAL THEME: ARCHETYPES OF
THE FEMININE AND THE MASCULINE

The stories about Saint Elizabeths Hospital that seemed to recur most regularly concerned the institution's founding; its meaning, purpose, and mission, and its special name; the character and deeds of the superintendents; and the attacks and criticisms on the quality of care given patients. These stories seemed to point to the dominant archetypal theme that characterizes the institution; the tension between masculine and feminine archetypes.

Jung identified several dialectical psychic functions in the human unconscious, each with potentially positive and negative characteristics. One set of opposing functions, the masculine and feminine, have various manifestations, including primitive femininity/masculinity, feminine receptivity/masculine action, feminine selflessness/masculine rationality, and feminine/masculine wisdom and spirituality (von Franz, 1964, 1986).

We recognize the personification of these archetypes in the images of the nourishing or evil mother, the nurturing or critical father, the wise old man or woman, the devil, the siren, and other figures. The archetypes appear also in individual personalities. Our feminine nature is subjective, other-oriented, concerned about relationship and values. It is our connective spirit, that allows us to love and nurture, to link, to feel, and to synthesize. Our masculine nature is objective, ego-oriented, concerned with power and control, mastery, order, and task. It is our power spirit, allowing us to know, to think, and to act.

The stories and symbols concerning Saint Elizabeths Hospital suggest that an archetypal dialectic enveloped the institution from the outset. In the organization's early stages, the feminine and masculine archetypes seemed to be entwined and to balance one another. The institution was to care for, shelter, protect, and heal those suffering from madness: a connective, relational, nurturing, and healing feminine purpose. The institution also was to cure mental illness efficiently and effectively and to serve as a model for the states and other nations: a rational, objective, task-oriented, and perfectionist masculine purpose. The institution enjoyed internal tranquility and external repute. In more recent times, the balance became disturbed. When the masculine purpose failed, the feminine was blamed for the failure. The masculine came to dominate the feminine and the institution suffered internal discord and external criticism.

Now let us look at the evidence that has led to this conclusion. What follows are five stories that highlight significant periods and events in the historical evolution of Saint Elizabeths: the founding, the selection of a name and location, the hospital's superintendents, the deinstitutionalization of the mentally ill, and the transfer of the hospital from the federal government to the District of Columbia. From a theoretical perspective, the stories also illustrate how archetypes can provide a new framework for understanding the meaning of organizational events.

THE FOUNDING, DOROTHEA DIX, AND THE
MODEL ASYLUM: ARCHETYPES OF FEMININE
WISDOM AND MASCULINE PERFECTION

The first story is about the birth of Saint Elizabeths. According to Jungian theory, birth is an archetypal event (1956, 1968a, 1968c, von Franz, 1972). Birth or founding stories are repeated over time because they represent important, specific aspects of the collective psyche. The characters and events serve as symbolic hooks for group projections. By retelling the accounts of their beginnings, individuals and groups come to understand and explain their existence and to attribute meaning to their current situations (Kerenyi & Jung, 1963). Psychologist Sam Keen (1988) suggests that the stories we tell about who we are, where we came from, and how we should behave, actually become what we are and what we believe, as individuals and as cultures. (p. 44).

For over a hundred years, the Saint Elizabeths' founding stories centered on a single figure, Dorothea Lynde Dix. Dix was a nineteenth-century humanitarian and social reformer whom many credit with establishing public mental asylums for the indigent, mentally ill throughout the eastern United States. In hospital accounts, she was singularly responsible for the birth of Saint Elizabeths. She lobbied Congress, session after session, until money was appropriated for the institution, despite the objections of conservatives and states rights advocates. She wrote the authorizing legislation. She approved and obtained the hilltop site on which the hospital was built. She recommended a man to be the hospital's first Superintendent, and he was appointed. Throughout her life she visited and "inspected" conditions at the hospital, ensuring that the level and quality of care remained high and that "human care and enlightened, curative treatment of the insane" was practiced (Houghton, 1971). Buildings were named for her, trees were planted in her honor, and the patients wrote stories and plays about her deeds.

Dix stood for more than a century as the great founding mother, a heroic feminine figure. President Millard Fillmore likened her to the Greek goddess of Wisdom, Athena (Snyder, 1975). Jung suggested (Campbell, 1971) that the feminine aspect of our nature is a powerful connective spirit whose ideals are relationship and completeness. The founding feminine, the Dix figure, was wise, aggressive, assertive, and effective, and the institution she founded embodied feminine wisdom and the feminine ideals of service, connection, balance, and dedication to others. In this respect, she is like the powerful Greek goddess Athena. The Athena archetype represents a positive feminine aspect of the human psyche: mature feminine wisdom (von Franz, 1964).

Besides the deeds of Dix, I found another theme in the institution's story of founding. The founding fathers, government officials and physicians, thought the government hospital for the insane should be a model institution. In Congressional documents of the 1850s, in reports from the Association of Medical Superintendents of American Institutions for the Insane, and in early institution accounts, one finds that besides being Dix's place of retreat and sanctuary for the mentally ill, the federal hospital was to be a model to the nation for asylum architecture, for staff composition and organization, and for treatment methods. Indeed, accounts suggest that not only was the government hospital to be a model for state asylums but it was also to be "worthy of the country" and a "shining example" to the world of the young nation's philanthropic nature (Davis, 1855). By 1855, stories were circulating to the effect that the hospital was a special, unique creation. It was to be a perfect model for the care of the insane, national in scope and purpose and international in influence, reflecting the character of the United States itself (Overholser, 1956).

Jung (Campbell, 1971, p. 566) suggested that the masculine aspect of our psyches is a vigorous power spirit whose ideal is perfection. If this is so, the early references I found to the institution as a model institution, that is, as a perfect hospital, reflects a masculine ideal. In fact, the idea that the hospital should be a national model persisted into the 1980s. This aspect of the founding image embodied the masculine ideals of perfection, mastery, model-building, and rational, scientific accomplishment.

From these stories of the institution's founding, two powerful archetypes emerge: one feminine, one masculine. These stories reminded both the storyteller and the audience that the place and its purpose were unique and that the hospital represented the nation's highest moral and scientific ideals. Legitimate management action had to (1) meet the feminine ideals of service; (2) achieve the masculine ideals of perfection by building a model institution; and (3) continue the myth that the hospital and the purpose it served were unique and special.

For many years, a balance seemed to exist between the feminine and the masculine. Dix's legislative objective, "humane care [feminine] and enlightened, curative treatment [masculine] of the insane," remained the institution's stated goal for 130 years. Mission statements, philosophies, histories, and annual reports usually began with her words. Actions flowed from those words and were justified by them. Staff conducted scientific research into the causes and treatment of mental illness. The federal psychiatric hospital enjoyed a national reputation for excellence. Management accounts reflected the perception that the institution treated its patients well, and at the same time furthered progress in psychiatry.

THE HEALING PLACE CALLED SAINT ELIZABETHS: ARCHETYPE OF THE SPIRITUALIZED, HEALING FEMININE

The second story is about the name and location of Saint Elizabeths and how the hospital reflected the meaning of both.

The Meaning of a Name

For nearly seventy-five years the federal institution had two names: a formal one, The Government Hospital for the Insane, and an informal one, Saint

Elizabeths Hospital. The formal name was authorized by Congress; the informal name was given by persons associated with the institution. In 1917, Congress recognized the informal name and officially renamed the institution Saint Elizabeths Hospital. It is an anomaly for a federal facility to be named for a Catholic saint. How did this come about and what did it mean?

Although many stories suggest that Union soldiers hospitalized for treatment of Civil War battle injuries first called the place "Saint Elizabeths," I found an earlier reference in a letter Dix wrote to the Superintendent in 1858. In it, she asked "How are things at St. Elizabeths?" (She spelled it without an apostrophe, as Congress would do three quarters of a century later.) Although there are two prominent Saint Elizabeths in Catholic tradition, the hospital stories depict only one patron, Saint Elizabeth of Hungary. This Elizabeth, despite a troubled life, cared for the sick and the poor and performed miracles. After her death, her dwelling place in Hungary became a shrine for healing. Elizabeth was patron saint of lepers and the insane, and of the sick, poor, and needy (Gorelick, 1986a). The hospital's superintendent insisted that the hospital was named for the Hungarian saint.

Saint Elizabeth represents a feminine archetype different from the one represented by Dix. Elizabeth is a manifestation of the spiritualized, healing feminine, the great healing goddess within. This archetype symbolizes the feminine sense of oneness and of meaning and connection to God and the Infinite. Elizabeth represents that aspect of the human psyche that heals the wounded and makes the afflicted whole again. Her power comes from the feminine power to create and give life. In her primitive form, she is Mother Earth, the creator and sustainer of all life. In her more highly evolved form, she is the spiritualized feminine capable of transforming love in men into spiritual devotion, connection, and meaning; and in women, changing love into selflessness in human relationships. In different times and cultures, this archetype has been represented as Hestia, Inanna, and the Virgin Mary (von Franz, 1964).

At the hospital, feminine archetypes of healing are manifested in two ways: by the name of the institution and by the physical environment. Not only is the feminine figure special but the environment itself is also special. Throughout human history, people have attributed mystical properties to certain place. At Saint Elizabeths, the magic begins with the story of the land. Several studies of Maryland land records reveal that the name Saint Elizabeths has been affixed to the land for more than 300 years (Gorelick, 1986b). The original English owner held two tracts of land, both of which he named Saint Elizabeths. Two hundred years later, the federal government purchased both tracts of land for the mental hospital. Through its name, the land has evoked the archetype of spiritualized, feminine healing since colonial times.

The Meaning of a Place

Von Franz (1986) suggests that we can tell from the "feel" of a place whether it is benevolent or malevolent. Temples of healing were benevolent and were sometimes built on hill tops or mountain tops as close to God as man could get.

Sometimes they were located in beautiful wooded groves filled with revered, holy trees such as cedar, cypress, olive, oak, and elm. Often these temples were near special rivers or had in them holy wells or cleansing pools. These temples of sanctuary and divine healing were surrounded by stone walls where one would find representations of the deity that protected the sanctuary. Sometimes that deity would be in the form of a person, for example, Apollo or Hestia, and sometimes the deity was an animal, such as an eagle.

In healing sanctuaries, one might also find symbols of psychic wholeness, the mandala, a perfect circle or square with great significance attached to its midpoint or center. The mandala is the universal symbol of the self and of psychic unity, completeness, and balance (Jung, 1968d). The other symbols—the mountain top, the wooded grove, the holy well, the stone walls, the eagle, the mandala—have regenerative qualities. From the earth comes life; from the trees, regeneration and transformation; from the waters, purification and regeneration; from the eagle, transformation and regeneration.

At Saint Elizabeths, symbolic representations of the archetype of the guarding and nourishing mother who can renew and transform the human psyche are everywhere. Like an ancient temple of healing, Saint Elizabeths Hospital was built on one of the highest points of land in Washington, D.C., "a shining city on the hill" that overlooked the nation's capital. The land stretched down to the banks of the Anacostia River and overlooked the Potomac. In organizational founding stories, considerable attention is given to the source of materials from which the old hospital was built. It was constructed from the land itself, from Saint Elizabeths' earth, wood, stone, and water.

For decades, meticulous attention was given to landscaping its 800 acres. Trees and exotic plants from all over the world were cultivated, as were gardens and crops. Pedestrian footpaths were constructed and fountains were built. Roses flourished. One superintendent wrote, "These grounds are among the most beautiful in Washington . . . I hope that the patients find healing in its touch" (Godding, 1892, p. 8). Another wrote that at Saint Elizabeths " . . . paths spread with green turf beneath the feet of the strolling invalid [who would] woo nature for the health that spurned nature had denied" (Overholser, 1956, p. 7).

Trees are feminine symbols of transformation, rebirth, and renewal (Jung, 1956, p. 219). The trees of Saint Elizabeths were greatly revered and carefully tended. Patient buildings and wards were named after trees, as were streets. Trees were planted as memorials to dead employees and patients. At one point, all the sacred trees of the Druids grew on the grounds. Today, circles of growing evergreens suggest sites of ancient religious practices.

At the entrance to the hospital are two golden eagles, the ancient symbols of rebirth and rejuvenation. Mandalas, the symbols of psychic wholeness, are found on many buildings and on the entrance. Like an ancient city, the hospital was surrounded by a protective stone wall—a symbol for the protective, healing feminine who, like a mother, harbored the inhabitants inside herself as if they were her children.

The symbols and the very setting of Saint Elizabeths Hospital offered reassurance about the frightening affliction of mental illness. Before psychotropic medications, mental illness had seemed beyond human control. Mental institutions were fearsome places. Because our knowledge was limited, we were compelled, I think, to turn inward, to the natural healing power of the feminine, to mother nature herself. At Saint Elizabeths, the feminine archetype was evoked and manifested in the name of the institution and in its physical symbols of rebirth and regeneration. Psychologically, the institution symbolically represented a place, and our best hopes, for psychic rebirth and transformation.

With this powerful symbol of feminine healing evoked, organizational activities at the institution focused on the connection between human beings and nature. Just as the hospital grounds were cultivated, contemplated, and conserved, so too were relationships between people. The spiritualized, healing feminine called for humane action. "Moral therapy" was practiced, a philosophy of treatment that stressed interpersonal relationships, respectful attention, and kindness. Physical restraints and drastic medical procedures were used sparingly. The humanistic and spiritual endeavor of the hospital required in the words of a former physician, the "almost devotional work of the superintendents" who lived always with and among the patients. Each manager of this institution had to be not only a healer but "a reformer, an active seeker for improvement, a relentless fighter of human prejudice in the hospital, in society, in the courts of justice, in human relations in general" (Zilboorg, 1956, p. 251).

THE SUPERINTENDENTS OF SAINT ELIZABETHS: ARCHETYPE OF MATURE, MASCULINE WISDOM, AND NURTURING, GODLIKE FATHERS

The third story is about superintendents of the hospital. Masculine figures are prominent in the hospital's history and in accounts of its contributions to psychiatry. Since men managed the institution, hospital histories were usually organized in terms of the superintendencies of specific physicians: Nichols, Godding, White, and Overholser. Each of these superintendents served for more than a quarter century, residing on the hospital grounds, ever present figures of male authority for staff, patients, and the community at large.

In the words of Zilboorg (1956), these men did devotional work. Not only were they prominent physicians who practiced moral therapy, they were also accomplished scholars, with musical or artistic talent, who championed the cause of mental health by fighting existing social and legal prejudices. Accounts of their lives depict them as above reproach in their conduct, and they were often described in paternal terms. For example, Nichols was the father of the secluded asylum household (Godding, 1890); Godding was "the kind of father and considerate ruler . . . beloved by all who knew him" (Simpson, 1899, p. 193); White was a "benevolent father" (Sullivan, 1940, p. 4); and Overholser was the "good daddy figure around here. Father implies an authoritarian presence. Daddy on the other hand is kindly, he can command you if he wishes, but he usually merely leads you, helping you to grow and be creative in your own right'' (Springarn, 1956, p. 14). These men were also national figures in psychiatry. White is credited with changing the course and practice of psychiatry in the United States and with managing the institution in such a manner that it achieved world renown. His successor, Overholser, was nearly as well regarded nationally and internationally as White (Springarn, 1956).

The superintendents represented not only the good father archetype but also the God archetype. By virtue of their role as physicians, the superintendents personified the Holy Healer. As superintendent of the national hospital, they were characterized as all-powerful, all-knowing Gods.

The aspect of the human psyche represented by these archetypes, good father/God, is the mature and wise masculine. In classical myth, these archetypes are represented by Apollo. One of the most important gods in both Greece and Rome, Apollo was the god of music, poetry, philosophy, prophesy, astronomy, mathematics, science and medicine. Apollo was the god of the Delphic oracle. He was the Healer who first taught mankind the healing arts. He was the god of light in whom there is no darkness, the god of truth in whom there is no falsehood. Apollo combined art with science and brought the light of rational thought to mankind (Hamilton, 1969, pp. 28–29). A bust of Apollo stands today at the hospital, in the former study of the superintendent's apartment. According to tradition, Carl Jung himself presented the bust to White in a visit to the hospital in 1919.

The father/God archetype evoked by and projected onto these men can be either a positive or a negative force. At the hospital, positive aspects of the archetype seemed to inform action. The archetype of the rational, yet moral and wise masculine, seemed to propel the superintendents to actions they might not have taken if they occupied lesser posts. Each man became prominent in reforming and advancing the care of the mentally ill. During the superintendencies of White and Overholser, 1905–1962, psychiatry matured as a field of medicine and they were in the forefront. Psychotherapy was established, somatic treatments were developed, and psychotropic medications were discovered and used. Much of the pioneering research was either done at Saint Elizabeths or introduced there as experimental treatment. In hospital accounts, this was the golden age, when the hospital was vibrant, active, and respected as a place of treatment.

The negative character of the father/God is two-fold. First, God's followers must submit to a God that demands perfection. When perfection is not attained, the God criticizes and punishes its followers. The followers either become more submissive and dependent or they blame God for what is going wrong. When this happens in groups, the God archetype projection is withdrawn from the leader, and the leader falls (Odajynk, 1976). Two of the four Superintendents did resign or retire when imperfections surfaced about the level and quality of care given to patients, Nichols in 1876 and Overholser in 1962.

INSTITUTIONALIZATION: ARCHETYPE
OF THE DEMON MOTHER

The fourth story is about changing attitudes toward the treatment of the mentally ill and the impact on Saint Elizabeths.

Public mental institutions have had many political, social, and legal critics over the years. Beginning in the 1930s, the criticisms about public asylums became increasingly vociferous. By 1961, a Presidential Commission denounced all large public institutions, suggesting that most should be closed down. These institutions, including Saint Elizabeths, became characterized not as places of retreat and rebirth for the mentally ill but as destructive, psychic prisons that were more harmful to the patients' psyches than the ailments they suffered from.

This conclusion was reinforced by a second event in 1961, the publication of I. Goffman's *Asylum*. Goffman, with the consent of the hospital's management, spent a year at Saint Elizabeths studying the social relationships between patients and between patients and staff. Goffman found the staff behavior toward patients to be inhumane and degrading, and he suggested that such behavior aggravated mental disorders. Relationships were depersonalized and patients were treated not as people but as objects. He coined the term "institutionalization" to describe patients' learned response to staff behavior and attitudes. Although I found no hospital accounts responding to Goffman's account of the socially debilitating effects of institutional life, he surely described an imperfect national model for the care and treatment of the mentally ill. The following year, Overholser retired.

Despite the efforts and technological progress made in the treatment of major mental illness, patients did not get well. Now those who treated them and the places of treatment came under attack. As many economic, political, social, and technological forces converged, Saint Elizabeths, like other asylums across the country, began the "deinstitutionalization" of its patients.

In the story of founding, we saw the masculine ideal of perfection reflected in the desire to have a model public institution. In the descriptions of the Superintendents, we found the archetype of the rational, moral, and wise masculine. According to Jung, the feminine side of the psyche has many virtues, but perfection and rationality are not among them. In Judeo-Christian cultures the feminine has been scorned for its imperfections and often made to serve the masculine (Campbell, 1971, p. 566). For centuries, the imperfect, illusion-spinning feminine had been blamed for insanity. The moon, a feminine symbol, struck human beings mad, made them lunatics. By the 1960s, sophisticated and elaborate psychological theories flourished that blamed women for insanity. If people were autistic, schizophrenic, manic-depressive, and had other major psychiatric illnesses, then their mother was the cause. These psychologically crippling women were described as demon mothers (Jung, 1956; von Franz, 1964).

The demon mother stalls psychic development, spins illusions, and casts spells that keep her child forever fused to her, forever dependent on her. She is the critical, engulfing, subservience-demanding archetypal demon, the polar opposite of the wise and healing feminine. By demanding dependence, the demon mother prevents psychological development and maturation.

It is my view that the demon mother came to be blamed for the failures of psychiatry. Mental hospitals across the country evoked and represented this feminine demon. At Saint Elizabeths Hospital, institutional defects were projected onto her, and the hospital itself became a demon. "She" (the hospital), like the archetypal demon mother, made patients dependent on her, institutionalized them, and then refused to let them go. And when the institution became "demonic," the people who worked there faced a moral and psychological dilemma of great magnitude. What does one do when one is accused of being possessed by a demon: deny it, admit it, or exorcise it? At Saint Elizabeths, the employees seemed consciously to deny being possessed, while at the same time they acted to oust all that was feminine in favor of the masculine. The feminine symbols of wisdom and spiritualized healing came more and more to be denied, as if all that were feminine was tainted. In stories of Dorothea Dix today, she is often characterized negatively, as a neurotic spinster or as an aggressive woman who badgered well-meaning men into creating insane asylums against their better judgment. In fact, she currently receives very little recognition for doing anything to aid the mentally ill. In 1987, on the 100th anniversary of her death, no official ceremony was dedicated to her honor at the hospital she founded. She was forgotten.

Management abased the feminine symbols at the hospital. The land was given away for highways, tourist attractions, and real estate development. The trees were cut back or cut down and few new ones were planted in their place. No longer were there orchards, gardens, and extensive flower beds. The fountains were filled in or removed altogether. The walls, built to protect this special place and to honor and harbor its goddess, began to be torn down, a symbolic emancipation from the demon mother.

When the District of Columbia assumed responsibility for the hospital in 1987, District officials "dissolved" Saint Elizabeths Hospital and renamed the entity the D.C. Commission on Mental Health Services. Legally, Saint Elizabeths Hospital no longer exists. Masculine rationality with its demands for perfection came to the forefront and there is little of the feminine left to temper its excesses.

CRITICISMS AND FEDERAL ABANDONMENT: ARCHETYPES OF THE DEMON FATHER AND THE CHILD

The fifth story describes the transfer of Saint Elizabeths from the federal government to the District of Columbia

Robert Denhardt (1981a) suggests that people tend to identify with their organizations, fusing part of their identity with the organization. Organizations give meaning to life and regulate and control human action. As individuals adapt to the organization, they suppress their personal views and sense of themselves. They come to view the organization, especially long-lived organizations, as an avenue to their immortality. For 135 years, Saint Elizabeths Hospital was a federal hospital, and at least part of the specialness employees felt about the hospital can be attributed to its national purpose and to their status as agents of the federal government.

From a psychological perspective, hospital employees tended to identify with one of the most powerful masculine archetypes, the Godhead of the state. As servants of the state, they carried out the will of this God. When their federal appointments terminated and they became city employees, the change in status was experienced as a denial and an abandonment by the all powerful father.

Hospital accounts suggest that after World War II politicians and others began to raise again the old question first asked when Dix lobbied for a national hospital. Should the federal government be in the business of giving direct service to the states, in this case running a public hospital in the District of Columbia? More and more frequently, the answer was "no." Steps began in the 1960s that finally culminated in the transfer of the institution to the District in 1987. The transfer by itself would have been psychologically difficult enough for the employees to handle. But the situation was complicated by two decades of federal criticism of the institution, criticism of its management and of the quality of its care. By 1987, the media were depicting the federal government as giving the District of Columbia not a prize gem, but a total mess (Boodman, 1986).

To make matters worse, even before the transfer, District officials began to attribute blame for problems in the developing mental health systems to the federal employees. In the year that followed the transfer, these officials continued to blame the former Saint Elizabeths employees for almost all problems that occurred. Collaboration between the employees and the District officials became impossible, mutual distrust resulted, and employee morale worsened. A negative masculine archetype appeared: the demon father.

By the mid-1980s, the employees of the institution were psychologically wounded. Their old stories and myths told them they were special people in a special place doing special work. Their history was known worldwide, their contribution to mental health had won renown, and the employees themselves were humanitarians serving the public good in service to the state. However, they had become identified with the godhead of the state, a masculine archetype that demands perfection. But they, like their hospital, did not attain perfection, and the Godhead criticized that imperfection as a transgression. Finally, they were cast out by the federal government and passed on to another critical, masculine, parental authority. Employees were angry about the way they had been criticized and abandoned by the federal government and about the way District officials characterized them.

Whenever the ego is wounded, a demon is always created to take the blame for the wound. In the story about the institutionalization of the mentally ill, we saw that when the collective ego was first criticized, the feminine was blamed, evoking the demon mother. In the 1970s and 1980s, the Godhead of the state became the demon. A demon father demands perfection while it criticizes, judges, blames, and wounds. As noted earlier, the God archetype has a dual nature, the perfectly good (God in Heaven) and the perfectly evil (the devil). Both these archetypes are dangerous to the human psyche. When a God archetype is evoked, it activates a "disciple" fantasy (Odajynk, 1976). Through deification of the God, the disciple-employee declines in stature, becoming dependent on the God for both self-definition and ego-recognition. This dependence activates the Child archetype. The disciple-child has only two choices. It must either kill the God or forever submit to it. At Saint Elizabeths, the employees did not kill the Godhead of the state; they instead submitted to it. Such submission produced rage that intensified when the Godhead criticized their imperfections and abandoned them.

In my view, when the demon father archetype emerged at Saint Elizabeths Hospital, the group psyche became infected with the Child archetype. In Jungian theory, the child evoked in this archetype blames all imperfections on external authority and refuses to assume responsibility for its actions, saying, in essence, "I did as I was told. Now look at the mess you made me cause" (Odajynk, 1976). This angry and petulant child is dependent and irresponsible. It makes messes and then denies its culpability, laying all responsibility at its master's door.

In organizations, activation of the Child archetype creates dependent employees who sometimes take irrational, irresponsible actions. At Saint Elizabeths Hospital, angry employees, like children, feigned dependence on the God/father, while simultaneously blaming the demon father for their pain and anger. Employees at this psychiatric facility became caught in deep-seated psychological conflicts that raised questions about the purpose and usefulness of their work, and about the purpose and meaning of their lives. In such a situation, positive organizational movement is stalled. Routine organizational activity continues, but these activities focus on surface matters, not on the underlying pain and anger.

After the transfer of the hospital to the District of Columbia, I heard no stories about rebirth, regeneration, or transformation. No mighty Phoenix has yet burned itself on its funeral pyre, to rise renewed from its ashes in the freshness of youth. The demons and the negative child seemed too strong and the feminine goddesses of wisdom and healing too weak to mediate and bind the wounds. Saint Elizabeth had died.

UNDERSTANDING ORGANIZATIONAL STORIES

As a result of my inquiry, I have come to believe that there are powerful stories in organizations that depict archetypal elements, reflecting what people are feeling, believing, and experiencing. If these stories are explored, they will yield their underlying psychological meaning.

Founding Stories

I think the easiest way to begin the mode of organizational analysis illustrated in this chapter is to look at the stories of organizational founding. The stories of founding tell the purpose and meaning of the organization. What was it created to do? What is its special place in society? How are its members expected to behave? In this case, Saint Elizabeths was a national hospital created to care for and treat the mentally ill wards of the federal government. It was to be a model of care for the nation and the world. Its employees were to behave humanely and rationally, to the credit of the nation. Masculine and feminine archetypes emerged, and they were equally powerful. They propelled those who initially managed the institution in positive directions that served both feminine and masculine ideals.

Heroes and Heroines

From the stories of organizational heroes and heroines, we get guidance about how members should behave in the organization and what values they should embrace. For example, what are the personal attributes of these figures? What special acts did they perform? What values do they represent? In this case, stories about Dix and the early Superintendents describe their selfless dedication to serving others, and their high moral character. They often acted against great odds, facing criticism and prejudices, to champion the cause of the mentally ill. Thus they evoked archetypes of heroic masculine and feminine figures.

Friends and Enemies

Are there stories about the organization's friends and enemies? Who are the friends and what values do they ascribe to? Who are the organization's enemies? What values do they hold? What actions do the stories suggest the organization take when encountering its enemies? What are the outcomes of these actions? Is the enemy converted, co-opted, coerced, tricked, or destroyed? In this chapter I did not go into detail about friends and enemies. However, Saint Elizabeths' friends and enemies were generally from the same groups: politicians, mental health advocates, patients' families, the media, and the courts. In the early days, stories suggest that enemies were often converted into allies because management addressed their concerns. But when the views of the critics came to be seen as correct, the Superintendent fell (Lombard, 1987). In more recent history, as criticism mounted, enemies were often ignored by the institution as ill-informed or malevolent. The archetypes of the demon mother and demon father emerged.

Physical Symbols

From the physical objects in the environment, what can we tell about the deities worshiped in an organization? Are they gods of money, power, service, science, progress? In public service, one would hope that the feminine deity of service would be prominent. At Saint Elizabeths in the early days, the feminine ideals of service and connection existed alongside the masculine ideals of perfection and accomplishment. This was evident in the Dix stories, in the hospital's name, and the characterization of the hospital's leaders. When the god of perfection turned demonic, criticizing imperfections, the demon mother and father came forth with a vengeance. Feminine symbols of healing and regeneration diminished.

Rituals

Rituals are the means to reenact myths. Are there any rituals (recurring practices) by which the organizational myths are acted out? I have described the rituals at Saint Elizabeths elsewhere (Lombard, 1987). The Dix figure was revered and honored in recurring ceremonies and citations. Mother Nature was celebrated annually in spring festivals, with music, dance, art, and games, when the hospital was afresh with green and the spring flowers were in bloom. As the land began to be given away in the 1960s, employees started a residential camping program in a nearby national park. There, patients could again be touched by the healing power of nature itself.

CONCLUSIONS AND LESSONS FOR PRACTITIONERS

Using Jungian theory to explore organizational behavior requires an understanding of the unconscious of individual human beings and a recognition that organizational stories, symbols, and rituals are products of unconscious internal psychic processes in individual human beings. These internal processes are projected onto external objects and events, where they are experienced collectively. Organizations progress, and regress, because of the dialectical tension inherent in the human psyche. The organization's stories, symbols, and rituals are our windows into what can be termed the organization's unconscious.

Many aspects of organizational archetypes remain unexplored in this chapter, and much remains to be done to bring this dimension of human behavior to consciousness. The first steps for administrators and organizational theorists interested in continuing this inquiry is to recognize the existence of archetypes in organizations, and to bring their manifestations (that is, stories, myths, and rituals) to conscious awareness. The second step is to understand what archetypes evoke and represent in the unconscious of human beings. This can be done by using the story lines suggested by archetypes (for example, the hero, the nourishing mother, and so on) to interpret behavior.

Some people will be concerned, and rightly so, about whether they are identifying the truly significant organizational stories and symbols and whether they are interpreting them correctly. We can say positively that all organizational stories are important. As for the validity of interpretations, do as some psychotherapists do: ask the patient, that is, the members of the organization. If the interpretation fits, there will an "aha" response or a vigorous denial. If there is neither, your interpretation may be wrong.

Probably the most important message I can leave with managers about this topic is my belief that we cannot control or manipulate the meaning of archetypes. We can only try to understand them once they appear. By bringing archetypes into conscious awareness, we can begin to deal with them and what they mean. Archetypes, if we are unaware of them, can propel us to the heights or dash us to the depths, and we never quite understand what happened. But brought to awareness, archetypes become a new and powerful way to understand the meaning of our lives and our organizations.

11

The Structure of Power in Public Organizations

Frank J. Nice

This chapter is about three dimensions of organizational power: overt, covert, and latent. While the three forms of power exist in almost all organizations, it has been my experience that administrators are usually aware of overt power, sometimes aware of covert power, and rarely aware of latent power. My central point in this chapter is that administrators can improve their ability to manage organizations by being aware of the structural dimensions of power.

POWER AND PUBLIC ORGANIZATIONS

Power is an indisputable fact of life in public organizations. It is what people use to get what they want in organizations. Yet it is often misunderstood by public administrators. One reason for this is the failure to recognize the multiple realities of public organizations and of power.

Public organizations can be understood in many ways: as problem-solving instruments, as sociotechnical systems, and as reward mechanisms. But they are also political structures (Boleman & Deal, 1984). They are made up of coalitions that compete among each other for material resources and influence. The coalitions are composed of people and groups who share common interests, and those coalitions will act to protect and advance their interest (Zaleznik, 1970).

Power has been defined in various ways. In its common language meaning, power can refer to the ability to perform effectively, the ability to exercise control, or the exertion of force. It can mean making decisions that affect other people (Bachrach & Baratz, 1962). Power is also a measure of the extent to which one person can get another to do something that he or she would not do otherwise (Dahl, 1957).

Individuals, groups, organizations, and societies can wield power. Power gives the user the ability to influence others' beliefs, emotions, values, and behaviors

(French & Bell, 1984, p. 309; Huse & Cummings, 1985, p. 567). Power can limit alternatives for action (Lukes, 1974, p. 22), influence organizational outcomes (Mintzberg, 1972, p. 4), or be the means for getting what one wants from the environment (Karp, 1986, p. 151).

Power has many forms: material resources, technical skills, knowledge, exclusive rights and privileges, access, visibility, energy, timing, trust, integrity, and likability (Smith, 1988). Administrators use these and other forms to exercise authority and leadership in organizations. They can also be used to manipulate, intimidate, or dominate. Power can be a means for achieving social good, or the method of gaining personal and organizational rewards.

Public administrators can increase their proficiency by understanding power. For example, it is important to realize that power stems from possessing a commodity that other people value. This knowledge helps administrators build a power base that they can use to maintain their organizational position and influence. Learning about the strategies and tactics of bargaining, negotiating, and office politics can further add to an administrator's effectiveness.

Understanding the theoretical characteristics of power is one place to start this study. Theory provides an intellectual framework to help make sense of one's experiences with power.

THREE DIMENSIONS OF POWER

I have found that power exists in at least three dimensions. First-dimension power can be seen in the overt behaviors exhibited by participants in decision-making situations, conflicts, and other organizational activities. It is the visible manifestation of power.

Second-dimension power is harder to see. It is related to a range of activity that is as much below the surface of activity as it is above. As I will describe later, the central idea in second-dimension power is the "nondecision decision," that is, the use of power to keep certain issues out of an organization's decision-making process.

The third dimension of power describes the forces that create an organization's power reality. The key issues in the third dimension are latent conflict and the "real" interests of the organization's members.

I recognize that these ideas are abstract, so my aim in the next section is to provide an example of how the three dimensions can be used to understand power dynamics in a public organization. Before I can do that, however, I have to say a few things about neurologists and neurosurgeons.

THE ORGANIZATIONAL REALITY OF NEUROLOGISTS AND NEUROSURGEONS

Neurologists are physicians who specialize in diagnosing and treating diseases of the nervous system. Neurosurgeons are also physicians, but they operate on the nervous system, in particular the brain. Thus neurosurgeons use a specific treatment, surgery, for nervous system diseases.

A neurosurgeon cannot operate until a neurologist diagnoses a nervous system disease or until the effects of earlier treatment are known. So neurologists play a key role in patient care. Neurologists are also important to neurosurgeons, since neurosurgeons depend on neurologists for their practice. But in the pecking order of the medical profession, neurosurgeons are considered the superspecialists, and they receive the highest respect and compensation for the work they do. Neurosurgeons who are in private practice can earn salaries several times higher than those of neurologists, and up to ten times higher than the salaries of general practitioners (Califano, 1986, p. 81).

Neurologists and neurosurgeons appear to have many interests in common. Both specialize in the same diseases, and their basic medical education and training are similar. When they are employed by federal organizations, the salaries of both groups are similar. If income is the same for government physicians, one would assume that their relative status and organizational power would be similar. The assumption turns out to be incorrect, however.

Several federal agencies employ neurologists and neurosurgeons, including the Department of Defense, the U.S. Public Health Service, and the Department of Veterans Affairs. In the federal agency I will describe below, the program administrators are neurologists, while the physicians who staff the program are both neurosurgeons and neurologists. Both groups compete for resources inside the organization to run their respective clinics and research programs. Because of the differences in the perceived value of neurologists and neurosurgeons, the people who administer neurology and neurosurgery programs soon find that they are not only managing physicians, they also are managing power and conflict.

Despite their nominally equal status in federal hospitals, the neurosurgeons have more organizational power than the neurologists. Neurologists outnumber the neurosurgeons by a large ratio, yet the neurosurgeons use a disproportionate share of the available resources. In addition, the neurosurgery program usually has priority in selecting available space, receives the largest number of hospital beds for its patients, has first choice in the types of patients that will be treated, and typically has the most influence on hospital and ward policies.

With the above as background, we are ready to discuss the three dimensions of power.

FIRST-DIMENSION POWER

The first-dimensional view of power has five elements:

- observable behavior
- a decision-making situation
- actual issues
- two or more competing subjective interests
- an obvious conflict among the interests

These elements form a matrix that can be used to analyze power in organizations.

Administrators who operate from a first-dimension perspective of power focus on observable behavior. If there are no visible signs of conflict, then the administrator assumes that no conflict exists. Power too has to be used visibly for the administrator to recognize it. For example, an individual or a group might have outside experts contact the administrator to try to influence a decision about budget allocations. They are using power overtly (Dahl, 1957).

Conflict in public organizations can arise over at least three scarce goods: budget personnel, and space. Managers typically have a set amount of money to divide up among competing interests; personnel ceilings are frequently imposed by higher authorities; and space is often limited to what is physically available in a building. In the federal hospital I have selected to illustrate my argument, neurosurgeons and neurologists both have to compete for their share of the budget, personnel, and space to support their programs. The program administrator's job is to allocate the resources, that is, to mediate the competition for resources.

An administrator who functions from a first-dimension perspective focuses on the visible. For example, the administrator would see that the central issues are what they appear to be: budgets, staff, and space. He or she would make a decision based on who had the most important wants and needs. Unless there is conspicuous evidence to the contrary, both camps are assumed to have equal access to the administrator. Each faction has equal opportunity to use their power to influence the decision-making process.

In the first-dimensional view of power, all the action leading to the resource allocation decision is out in the open for all to see and participate in. The winner of the conflict is the group that can make the best case, on the merits, to the administrator. The first-dimension perspective is, at best, a naive view of organizational power.

SECOND-DIMENSION POWER

A second-dimension view of power throws out the assumption that all the players in the contest have equal opportunity to access and to use power. From this perspective, there is more to the power arena than meets the eye. Power can be used to suppress issues. Conflict, which was overt in the first dimension, can also be covert.

Those with more power can prevent the less powerful from participating effectively in decision making with the "nondecision" strategy. If one sees a decision as a choice among alternatives, then a "nondecision decision" is a decision that "results in the suppression or thwarting of a latent or manifest challenge to the values or interests of the [dominant interest group]" (Bachrach & Baratz, 1962). Nondecision making is a way in which demands for change (that is, potential issues) can be killed before they get on the active decision agenda.

The second-dimensional view adds three ideas (italicized) to the first-dimension framework for analyzing power:

- observable behavior
- a decision-making situation *and a nondecision-making situation*
- actual issues and *potential issues*
- two or more competing subjective interests
- an obvious conflict among the interests, *and a covert conflict*

From a second-dimension lens, the federal hospital program administrator can influence or be influenced by power to prevent an issue from being raised. Consequently, the members of the organization with the least power are the least effective in political or conflict situations.

Let us say that the program administrator believes, for reasons we will discuss later, that neurosurgeons are indeed the most important members of the organization. This attitude is translated into a philosophy that "whatever the neurosurgeons want, the neurosurgeons get." When the yearly budget decision has to be made, explicitly rational decision-making processes give way to the nondecision. It is now an unquestioned given that the interests of neurosurgeons come first in the organization.

In effect, the program revolves around the perceived needs of this powerful group, at the expense of the less powerful groups. Except for its symbolic value, a formal decision process to allocate the organization's resources is no longer necessary; everyone knows how it will turn out. Because the weak groups do not challenge the strong ones, there is no overt appearance of conflict. It seems as if resource decisions are made through consensus.

One significant effect of second-dimension power is that issues of importance to the future of the organization are not raised unless they are supported by the dominant group. For example, concerns about the direction of research or the philosophy of patient care that the less powerful want to raise, remain potential rather than actual issues.

It is important to emphasize that power is being used to keep these issues dormant. Power in this instance is the ability to control the premises of decision making. Because there is no conspicuous opportunity for overt conflict, conflict becomes covert. In the example I am using, neurologists are reduced to complaining to other neurologists or to officials outside the program how it is that neurosurgeons get everything they want and neurologists get nothing. But the complaints are not translated into action.

THIRD-DIMENSION POWER

The third-dimension view argues that power can be used not only to prevent issues from reaching the decision-making agenda but also to prevent anyone from even *perceiving* that there is an issue that would give rise to conflict. In this sense, power is used unobtrusively to shape perceptions and cognitions (Hardy, 1985).

Individuals on the receiving end of third-dimension power placidly accept their role in the existing order. They cannot conceive of a different state of reality.

They view their organizational role and their conception of their interests as natural, beneficial, and unchangeable (Lukes, 1974, p. 24). Conflict is latent but is currently neither felt nor perceived.

The subjects of third-dimension power are not conscious of their real wants and interests. They docilely support the organization's existing power structure, regardless of their rank in it. Thus public managers cannot assume that the absence of complaints indicates that the organization is ruled through the harmony of consensus. But the latent conflict has to be brought to the surface, meaning it has to be felt or perceived, before the subjects of third-dimension power can improve their power position.

The third second-dimensional view adds two ideas to the first- and second-dimension framework for analyzing power:

- observable behavior
- a decision-making situation and a nondecision-making situation
- actual issues and potential issues
- two or more competing subjective interests and *real interests*
- an obvious conflict among the interests, a covert conflict, *and a latent conflict*

People who use unobtrusive power rely on a variety of mechanisms to secure their preferred outcomes, including symbols, language, myths, rituals, and ceremonies (Hardy, 1985). For example, medicine is a highly regarded profession; it offers the promise of extending life and delaying death. Neurosurgery is the epitome of medical practice, and neurosurgeons affect life in dramatic ways. The rituals of brain surgery inspire awe to anyone who has witnessed the complexity and sophistication of neurosurgeons at work. At the level of myth, neurosurgeons are godlike; when the brain is dead, the person is dead.

The symbolic authority of neurosurgeons affects program administrators just as it does people in other parts of society. Even administrators who are neurologists, and who thus would be expected to support other neurologists in conflict situations, can allow neurosurgeons to dominate an organization's political process. Domination occurs through inaction by administrators who subscribe unthinkingly to institutional and societal biases, and by other neurologists who unquestioningly accept the status quo. Any possibility of conflict remains latent, and, for many participants, buried below conscious awareness. As a result, disagreements among interests that could help an organization grow and perform more effectively remain unrecognized and unarticulated.

APPLYING THE PERSPECTIVES

Public administrators frequently think that power is being used only when there is a conflict. If conflict does not exist, administrators usually believe the organization has achieved consensus. The second- and third-dimensional views of power contends that this assumption can be wrong. Power can be in use even when conflict is not visible. Political inactivity no longer automatically equates with satisfaction. It can be the result of political strategies used by others to insure the dominance of their interests. The three-part model of power presented in this chapter offers public administrators a way to see organizational power in new perspectives.

The main lesson of the three-dimension view of power is that public administrators can raise an organization's consciousness of power and conflict. The administrator can point out potential issues and conflicts, clarify the wants of the competing interests, and, by redirecting complaints and grievances, bring covert conflict to the political agenda.

Managing the structure of organizational power can help administrators solidify their own power. Understanding the different manifestations of power can better enable administrators to recognize and to confront the power of others. If administrators see power exclusively through a first-dimension lens, they will tend to use their power only during overt conflicts. In effect they have abandoned the political responsibilities of management to those who wield second- and-third dimension power.

Becoming aware of the multiple dimensions of power can help administrators raise the consciousness of all interests, allowing for a richer and more inclusive decision-making process. By facilitating organizationally constructive conflict, administrators can broaden their base of power and can play an active role in creating a dynamic organizational power structure.

USING THIRD-DIMENSION POWER TO CHANGE A POWER STRUCTURE

In the neurology example cited throughout this chapter, the administrator was eventually able to look at the power dynamics through a third-dimension lens. He realized that the myth of the neurosurgeon's social value suffused the organization's culture and dominated the resource allocation process. So he created a different arena and a different myth to attempt to bring the latent conflict implicit in the neurosurgeon's dominance out into the open.

The program administrator was an expert in patient-care matters. He used this expertise to institutionalize norms and biases that favored patient care. The administrator established a patient-care committee to monitor the treatment that patients received. The committee was made up of administration, nursing, neurosurgery, neurology, and other organizational interest group representatives. The new organizational myth the administrator championed was that the patient was the most important element in the health-care arena.

The myth was supported by changes taking place in the environment of health care. External accreditation groups were playing a larger role in monitoring the way government institutions provided patient care, so the committee's importance increased as the status of patients became more important to the organization.

New accreditation standards were introduced, including peer review of physicians. Neurologists and neurosurgeons were given the joint responsibility for reviewing each other's professional performance.

Other groups in the organization that had been politically inactive had new opportunities to use power. The patient-care committee determined how hospital beds would be used. Nurses, who lacked a role in the budget allocation process, were now an important part of patient-care decisions.

The institutional biases and social myths surrounding neurosurgeons came into open conflict with the norms and biases of proper patient care, as articulated by accreditation groups and by nurses. Although the neurosurgeons retained their high status in the medical profession, they were equal to other providers when the issue was how to provide proper care to patients.

The program administrator was able to raise latent and covert conflicts to consciousness through strategic action. He made a unilateral decision that outside standards (from the accreditation body) would be used to determine the organization's policies and procedures. He changed the focus of the organization from what was good for program administrators to what was good for patients. This change was compatible with the personal and professional interest of physicians. He used peer review as the basis for resolving professional conflicts, instead of relying on the hierarchical norms of the hospital and of the medical profession. He opened the decision-making process to all interests in the organization, through the patient-care committee.

By being aware of second- and third-dimension power, the administrator was able to surface and redirect conflict so that the organization benefited. There is a greater sense of community in the organization now, since administrators, neurologists, and nurses can compete openly with neurosurgeons on the issue of what constitutes good patient care. Patient care has improved. As a reward, the administrator broadened his personal and organization power base.

CONCLUSION

I will close this chapter with eight specific suggestions that administrators can use to broaden their ability to manage power in organizations:

1. Do not avoid conflict. See it as a potential source of organizational growth.
2. When important issues are dominated by strong interest groups, change the organization's power dynamics by raising the power consciousness of interested parties.
3. Point out covert and latent conflicts in the organization.
4. Raise latent conflicts to consciousness by intervening in issues where real interests are being submerged.
5. Assist organizational members in clarifying and articulating their wants and needs.
6. Discuss with other members of the organization the norms concerning power.
7. Establish mechanisms to resolve conflicts.
8. Stay focused on the results you want and use any ethical process that gets you there.

As is true for other ideas offered in this book, the concepts presented in this chapter are offered for the reader to experiment with. Organizations are more than political structures, so looking at all issues through a power framework will be as misleading as seeing the organization only as a problem-solving instrument. The suggestions for practitioner-learning provided by Waldo, Boyd, and others in this book are also applicable here. The three dimensions of power and the suggestions for managing power are concepts that can assist administrators to organize their experiences. They are also a foundation for creating your own ideas about how to manage power in public organizations.

PART IV

SKILLS AND PUBLIC ORGANIZATIONS

As the first author in this section notes, people who are effective in public organizations are also skillful. Some skills can be learned in a classroom or a workshop. Other skills are learned only through practice. Part IV describes three approaches the authors have used to become skillful at understanding organizations.

William F. Pilkington is the Health Director of the Cabarrus County Public Health Department in Concord, North Carolina. He is interested in what determines the effectiveness of public managers. His search through the literature did not provide much help. The conventional wisdom holds that once you have located an effective organization, you have also found an effective manager. Most of the research he consulted described what the effective manager did, not the causes of effectiveness.

In chapter 12 Pilkington reports the results of a study he conducted to discover the determinates of effective management. He asked an expert panel to group seventy-eight local government managers as effective or ineffective. He then surveyed and interviewed the managers to identify what part skills, personality, and several other variables played in a manager's success.

He found that the effective managers tended to have high technical skills, an educational background appropriate to the job, experience, and a particular personality style. His study also found that training courses were not significantly associated with managerial effectiveness. Pilkington's study identifies areas for further research and offers administrators guidance about what they can do to become more effective.

Pilkington received his public administration doctorate from the University of Southern California in 1987. He began his career in 1974 as a policy analyst for the governor of North Carolina, became an assistant director of a health systems agency in 1977, and assumed his present position in 1981.

Organizations often send their managers and executives to courses to improve or to develop new skills. Barbara Bertsch Boyd, author of chapter 13, designs management development programs for the U.S. Department of Health and Human Services. In Boyd's experience, development programs frequently ignore the theoretical basis of the program's content and design. She discusses why program designers should pay attention to theory. In presenting her argument, she outlines the theoretical perspectives that inform her work.

Boyd starts the chapter with a description of the dysfunctional split between theory and practice and, by implication, between theoreticians and practitioners. She then explains how public administrators can benefit from theory. After reviewing evidence about paradigm shifts that affect practitioners, she discusses why traditional approaches to understanding organization and management cannot be expected to provide much practical guidance in postpositivist world.

With the foregoing as background, Boyd explains the theory she constructed to guide her in designing and evaluating management development programs. Her approach is based on adult-education principles, and on critical and interpretive theories of organizing. For Boyd, management development means helping managers grow toward independence and personal responsibility. Her chapter is especially valuable to people who design and participate in development programs.

As a manager of the Human Resources Development Institute at the Department of Health and Human Services, Boyd is responsible for the design and implementation of executive, management, and other employee development programs. She has been with the Department for fifteen years, during which time she has worked for the Social Security Agency, the Office of Human Development Services, the former Office of Education, and the U.S. Public Health Services. She is a doctoral candidate in public administration at USC.

Peter Wheeler is the Deputy Associate Commissioner for the Social Security Administration in the Department of Health and Human Services. He began his career with Social Security working in the Bronx, New York. He has been a public administrator for twenty-nine years, and a member of the federal Senior Executive Service since 1973.

In chapter 14, Wheeler describes the transforming skills of public leadership. He believes that effective leaders must be anchored intellectually to an understanding of administrative and political theory, for example, the origins and legitimacy of social institutions, political economy, and institutional design. Additionally, as other contributors to this book have maintained, the leader needs to articulate the personal theory that guides and reflects action.

Wheeler's leadership theory incorporates a clear understanding of his assumptions about human nature, and about the normative premises of public organizations and individual ethics. His desire to balance what he terms the "quest for internal and external goods," and to integrate that quest with his understanding of contemporary political theory, led him to James MacGregor Burns's idea of the transformational leader. The author concludes his chapter by describing the vision that transformational leadership offers to the public leader.

Wheeler presently manages the Social Security Agency's nationwide Quality Assurance and Payment Integrity Systems. He is also completing his doctorate in public administration at the University of Southern California.

12

Understanding Effective Management

William F. Pilkington

Managerial effectiveness is a crucial element in the study of public administration. Despite the recent attention given to effectiveness in the public administration literature, however, many questions remain unanswered and many related issues remain unresolved. For example, what do we mean when we say that a manager is effective? Can personal effectiveness be separated from organizational effectiveness? Is effectiveness learned or is it intuitive? What type of manager will be effective in a specific job?

These questions illustrate the gap between knowledge and the application of knowledge about managerial effectiveness. It is obvious that additional research is needed before we understand the relationship of certain variables to effectiveness.

SEARCHING FOR THE MEANING AND DETERMINANTS OF EFFECTIVENESS

A logical place to begin is to examine the various definitions of managerial effectiveness. However, there is no clear consensus in the literature on a definition, and it also not clear at what level—organizational, departmental, work unit, or individual—effectiveness is measured. The only consistent theme to any of the definitions is that effective performance, at some level, leads to the achievement of positive results. These "performance" definitions of managerial effectiveness are grounded in the philosophical perspectives associated with business administration and economics.[1]

In many public organizations it is difficult to agree upon the indicators that can be used to measure effectiveness. It is even possible that the effectiveness of the organization can be unrelated to the effectiveness of its managers. For example, a manager may be impeded by organizational forces, such as inadequate budget or staff. Are these managers truly ineffective if their organizations do not achieve the expected goals? Can it be truly stated that organizational effectiveness is *the* factor that determines managerial effectiveness?

Research generally indicates that managerial effectiveness is associated with personal and environmental factors. Among these are the individual's competencies, the job's demands, the specific actions or behavior of the manager, and the organizational environment (Boyatzis, 1982, p. 30). The most prominent of these factors are individual competencies. The competencies include skills; personal characteristics or personality; special education, training, and experience; the use of power; and personal faculties, such as self-confidence, self-image, and self-control.

Richard Boyatzis has developed a definition of managerial effectiveness that incorporates both organizational performance and individual competence and abilities. For Boyatzis, "Effective performance of a job is the attainment of specific results (i.e., outcomes) required by the job through specific actions while maintaining or being consistent with policies, procedures, and conditions of the organizational environment" (1982, p. 12).

The requirement for "specific results" in Boyatzis's definition is consistent with other definitions of managerial effectiveness and allows for the use of outcome measures. These outcome measures can provide important information on organizational effectiveness.

The phrase "through specific actions while maintaining . . ." adds an important dimension to the meaning of effectiveness. The implication of Boyatzis's formulation is that it is not enough to relate effectiveness to one variable, that is, organizational performance, without examining the roles of other variables. These variables may be acting in concert or separately to produce effective management. For example, a manager's competencies and abilities (for example, skills, education, experience, and training) influence the actions he or she will take to move an organization toward specific results.

THE EFFECTIVENESS OF GOVERNMENT MANAGERS

To evaluate the view that managerial effectiveness was related to more than organizational performance, I conducted a study to investigate the relationship of individual attributes to effectiveness. The study involved seventy-eight local government managers in North Carolina and was conducted during 1986–87.

The study tested the relative impact of six variables (skills, education, training, experience, personality type, and management style) on the managerial effectiveness of a select group of public administrators. Other variables, such as organizational resources, were not examined in this study and are not a part of this research design.

The study provided the opportunity to reduce some of the mystery that has surrounded the question of what makes one manager more effective than another. The first step in this study was to develop a means for evaluating the effectiveness of managers. Next, the relationship between effectiveness and the education, train-ing, and experience of these managers was analyzed. Then, the differences in management style and personality temperaments were examined to see if rela-tionships between these variables and managerial effectiveness could be found. Finally, the management skills of these participants were examined to identify any relationship between effectiveness and skills.

To select the participants for the study, I asked people who were familiar with local government managers in North Carolina to identify the people they believed to be the most and the least effective managers. This is known as "the reputa-tional approach" and was developed as a method for studying community power structures (Rose, 1967). I based my selection of participants for the study on the number of times they were identified by the expert panel as effective or ineffective.

Conceptualizing a Manager's Skills

The study focused on the skills, education, training, experience, personality, and management style of the participants. Each of these variables can take on a range of values, depending on how they are defined and measured. Table 12.1 provides a summary of how I defined and measured these variables.

Skills are the actions that managers take in carrying out their jobs effectively (Katz, 1974, p. 90). According to Katz, "a skill implies an ability which can be developed, not necessarily inborn, and which is manifested in performance, not merely in potential" (p. 91). Katz further suggests there are three basic skills: technical, human, and conceptual. I measured management skills by administer-ing a survey instrument that I designed using Katz's framework.

Technical skills involve methods, processes, procedures, or techniques. Budgeting, performance appraisal, time management, planning, and forecasting are examples of dimensions of technical skills that can be measured. The measure of technical skill is how well the manager performs the essential activities associated with his or her job.

"Human skill is the executive's ability to work effectively as a group member and to build cooperative effort within the team he leads" (Katz, 1974, p. 92). Katz distinguishes technical skill from human skill by noting that technical skill involves working with things while human skill involves working with people. Some measures of the manager's human skill include communication, under-standing, and sensitivity to individual needs.

Conceptual skill involves the ability to see the "big picture." Katz describes conceptual skill as "seeing the enterprise as a whole, recognizing how the various functions of the organizations depend on one another, and how changes in one part affect all others" (p. 93). Measures of conceptual skill include attitudes, perception, insight, and flexibility.

For the purposes of this study education was defined by the type of graduate degree the respondent possessed. Education was measured by whether the respondent had the appropriate degree prescribed by personnel requirements (for

Table 12.1
Variables That Influence Managerial Effectiveness

Variable	Definition	Measure
Skills	Ability to perform essential management functions.	*Level* of human, conceptual, and technical skill as determined through the administration of a survey instrument.
Education	Formal education leading to a specific graduate degree.	*Possession* of appropriate educational degree(s).
Training	Participation in management development training outside of traditional educational training.	*Absence* or *presence* of management development training from survey of individuals involved in this study.
Experience	Service as a local government manager.	*Number* of years of service as a local government manager.
Personality	Preferred way of dealing with the world, reaching decisions, and handling problems.	*Scores* on Kiersey-Bates Temperament Sorter.
Management Style	How a manager behaves with respect to the competing concerns of people needs and production needs of the organization.	*Scores* on the Styles of Management Inventory, based on the Managerial Grid Concept of Blake and Mouton.

example, a degree in management or administration). I considered the absence of the appropriate degree as evidence of inadequate preparation for the job.

I defined training as participation in management development seminars. The seminars did not include courses taken as a part of a degree granting program. For data collection, training was measured as a yes/no variable—either the manager had some exposure to training or he or she had none.

I measured experience by the number of years a manager served as a local government administrator. Supervisory experience is generally a primary basis for selection as a top manager (Young, 1977, p. 46). However, experience may or may not be indicative of competence (Young, 1977, p. 47). Nevertheless, I considered experience to be an important variable in determining the factors that influence managerial effectiveness.

I defined management style by using an instrument that depicts five basic leadership approaches. These are: the 1/1 manager who has little concern for people or production; the 9/9 manager who has maximum concern for people; and the 9/1 manager who has extreme concern for production. I used the Management Style Inventory to measure the management style of each respondent (Hall, Harvey, and Williams, 1980).

Finally, the personality of each respondent was defined by the Kiersey-Bates Temperament Sorter. The inventory identifies sixteen personality types, each with distinctive characteristics (Keirsey and Bates, 1978, pp. 5–11).

STUDY FINDINGS

In the study I found that effective managers tended to have high technical skills. There was a positive relationship between effectiveness and the two other skills: people and conceptual, although the association was not as high as it was for technical skills. A manager's education and experience were also related to effectiveness. Managers who had a particular personality type were more likely than the other managers I studied to be effective.

The Importance of Skills

The most effective directors were those with high technical skills. Seventy-seven percent of the managers with high technical skills were effective managers, while only 27 percent of the managers with low technical skills were effective managers. The obvious inference is that it is more difficult for a manager with low technical skills to be effective. If high technical skills are the most closely associated with effective management and if technical skills are indeed learnable and teachable, it is then possible to improve the technical skill level of ineffective managers, thereby increasing their chances of becoming more effective managers.

People skills also appear to be associated with managerial effectiveness, although the relationship is not as strong as it was with technical skills. Sixty-seven percent of the managers with high human skills were effective managers, while 42 percent of the managers with low human skills were effective managers. The data suggest that high human skills may lead to effective management but low human skills do not necessarily lead to ineffective management.

Conceptual skills were also associated with managerial effectiveness. Sixty-four percent of the managers with high conceptual skills were effective managers; 40 percent of the managers with low conceptual skills were effective. From these data, one could arrive at the same conclusion that was reached on human skills. That is, high conceptual skills may lead to effective management but low conceptual skills do not necessarily lead to ineffective management.

Education and Training

A manager's education was also associated with effectiveness, although not as closely as skills. Sixty-four percent of those managers with appropriate educational backgrounds were effective managers, and 80 percent of the managers without appropriate degrees were ineffective managers.

Training was the only variable I studied that was not associated with effectiveness. Fifty-eight percent of the managers with some training were effective managers, but 55 percent of the managers with no training were also effective managers. The data suggest that training may not significantly affect managerial effectiveness. However, it was not easy to define training as a variable, and a better definition might yield a different result.

A Manager's Experience

I found that manager's experience was related to effectiveness. Sixty-five percent of the managers with five years or more experience were effective managers; only 40 percent of the managers with less than five years experience were effective. There seems to be some relationship here between experience, technical skills, and effectiveness. Presumably, a manager with more years of experience will acquire more technical skills and become more effective. Conversely, the manager with less experience will not possess the technical skills needed to be effective.

A Manager's Personality

I also found that personality was related to effectiveness. Specifically, the ESTJ type was most frequently associated with effective local government managers. Seventy-three percent of the managers who were categorized as the ESTJ personality type were also defined as effective. The ESTJ type is described as follows: extroversion (E); sensation (S); thinking (T); and judging (J). ESTJs are especially well-suited to organizations that are structured along hierarchical lines of authority. The personality types of other managers in the sample were distributed broadly among the remaining fifteen personality categories.

As one might expect, a management style that showed equal consideration for people and production (the 9/9 style) was strongly associated with effectiveness. I found that most of the *ineffective* managers were 5/5 and 9/1 managers. The result is not surprising. The 9/1 manager focuses on the needs of the employees at the expense of organizational goals and organizational production. This manager is excessively people oriented. The 5/5 managers tend to overcompensate in balancing the needs of the organization against the needs of the employees, often leading to dissatisfied employees and poor production.

THINKING ABOUT MANAGERIAL EFFECTIVENESS

I have been a local government manager for almost fifteen years. In the past three years, I have been formally studying the determinants of managerial effectiveness. In reflecting on my experience and my research, I believe what I have learned has specific consequences for the way we think about the subject of effective management. I will present my ideas in six propositions.

Proposition 1: *Managerial effectiveness can be defined and measured.* Although there are many different definitions of managerial effectiveness, it is possible to develop a definition that considers the components of the various definitions.

To help clarify the concept, I suggest that managerial effectiveness means attaining a specific result through the simultaneous interaction of skills, education, training, experience, personality, and management style. Additional situational variables, such as organizational resources, were not included in the design of my study. Consequently, the definition I offer is a partial one. Nonetheless, the definition reflects the importance of the factors that I found to influence managerial effectiveness. In my view, a measurable way to define the effective manager has been missing from the literature.

Proposition 2: *Linking managerial effectiveness to organizational effectiveness limits our view of managerial effectiveness.* In the conventional wisdom, once one has located an effective organization, one has also found an effective manager. Typically, the next step in the inquiry is to identify the work activities of the effective manager to understand how managers spend their time.

Although this approach has its advantages, the resulting product is little more than a "portrait" of *what* the effective manager does. Unlike the study reported in this chapter little if any effort goes toward understanding *why* these managers are effective.

Proposition 3: *The "whys" of managerial effectiveness are more import than the "whats."* The "whys" look to explain the causes of effectiveness. The "whats" seek only to demonstrate consistent work activities among effective managers. We should be more interested in how effective managers do what they do, instead of simply knowing what they do.

The present study focused on several individual managerial abilities and competencies, and demonstrated a relationship between the characteristics and effectiveness. It is an approach to understanding why managers are effective that is strikingly absent from much of the literature.

Proposition 4: *No single factor leads to managerial effectiveness in every situation with every manager.* Consequently, to understand effectiveness it is necessary to look at many factors simultaneously. For example, this study involved looking at the association between education, training, experience, skills, personality, and management style effectiveness.

Proposition 5: *Environmental forces may play a key role in explaining managerial effectiveness.* Among these environmental forces are organization resources, organizational climate, and organizational culture. I did not test for any relationship between the environment and effectiveness, yet my experience as a manager tells me that there is one. An organization with adequate staff, finances, and facilities is probably more likely to succeed in accomplishing its goals than an organization with inadequate resources. However, as I indicated earlier, organizational success does not automatically equate to managerial effectiveness.

Proposition 6: *Additional research can help clarify the factors that are situationally associated with managerial effectiveness.* I was surprised during this research to discover the paucity of work done in conceptualizing and measuring the factors associated with managerial effectiveness. I was particularly struck by the absence of data linking effectiveness with the variety of situations and conditions a manager or organization might encounter. Clearly there is room in this area for additional empirical work.

THE EFFECTIVE MANAGER

From a practitioner's perspective, I think that the study has yielded results that are especially interesting to those seeking to become more effective managers.

Knowing that technical skills are clearly associated with effectiveness, and that human skills, conceptual skills, education, experience, personality type, and management style may be associated with managerial effectiveness, is a significant step toward understanding why certain managers are effective or ineffective. Understanding the degree to which each of these factors is associated with one's own effectiveness is an important part of becoming a better manager.

High technical skills had the strongest relationship to effectiveness. These skills involve such activities as planning, budgeting, and forecasting. They can be taught and learned. Obviously, the manager seeking to become more effective must be interested in achieving technical proficiency.

The personality type ESTJ also appeared to be strongly associated with effectiveness. Although it is probably impossible to alter our basic personality preferences, it is possible to use our auxiliary, or secondary, preferences. Since the ESTJ-type manager seemed most effective, other managers with different preferences can use their auxiliary preferences to gain more balance: for example, to become more focused on the outer world (E), more fact-based (S), more logical (T), and quicker to reach decisions (J).

Effective managers used the 9/9 management style, showing equal consideration for people and production. People with other styles of management should analyze their styles and decide whether attributes of the 9/9 style would help them become more effective.

Education in fields related to management or administration and experience of five years or more also appeared to be associated with effectiveness. The implication for the practicing public administrator is clear: get the appropriate education and stay in the job long enough—at least five years—to become effective.

High human skills and high conceptual skills also appeared to be associated with effectiveness although not as closely as these other variables. According to Katz, conceptual skills are probably developed early in life and it is unlikely that much change in conceptual skill level can be attained. Managers seeking to improve their human skills must learn to work more effectively with people in such areas as personal relations and communications.

Effectiveness is not as easily achieved as the preceding paragraphs might suggest. Managers are not chameleons. Some are more flexible than others. Some simply lack the ability to change. Some changes, such as to one's personality, are not very likely. However, it is possible to evaluate those factors associated with effectiveness and make changes where change is both possible and comfortable for the individual.

NOTE

1. A review of this literature and of the data supporting the study results I will discuss below are contained in William F. Pilkington, "Selected Determinants of Managerial Effectiveness" (Doctoral Dissertation, University of Southern California, 1987).

13

In Search of the One-Minute Megatrend: Theory and Practice in Management Development

Barbara Bertsch Boyd

Those of us who design and implement programs to develop public sector managers for a complex and turbulent world face a dual challenge. While we create programs to help managers in the midst of unprecedented change, we must conduct our own practice in the same chaotic environment. In the past we could afford to be unaware of the assumptions and theories that guided our practice. However, with both the content and context of our practice in turmoil, such ignorance may make us ineffective at best, and irrelevant at worst.

I believe that theory should be an integral part of public sector management development programs. Most of the time, however, its role is inconsequential. This chapter discusses why theory tends to be neglected, the consequences of neglect, and how explicit attention to theory can improve management training programs. I conclude by offering a theory of practice, derived from my experiences, that guides the work I do in designing public sector management and executive development programs.

I do not offer these ideas with the aim that they should be adopted by others. I include them in the hope that my discussion will encourage others to begin, or to continue, their exploration.

THE SPLIT BETWEEN THEORY AND PRACTICE

Praxis is the synergistic intertwining of theory and practice. All the chapters in this book are about praxis. They each describe how practitioners use theory to improve their practice, or how their practice has helped them to develop their theory about some aspect of the public administrator's world. Praxis is also a concept that is notable for its absence in much of what passes for public sector management development.

It is rare to find people who are comfortable both with theory and with practice. For example, the split between the way academicians and practitioners view the world is apparent to anyone attending a national public administration conference, such as the American Society for Public Administration or the Association of Policy Analysis and Management. Academicians tend to "talk down" to practitioners, as if they were a lower species. Practitioners frequently come away from conferences with the view that academicians do not understand "the real world."

In actuality, the two groups are not very different. Practitioners develop and use theories every day, although they are rarely aware that they are doing so. Academicians are also practitioners of education, although they seldom view themselves explicitly in that role.

The content of management development programs in many public agencies contributes to this dichotomous view. Sometimes theory is ignored completely. For example, seminars on the legislative process may provide practical knowledge about "how Congress really works," but they avoid broader Constitutional and societal issues. When theory is discussed, it is frequently treated as a separate (and often boring) ideal that practitioners find difficult to apply to their environment.

The theory-practice split is also apparent in the attitudes of the people responsible for designing management development programs. A 1987 survey of Fortune 500 companies (Stephan, Mills, Pace, & Ralphs, 1988) showed that human resource development (HRD) practitioners are often unaware of the theories (for example, behavioral experiential, rational) on which their programs are based. The same survey also shows that practitioners consider knowing about such theories somewhat unimportant. In my experience, many public sector HRD practitioners would, unfortunately, respond in a similar fashion.

THEORY OFFERS MEANING AND ALTERNATIVES

A review of development courses offered to practitioners over the past several years would turn up a rapid succession of "hot" management topics: productivity improvement, Japanese management, excellence, peak performance, total quality management, and so forth. The latest management fad is quickly turned into a seminar. There is little evidence in these programs, though, that the designers gave any significant thought to the theories on which the programs are based, or to the outcomes, if any, they were intended to produce.

While theory may appear to be irrelevant to getting a job done, a leading adult educator, Malcolm Knowles, warns HRD practitioners that it is unrealistic to think that they can ignore theory:

The fact is that there are assumptions, concepts, and principles—theories—behind everything you do, whether you are conscious of them or not. . . . If you aren't clear about what your theory is—or even whether you have one—the chances are that you will end up with hodgepodge. You will use different theories in different times or situations, or conflicting theories for different decisions in the same situation (1984, pp. 106–7).

Boyd and Levinson (1989) note that if planners ignore the leadership theories they are using in curriculum design, the program outcomes may be surprising or disappointing. They make the obvious, but often ignored, point that designers should be clear about the purpose of their programs. For example, if the purpose is to reinforce existing organizational leadership styles, a design that is based on a different theory than the one currently in use may produce unwanted change.

Robert Denhardt (1984) believes that practitioners want two things from theory: ideas they can use to fashion alternative approaches to their work, and frameworks that can help them see their experiences as a meaningful part of something broader and more significant. This argument clearly applies to the people who design management development programs.

Brookfield (1986) asserts that because the people who facilitate adult learning have not articulated their own theories of practice, they often accept their agency's mission or objectives as the general definition of what they are about. Or they believe that good practice means simply satisfying the program needs or wants that have been identified. "Without some sense of what is both effective and desirable," Brookfield argues, "we may begin to shift with whatever professional wind is blowing at the time or become subject to the dictates of political office-holders who can use us to achieve whatever ends they deem desirable" (p. 199).

The apparent indifference of those in the human resource development field to understanding and articulating a theory of practice may stem from ideas about the origins and functions of theory. There is a dichotomous view that theories are developed in the academic world and then passed on to practitioners to use if they can. Theorists do not practice and practitioners do not theorize.

Removing the division between theory and practice can illuminate and clarify alternative approaches to management development. However, it does little to provide managers with a deeper sense of meaning. In my view, management development practitioners will begin to see their work as meaningful only when they construct personal theories of practice. To illustrate the point, I have written this chapter to share the personal theory I have constructed.

THE CONTEXT OF CONTEMPORARY MANAGEMENT DEVELOPMENT

The first step in developing a theory of practice is to understand the context of practice. Naisbitt (1984) contends that Americans now live in "the time of parenthesis," a time between the old era of an industrialized society and the new era of an information society. We have come to realize that many characteristics of the past—centralized hierarchies, representative government, nationalistic thinking, short-term solutions—are inappropriate in the contemporary world. Yet we have been unwilling to embrace fully a future of decentralized networks, direct democracy, global interrelationships, and long-term processes.

Thomas Kuhn (1970) introduced the idea of paradigm as a way to understand changes of the magnitude described above. As Nancy Eggert discussed in an earlier chapter, paradigms refer to basic ways of looking at and acting in our world. From this perspective, the time of parenthesis can be viewed as living in the midst of a paradigm shift.

A study conducted at the Stanford Research Institute (Schwartz & Ogilvy, 1979) identified the paradigm shifts that are occurring in a variety of fields, from quantum mechanics and physics to religious studies and the arts. This movement from a positivist (or "what you see is what you get") to a postpositivist world view is characterized by the seven major shifts summarized in Table 13.1.

The Traditional Paradigm

The traditional paradigm assumes that reality can be broken down into simple units and that we can understand the whole by adding our knowledge of the parts. In this simplified world, people and ideas can be ordered in pyramidal hierarchies, with the "best" or most important at the top. The metaphor of the machine fits naturally the traditional paradigm, in that machines can be taken apart, their pieces studied or repaired, and then put back together again to form the whole.

The traditional paradigm assumes that if enough information is gathered about past and present behavior, future behavior can be predicted or controlled. Moreover, it assumes that events and their causes are direct, linear, and knowable. Consistent with the metaphor of the machine and this pattern of linear thinking is the notion that systems are constructed and modified by assembling the pieces

Table 13.1
Toward a New Paradigm

Construct	Traditional Paradigm		New Paradigm
Ideas About Reality:	Simple	→	Complex
How The World Is Ordered:	Hierarchy	→	Heterarchy
Metaphor To Describe Reality:	Mechanistic	→	Holographic
The Nature Of Reality:	Determinate	→	Indeterminate
The Nature Of Causality:	Linear	→	Nonlinear
How Change Happens:	Assembly	→	Morphogenesis
How To Understand The World:	Objectivity	→	Perspectival

in the proper sequence. Finally, the traditional paradigm assumes that inquiry about the world, that is, science and research, should and can be objective.

The New Paradigm

In contrast, the new paradigm recognizes that breaking a thing down into simple pieces can not only make the thing less understandable but can change the relationships between its units. The whole is often different from the sum of its parts. Such a highly complex world may have many "bests" and thus requires multiple ways of talking about and organizing this diversity. The old machine metaphor cannot support or illuminate this emerging world view. Holograms provide one possible alternative. With a hologram, each piece contains information about the whole. If a section is missing or removed, the remaining pieces can be used to regenerate the whole.

In a complex world of diversity and heterarchies (or multiple structures), the future is ambiguous, and the relationship between an action and its outcome is unclear. We often know what will happen only after it happens, and even then we may not know what caused it to happen. For this reason, attempts to create new systems by tinkering incrementally with what is in existence may produce unexpected and unwanted outcomes. Morphogenesis, by contrast, is the creation of a new form that is qualitatively different from its originating elements, as, for example, butter is different from cream. Finally, the new paradigm requires multiple points of view and modes of inquiry to understand the world adequately.

APPLICATIONS TO PUBLIC ORGANIZATION AND MANAGEMENT THEORY

The paradigm changes described by Schwartz and Ogilvy are reflected in recent approaches to understanding organizations and management. The titles of several recent management books make the point vividly—*Managing as a Performing Art: New Ideas for a World of Chaotic Change* (Vaill, 1989); *Riding the Waves of Change: Developing Managerial Competencies for a Turbulent World* (Morgan, 1988); *Beyond Rational Management: Mastering the Paradoxes and Competing Demands of High Performance* (Quinn, 1998). All explicitly or implicitly acknowledge the shifting paradigm and the need for a new approach to management. However, the most widely accepted ideas about public organizations and management remain grounded in traditional, positivist schools of thought. In the next section I will summarize what I see as the main assumptions of traditional organization theories, and of alternative theoretical perspectives.

The Positivist Perspective

Although there are significant differences among the theories of organization that have traditionally been applied to the public sector (for example, human relations theory and systems theory), they share at least six basic assumptions. These assumptions frequently inform contemporary discussions of public organizations and management (for example, Lynn, 1987a; Gortner, Mahler & Nicholson, 1987).

The first assumption is that activity in organizations is and should be directed toward and evaluated in terms of a known purpose. People's actions are viewed as instrumental means to accomplish the organization's goals. Thus, for example, we have management-by-objectives systems for tracking activities and appraising employee performance. In most MBO systems, achieving the stated organizational goals is the ultimate determinate of success.

A second assumption is that government efficiency is the proper focus for the study of public administration. Public managers are often rewarded for finding the least costly (usually defined in terms of direct dollars saved) means to the stated ends.

The third assumption is derived from the first two. It is the belief that all behavior in organizations is and should be rational. Rational behavior is defined as actions that contribute to the stated objectives. The rational individual obeys the directives of those farther up in the hierarchy. Behavior is simply a response to environmental demands.

Mainstream organizational theories also share the fourth assumption, that individual interests and organizational interests can be made congruent with one another. It follows that, ultimately, no conflict need exist between the goals of the organization and the goals of the individual. Most organization development interventions are designed to help managers assure the alignment of individual and organizational goals.

The fifth shared assumption is that social science, the preferred mode of organizational inquiry, is fundamentally the same as natural science. The scientific method may be used to reveal objective, value-free descriptions of life in organizations.

Finally, values and facts are assumed to be logically separate concepts that can and should be kept apart. Public administration's long-standing distinction between politics and administration is an indication of this dichotomy. Similarly, theory and practice are also seen as distinct categories of activity.

Theoretical Alternatives

Critical and interpretive social theories reflect world views or paradigms that differ significantly from positivist view. Critical theory is most often associated with the Institute of Social Research, founded in the early 1920s at the University of Frankfurt. The "Frankfurt School" was designed as a center for the study of radical scholarship, especially the early works of Marx, and attracted such scholars as T. W. Adorno, Erich Fromm, and Herbert Marcuse.

Critical theory maintains that a tension exists between our true consciousness and the limitations placed on us by society. Because we are often unaware of these constraints, we develop a "false consciousness" that keeps us from realizing human fulfillment. The major concern of critical theory is the release of these constraints through critique of the status quo. Critical theorists seek a radical change in the social world through a change in human consciousness.

Interpretive theory provides a second alternative to the positivist paradigm. Based on the German idealism of Immanuel Kant, interpretive theory argues that the social world can be understood only in terms of the subjective meanings, or interpretations, that people give to their everyday experiences. Human beings are seen as conscious *of* something, and our social reality is created by the reflections of our consciousness. The social world created through this process is held together by intersubjective agreements among people about what is to be considered as real (Berger & Luckmann, 1966).

In contemporary American public administration literature, a synthesis of critical and interpretive theory is emerging. Harmon and Mayer (1986) outline six elements of this unified perspective that challenge the assumptions of traditional organization and management theory.

The first element is that the rational model of goal-directed activity misrepresents and limits the understanding of action in individual, social, and organizational contexts. Second, the primary problem for theorists is to understand how organizations reinforce social processes of domination that produce individual alienation. Basic to this is understanding the relationship of social structure to forms of language and discourse.

The third element is that the traditional social science notion of behavior is an inadequate basis for understanding the social world. The concept of *action* can replace behavior, since it includes the subjective meaning that people give to their social activities.

Fourth, individual and organizational interests are inherently in tension with each other, and therefore, involve issues of political power. The question is not how individual interests can be made congruent with those of the organization but how the individual may transcend the organization.

The fifth element holds that the distinction between empirical theory (what is) and normative theory (what ought to be) is misleading and unproductive. The two are inextricably tied together. The final element is that the purpose of theory is fundamentally practical. A practical theory enables self-understanding leading to responsible and autonomous action.

Praxis Revisited

The term *praxis* comes from the Greek. Aristotle made the distinction between *theoria*, the life of theoretical reflection, and *praxis*, the tasks of daily life. Thus theory and practice were separate spheres. Marx, however, believed that the point of social theory was not just interpretation but change. In reconnecting theory with practice, he chose to use the old term *praxis*. For the critical/interpretive theorists, theory and practice are complementary modes of action. Praxis provides a bridge between personal reflection and social action (Denhardt, 1981b).

Denhardt and other scholars believe that the theoretical alternatives to the positivist perspective lead to a new style of management. Instead of being focused on control, the emerging approach to management aims to help individuals discover and pursue their own developmental needs. This new frame of reference would emphasize not the extrinsic rewards of technical productivity and efficiency but rather the intrinsic values of autonomy, responsibility, individuation, and praxis. In the next section, I discuss how people who write about and practice adult education also see the merit of this approach to management development.

ADULT LEARNING THEORY AND PRACTICE

Standard approaches to the designing of learning programs for adults have been grounded primarily in the positivist paradigm. These programs usually have three features: purpose, order, and finiteness (Brookfield, 1986). The widely accepted model of program development has a five-step linear process: assess needs, define objectives (preferably in terms of specific behavioral outcomes), select teaching and learning methods to meet the objectives, arrange the learning activities in a particular sequence, and evaluate the program based on whether the behavioral objectives were met.

This "institutional" approach to program design ignores "the domain of the most significant personal learning—the kind that results from reflections on experiences and from trying to make sense of one's life by exploring the meanings others have assigned to similar experiences" (p. 213). Stephen Brookfield argues further that the institutional approach is an attempt by educators or program designers to control and confine participants' learning, rather than to free or broaden.

Traditional management development programs all have specific goals and objectives. The predetermined objectives may devalue or ignore the unanticipated learning that can occur. They also tend to reify the objectives.

Andragogy, or the practice of adult education, has been offered as an alternative to traditional modes of teaching. Malcolm Knowles (1984), who popularized the term, identifies andragogy's four guiding assumptions:

1. Adults are and want to be self-directed.
2. Adults' experiences are a source of and a technique for learning.
3. Adults' learning needs are generated by life tasks and problems.
4. Adults are interested in learning competencies, or skills, that they can apply to their immediate circumstances.

Brookfield (1986) critiques andragogy from a critical/interpretivist perspective. He notes that little evidence exists that adults are actually self-directed and autonomous. Brazilian educator Paulo Freire (1970) bases his work on the premise that many Third World adults live in a culture of silence, in which alternatives to their current circumstances are never contemplated. Erich Fromm (1941) has documented the fear of freedom that characterizes adults living in modern democratic societies. Almost a century ago, Emile Durkheim found that individuals often became neurotic when they realized that there were no fixed moral codes or divinely ordained "truths" (Durkheim, 1952, cited in Brookfield, 1986). Brookfield argues that because self-directedness is an empirical rarity, the proper purpose of andragogical education should be to pursue self-direction, not accept it as a given for all adults.

Brookfield (1986) agrees with Knowles' second assumption about andragogy, regarding the importance of adult learners' experience base. One of the most significant forms of adult learning is the "development of critical reflection of experiences, along with the collaborative interpretation and exchange of such experiences" (p. 98). However, he is in less accord with the last two assumptions of adult learning: the origin of learning needs and the desire for skills. Those assumptions can lead practitioners to equate all learning with instrumental learning that is, increasing skill in some predetermined area. These two assumptions tend to ignore the complexity and diversity of learning.

For Brookfield (1986) the facilitation of learning is a complex, often turbulent, psychosocial drama involving the personalities of the actors, the context of the learning, and the prevailing political climate. It is "a value-laden activity in which curricular and programmatic choices reflect normative preferences" (p. 283). Adult learning experiences can be used to confirm existing world views or to challenge those views and encourage thinking about alternative perspectives.

This returns us to the importance of developing a clear and thoughtful theory to guide practice. If the people who practice adult education fail to clarify their rationale, their programs and activities can be morally bankrupt, and they can fall prey to the continuing waves of new techniques and fads.

A PERSONAL THEORY OF PRACTICE: DESIGN FOR MANAGEMENT DEVELOPMENT

Brookfield (1986) suggests that a "philosophy of practice" is comprised of three basic elements: a clear definition of the area of activity, the purposes that are derived from the definition, and a set of criteria by which the success of practitioner efforts can be judged. His framework guides the following discussion.[1]

The Meaning of Management Development

A clear definition of management development requires a discussion of both development and management. To clarify terms used by human resource development professionals, Nadler (1979) distinguishes three types of activities: training, education, and development. Training focuses on improving performance in a current job; education prepares individuals to move into different but existing positions; development helps people grow to meet unspecified future needs of the organization. In practice, all three types of activities frequently masquerade as management development, because practitioners and managers are either not aware of the differences or are not concerned about the precision of their language.

While I generally agree with Nadler's distinctions, his conception that management development should serve organizational needs places us face-to-face with a major problematic of the positivist world view. Seeing development in organizational terms equates the totality of individual existence with an organizational role. In my view, development should enable the individual to critically recognize and to transcend the organization.

I use management in this section to include supervisors, managers, and executives. While training and education may require distinguishing between these three levels (for example, the skills needed by new supervisors may differ from those required by an experienced executive), development does not. The specific content or techniques of programs may vary depending on the organizational level of the participants, but the definition of management development remains the same.

My professional practice involves me in both training and education programs. So I obviously do not believe that management training (for example, learning to use data base management software) and management education (for example, learning about the budgetary process to move into a more general or higher level management position) are unimportant. However, facilitating and fostering individual growth toward independence and personal responsibility is what defines and gives meaning to what I do as a practitioner.

Four Purposes of Management Development

Defining management development as "facilitating and fostering the growth of managers toward independence and personal responsibility" leads me to four specific purposes: to model praxis to foster critical thinking to create opportunities for dialogue, and to encourage learning communities.

Model of Praxis

Management development programs should provide a model of praxis. This implies that the content of development programs should include explicit attention to both theory and practice.

One popular method of teaching management skills is behavior modeling. This consists of describing the steps involved in a skill, such as coaching an employee, showing the participant an example of "good" coaching (often on video tape), providing an opportunity to practice the skill, and offering constructive feedback on that practice.

The best examples of programs based on behavior modeling do result in changes in participant skill levels. However, because these programs do not usually include any related theory (such as, in the coaching illustration above, personality preferences, organizational culture, or the impact of values on communication), participants can quickly become discouraged with their attempts to use the new skill. They may not understand why a coaching session does not accomplish what they thought it would, although they followed all the steps. The result may be that they "blame" the skill and discard it as useless.

By including related theory and encouraging program participants to reflect on their experiences in light of that theory, program designers are giving managers an opportunity *to build their own theories* to guide the use of the new skills. This allows them to be self-directing and supports acceptance of responsibility for their actions.

Management development practitioners also should model praxis in the way they manage their programs. By reflecting on what supported or hindered participant learning during a given program, and by understanding the theoretical basis for those occurrences, practitioners can make significant improvements in program design and content.

The best HRD practitioners often make these adjustments in the midst of facilitating or managing programs. At the very least, the next program can be adjusted or redesigned to incorporate what is learned. The process I am recommending differs from the traditional way of evaluating programs and using the data to make program changes. In my approach, praxis demands reflecting on underlying assumptions.

For example, if executives give a speaker on leadership a low rating, the traditional approach would lead the program designer to not use that speaker again. The designer would use a different speaker the next time that program is given. The new speaker may or may not be more "popular." Raising the issue of why the first speaker was given poor ratings, and examining that question at the level of assumptions and theory, may reveal some nontraditional alternatives to finding a new speaker. For instance, what theory or model of leadership was the speaker using? Does that theory support or conflict with the values and assumptions of the participants? If there is conflict, maybe that speaker should be invited back, but with the differing assumptions highlighted and used to foster learning.

As another example of practitioner praxis, consider the situation of a week-long orientation for new management interns. The program designer became aware that the interns apparently were not interested in the presentations by top executives about the agency's legislative agenda and policy initiatives. What theories might help make sense of this observation?

Looking at the schedule for the orientation program revealed that discussions about the intern program itself were scheduled on the last day of the week. Reflecting on the negative relationship between stress and listening may lead an HRD practitioner to move the discussion of the internship program's requirements and expectations earlier in the week, to reduce anxiety and increase the interns' ability to focus on the broader issues. Applying something as basic as Maslow's theory of the hierarchy of needs also may have the same result. The interns may not be ready to "self-actualize" until their security needs are met, by, for example, information about performance expectations, and therefore their income. Programs that model praxis may never be done the same way twice since the program designers and/or facilitators are constantly reflecting on what is going on and making adjustments to their theories of content and design.

Critical Thinking

The second purpose of management development is to foster critical thinking. Brookfield (1987) suggests four components of critical thinking: identifying and challenging assumptions, understanding the importance of context, imagining and exploring alternatives, and exhibiting reflective skepticism.

Critical thinking is sometimes portrayed as cynical and negative. However, the opposite is true. Thinking critically opens up possibilities, encourages the recognition and valuing of diversity, and is at the core of true democracy. While critical thinking historically has been relegated to the academic setting, the recognition of its wider importance is growing. For instance, an article in *McCall's* (Schoumacher & Cadden, 1989) adds critical thinking to the list of skills, including computer literacy and language arts, that children need to learn to prepare themselves for the twenty-first century.

Although it may seem obvious that critical thinking will be required in a postpositivist world, it is generally not valued or encouraged by modern organizations or traditional management theory. Hierarchy, control, and obedience to authority are all challenged by the critical thinker. Encouraging managers to think critically puts them at risk, and they should be made aware of the potential dangers. For example, after completing a long-term executive development program, several participants have left the sponsoring agency, or turned down offers of promotions, because they had the opportunity to critically assess and clarify their priorities and what they wanted from their careers. Many people in the organization saw their decisions as disloyalty or insubordination, instead of a reflection of autonomy and the willingness to live their values.

Opportunities for Dialogue

A third purpose of management development is to create opportunities for dialogue. Managers learn about themselves and add meaning to their experiences through conversations with others. Verbalizing assumptions and opening them to the critique of others often clarifies, supports, or negates their validity. Traditional management development programs focus on assessing the content needs of participants, not on designing settings for dialogue. When managers are given time during the program to interact reflectively with their peers, they frequently report that interaction as the most significant aspect of the program. The value of such dialogue is so great that at times it appears the content is irrelevant.

Learning Communities

The final purpose for management development is to encourage communities of learning. Development is not synonymous with "entertainment." It often creates discomfort in both the persons who are learning and growing and in the people who knew them and liked them the way they were. The active encouragement of support groups, learning teams, networks, and other collaborative arrangements can help to alleviate the stress encountered when managers are involved in the development programs.

Learning communities also support and enhance the learning process. Discussing a developmental experience with someone who shares the same language and knowledge base builds on and clarifies the learning that the experience stimulated. Often groups or relationships will continue long after the management development program is completed. In addition, once managers have experienced a meaningful learning community they are more likely to want to recreate that experience in their immediate organizations or in other settings.

EVALUATION CRITERIA

Given the four purposes that currently guide my management development practice, I use six criteria to judge my success.

First, *the program is noncoercive in both design and content.* Participation in specific activities is not mandatory. If one believes that certain elements are an integral part of a program, one should explain the rationale to the participants. Those reasons can then be challenged, and alternatives explored.

While noncoercive program design is not unusual, noncoercive content is much less so. Most management development programs present one theory or viewpoint. For instance, many current books on leadership put forth a prescription for how to be a leader. The implication is that anyone who does not do the things touted cannot possibly be a leader. Presenting such a theory to a group of executives who already think of themselves as leaders can generate several reactions. They may decide that they do the things leaders do, in which case no learning is likely to occur. They may decide they do things differently, but since they are leaders the theory must be wrong. Again, not much learning takes place. They may accept the model as the right way to be a leader and work to change what they do. In this case learning has occurred but they may or may not be "better" leaders.

A noncoercive approach to leadership might include exposure to several theories, with dialogue about the assumptions underpinning each. If only one model is used, its assumptions and values should be made clear and the existence of other theories at least acknowledged. A third alternative is to use a theory that is inherently nonprescriptive.

The second criterion is that *all assumptions are made explicit and are open to challenge.* This does not mean that the facilitator or instructor cannot take a stand or express a preference. It does mean that it should be clear that it is a personal viewpoint, and that it is open to critique.

It also implies an equality between the facilitator and the participants and among participants, despite "status." The facilitator is not there to give the right answer or indoctrinate participants. He or she is there to guide the developmental process.

This should be emphasized early in a program since most of our educational systems establish the teacher as the ''boss.'' For example, during a discussion of power half-way through a fifteen-day program, a group of supervisors argued strenuously that they had to do whatever the instructor wanted them to do, because the instructor was in a position of formal authority.

The third standard is to *recognize the importance of context*. Participants are encouraged to reflect on their individual circumstances, whether personal or organizational, and the effect these circumstances will have on how or what they do. This can often be enhanced by increasing the heterogeneity of the group. During dialogue with other participants they learn that the context in which they work shapes and constrains their assumptions, attitudes, and actions. They also can then critically assess their own beliefs and theories.

The fourth criterion is to *use experience*. The developmental process draws heavily on participant experience. This can be prior experience or experience while in the developmental program. Drawing on experience does not mean sharing war stories. It means fostering a cycle of critical self-reflection, experimentation, reflection on that experimentation, refinement of the experiment, reflection, and so on.

The fifth standard is to *challenge rather than entertain participants*. Often management development programs are evaluated on what are called ''happiness'' ratings. Participants are essentially asked whether they like the program. The highest ratings therefore may go to programs presented by motivational, charismatic speakers who reinforce the participants' beliefs. A better indicator of development is the degree to which participants feel challenged by the facilitator, by the content, or by each other. This can cause varying degrees of discomfort as people reassess their beliefs, assumptions, and personal actions. While feedback and critique are essential to the process, they must be done in a way that supports the recipient's self-esteem.

The sixth criterion I use is whether *participants report that they learned something meaningful to them*. What actually was learned may or may not be what traditional course objectives indicated should be learned. For example, participants in a supervisory development program often report that they have more self-confidence in what they do. Typically this does not appear on a list of the program's behavioral objectives.

CONCLUSION

In this chapter I have discussed the importance of theory to public administrators and, specifically, to the people who design management development programs for the public sector. Theory is more than an ivory tower exercise in abstraction. It is a way of learning to understand one's world. It is an indispensable part of the learning process.

Robert Denhardt summarized the spirit of what I intend to communicate in this chapter:

Theory and practice seem to be connected in the process of personal learning. As individuals live and work in public organizations, as they read and inquire about the work of others in such organizations, they build a body of experience that is extremely valuable for practice. However, until that body of material is analyzed, reflected on, and generalized into theory, it is really not useful for action. To build a theory is to learn a new way of viewing the world. . . . The process of theory building is a process of learning. (Denhardt, 1984, p. 179)

The theory I have presented here is a personal example of learning and praxis. It was derived from a reflexive exchange between my practice as a public sector human resources development professional, and my interest in the world of theory.

As public administrators become aware of the changes implied by a postpositivist world view, individual learning skills will take on added importance. Learning will be recognized as an essential ability for the effective manager. Sometimes what an individual learns will be immediately beneficial to the organization. Other times, benefits may not be apparent and, in some sense, may be seen by some as detrimental to the organization. That is part of the risk of learning. However, in my view, only by embracing reflective learning can we begin to see our actions as truly meaningful in a free society.

NOTE

1. I am sure that I have implicitly "borrowed" many of my ideas from people who have influenced my thinking about my practice over the past several years. These include authors already cited (Brookfield, Denhardt, Morgan, & Vaill), and people I have worked or studied with, including Michael Harmon, Cynthia McSwain, and Frederick Thayer. Most important, the colleagues and friends I see at work every day are a constant source of both support and challenge for my ideas about the practice of management development. To anyone in any of these categories from whom I appear to have borrowed without credit, my sincere apologies for missing the connection, and my heartfelt thanks for your stimulating ideas.

14

The Transforming Power of Public Leaders

Peter M. Wheeler

Early in my career, I supervised a small group. Now I lead over 1,400 people, spread throughout the United States. My understanding of leadership has grown over the past several years as I studied administrative theory and behavior. My experience and study have taught me that having an explicit theory of leadership is critical for those of us who labor in the public vineyard.

I am using "leader" in this chapter to mean anyone who supervises other people. It is self-evident but necessary to state up front that it is difficult to be a good public leader. But having a theory helps. A theory of leadership is a critical determinant of the decisions and judgments leaders make each day, and it helps one to place the public interest before personal gain.

The purpose of this chapter is to describe the ideas that inform my leadership style. In the pages that follow I will identify some issues that I believe are important for public leaders, at all levels of government, to think about regularly. Continuous reflection will help to sustain a clear image of what role we play in public life. Those areas include: the origins of public administration, the legitimacy of social institutions, the political economics of growth and redistribution, and organizational theory. After briefly treating each area, I will devote most of the chapter to describing the leadership theory that, for me, meshes and connects the other themes.

THE INSTITUTIONAL CONTEXT OF PUBLIC LEADERSHIP

Leaders affect the design of public institutions through their ability to formulate agendas, to execute policies and procedures, and to influence the behavior of subordinates. In turn, leaders are affected by their institutional context. By institutions, I mean a system of roles, norms, and structures that shape human behavior. For the purpose of this chapter, institutions include the family, the church, and the economic factors that drive government and business behavior, such as inflation, interest rates, and unemployment. They also include public entities such as the Office of Management and Budget, the Social Security Administration, the press, and the nightly news. Institutions are human creations to bring order to what otherwise would be chaos.

Four institutional themes provide a foundation for understanding the nature of public leadership. These themes are (1) the origins and purposes of public social institutions; (2) their basis for exercising legitimate power; (3) the political economy of the institution's social context; and (4) the design of responsive social institutions.

ORIGINS AND LEGITIMACY

In the United States, a review of the works of Locke, Hobbes, Hume, and Montsquieu, and their impact on Madison, Hamilton, Jefferson, Wilson, and others, would provide public leaders with a base of knowledge about the origins, purpose, and legitimacy of the administrative state (Rohr, 1987; Chandler, 1987). Aaron Wildavsky also has searched for the institutional roots of public leadership. In his book *The Nursing Father* (1984), he tells us that:

Social structure, including the structure of the State, is a product of human interaction. . . . No one is to be in the grip of impersonal forces that he or she cannot control, nor subject to the inexorable forces of a history apart from human will. . . . Government, of, by, and for the governors, regimes for rulers, are inevitable unless the self absorption of rulers, self worship through the state, is countered by submission to the community, whose collective experience is contained in the laws of their God. . . .

As one reads through Exodus, one senses that a social institution is beginning to emerge, as people perceive that as individuals they are too weak to be anything more than animals struggling for survival. A people who complain about and sin against each other are deciding to become something that could assure protection, security, and a better life.

Wildavsky is offering a message for contemporary public leaders. To construct a lasting institution that will serve all its members, Wildavsky is saying, leaders need to be attuned to and constrained by the collective will of the community, what we might term the "public interest." For in that will rests the legitimacy of leadership.

POLITICAL ECONOMY

Contemporary understandings of public leadership would be incomplete if we did not discuss the impact of declining resources, declining per capita worker earnings, and the significant downsizing of social institutions. Some people argue that the growth of capital, earnings, and consuming power can be achieved if government restraints on the economy are loosened. In another camp we have those whose economic goal is to use the political system to redistribute wealth.

Higher taxes, regulation and liberal policies toward minimum incomes, tax credits, and direct subsidies to low and middle classes are the usual tools of redistribution. However, if taxes draw huge sums from profits in the private sector, it is generally agreed that growth will suffer. Investment in new ventures could be stifled and growth will stagnate. How then can we reconcile redistribution and growth, and how can public administrators influence the problem in a positive way, and in harmony with democratic constitutional principles?

Mancur Olson (1983) argues that interest groups substantially alter economic evolution and slow its rate of growth. Though the economy evolves, it centers increasingly on organization or on political struggles over distribution, rather than on the search for new revenues or lower costs. As powerful interest groups gain control over political subsystems, government as a whole becomes increasingly paralyzed. Olson suggests that "the more that pushy entrants and nonconforming entrants are repressed, the rarer they become and what is not customary is not done."

Bowles and Eatwell (1983) take issue with Olson's analysis and argue that interest groups are fundamental to a democratic society. They describe labor unions, for example, as essential partners of an effort to increase economic growth and redistribution. In their model, economic and political systems should be integrated.

Elites who control most of the capital want to preserve the deregulation and monopolistic institutions that prevent labor from establishing new institutions, such as national health care or full employment. The existence of powerful interest groups to support redistribution efforts is therefore a very important strategy to Bowles and Eatwell. In their view, if people are healthy and working, they will be more productive and will provide a broader supply of labor for new capital ventures.

John Kirlin (1984) seeks to shift the terms of the debate. He wants to strengthen and make more visible the choice-making role of the political system. He notes that from 1965 through 1975, government expanded its service role. As a result, single-issue interest groups dominated policy making and implementation. These groups successfully sought favorable policies at local, state, and federal levels. Their successes strengthened functionally specific institutions. The interest groups (made up of federal, state, and local power centers such as housing, social services, and so forth) have a support system that ensures stability of resources. Kirlin argues that where resources are limited we have an opportunity to return to more democratic practices, where priorities can be more readily chosen. He offers this as an alternative to the current system, which builds a floor under much government spending, buttressed by powerful public and private interests that support specific programs.

Public administrators are in the middle of this debate. That is why it is important for public leaders to reflect on the classic writings of the Founding Fathers, and on the contemporary works of people like Olson, Bowles and Eatwell, and

Kirlin. Their ideas create and reflect the institutional context of public leadership, and stimulate leaders to think about what role they should play in public institutions.

HUMAN NATURE AND ORGANIZATIONS

Part of the process of constructing a personal leadership theory is to clarify one's assumptions about human nature and human behavior. The task can be illustrated by contrasting two very different views of organizational life. The first organization is a religious community of lay people who share a close-knit life and are dedicated to serving the poor, especially the handicapped. Jean Vanier, the leader of this community, tells us of the experience of people who first join (1978, p. 34–36):

Those who come close to the poor do so first of all in a generous desire to help them and bring them relief; they often feel like saviors and put themselves on a pedestal. But, once in contact with the poor, once touching them, establishing a loving and trusting relationship with them, the mystery unveils itself. The poor seem to break down the barriers of powerfulness, of wealth, of ability and of pride; they pierce the armor the human heart builds to protect itself. . . . When people start the journey toward wholeness, the pilgrimage to the promised land, there is a moment when their deepest being has been touched. They have had a fundamental experience, as if the stone of their egoism had been struck by Moses' staff and water had sprung from it.

Such experiences, Vanier tells us, can happen in many ways besides seeking out the poor. It can happen in a meeting with individuals in a community:

In listening and watching them, we discover what we want to be; they reflect our own deepest self, and we are mysteriously attracted to them. . . . It makes us feel that we have glimpsed the promised land, found ourselves "at home," found "our place." The experience is often such as to take someone into a community or change the orientation of their life (Vanier, 1978, p. 37).

Human behavior that is loving, outpouring, and generous is the result of this organization's purpose and day-to-day ministries. But humans are also full of conflicts and doubts of "is this what it's all about." We are sometimes urged from within to "pack it in" and enjoy some of the worldly lusts that are ever present in every individual. In Vanier's community, there is a peace and a wonderful stillness of spirit that serves as a foundation for human strength.

Now let us listen to an observer of the secular world and his observations about our more numerous organizations. Charles Perrow's critical essay on *Complex Organizations* (1986) is an attempt to unmask the realities that pervade our society because of the spread and influence of large organizations. He tells us that:

bureaucracy is a [social] tool . . . that legitimizes control of the many by the few, despite the formal apparatus of democracy, and this control has generated unregulated and unperceived social power. This power includes much more than just control of employees. As bureaucracies satisfy, delight, pollute, and satiate us with their output of goods and services, they also shape our ideas, our very way of conceiving ourselves, control our life chances, and even define our humanity (pp. 270–71).

After carefully weaving an analysis of the organizational theory and behavior literature, he synthesizes his conclusions:

Our society is creating a permanent underclass of people who may never have any need for the skills they learn in the eleventh and twelfth grades, if they last that long, and whose functional illiteracy is hardly a handicap in a life on the welfare rolls or in the world of crime. . . . Better education should produce a more informed citizenry, ready for lifetime learning, but if I were an elite concerned with my income, class position, and the opportunities of my offspring, I would think twice about a more informed citizenry in an economy that survives on defense and service jobs with an increasingly polarized income distribution and growing permanent underclass.

Organizations and their cultures play an important role in establishing the identity of a public leader. The Vanier-Perrow comparison illustrates that there are organizational ideas that enthrone the dignity of the human spirit and are life giving and there are ideas that drain life from the individual. Public leaders need to decide which view they subscribe to.

DEFINING ONE'S ORGANIZATIONAL REALITY

Public leaders are the products of their organizations (Scott & Hart, 1979). Long-held assumptions emanating from the culture of one's organization often drive behaviors and beliefs. If, as Robert Denhardt asserts, public administration is concerned with managing change processes in pursuit of publicly defined societal values (Denhardt, 1984, p. 17), then public leaders must confront the organizational assumptions that might deter them from pursuing change that serves the public interest.

As a member of a religious lay community and as a senior executive of a large federal bureaucracy, my behavior has been affected by many organizations. I have found it valuable to have a conceptual foundation to help frame my organizational reality. The framework is derived from ideas about the function of public organizations and about the theoretical perspectives that guide one's behavior in organizations. The framework can offset the tremendous pressures generated by people and cultures that see the world only as an economic reality and that regard public service as foolish.

I believe that a public organization is a servant to democratic ideals. Denhardt discusses the implications of this view: "If public organizations are . . . committed to the pursuit of publicly defined societal values, their members carry a special burden that others do not—always to act in keeping with democratic norms" (1984, p. 40).

In a democratic society, public leaders are responsible for assuring that democratic values permeate the social institution in which they work. In my view, the values embedded in constitutional principles provide the ethical frame to guide the moral behavior of public leaders. Operationally, this means that public leaders should understand: (1) the individual dignity of those they serve and those they work with; (2) the right of individuals to be recognized as equal by social institutions, not matter what their social and income status may be; and (3) the right of people to participate directly in decisions that affect them, or to be part of a constituency that can remove, if necessary, those who represent them in such decisions (Redford, 1969, pp. 3-9).

As other authors in this book note (for example, Boyd; Eggert), public administration's concern with organizations has been dominated by the positivist-rationalist view of the world. The view is often at odds with democratic ideals, since the efficient way to create a better world justifies treating people as means to the desired end.

The dominant view has been expressed by authors who write about organizations as systems (for example, James D. Thompson), decision arenas (Herbert Simon), social systems (Chester Barnard), and bureaucracies (Max Weber). Other writers note that the similarity should not be surprising, ". . . given the history of the increasing bureaucratization of society. . . . Again and again for organizational theorists, the question was clear: how can human activity best be organized to achieve given societal goals in an efficient and effective manner" (Harmon & Mayer, 1986, p. 197).

In the early twentieth century, the idea that organizations could be based on democratic norms and personal growth and development, and that the needs of people and organizations could be integrated, was a minority view. Follett, McGregor, Argyris and a few other writers stimulated organizational theorists to focus on the personal development of their employees. Their efforts have broadened the rationalist view of strict efficiency, although they certainly have not supplanted it. Some authorities even believe that the human relations approach is another way for managers to control workers (Denhardt, 1984, p. 97). It is my view, however, that thanks to these scholars, the concern for personal growth and development is a much greater part of organizational life today than in the past.

My bias for the sacredness of life and the sanctity of the human spirit places me in sympathy with what might be called the "life-enhancing" theorists. The scriptures are as instructive as the organizational theorists are on what my relationship, as a public leader, should be to institutional and human concerns:

Again he entered the synagogue. There was a man there who had a withered hand. They watched him closely to see if he would cure him on the Sabbath so they might accuse him. He said to the man with the withered hand, "Come up here before us." Then he said to them, "Is it lawful to do good on the Sabbath rather than to do evil, to save life rather than to destroy it?" But they remained silent. Looking around at them with anger and grieved at their hardness of heart, he said to the man, "Stretch out your hand." He stretched it out and his hand was restored. The Pharisees went out and immediately took counsel with the Herodians against him to put him to death (Mark 3: 1–6).

ETHICAL LEADERSHIP

Ethical principles and moral behavior are critical to the survival of public organizations as effective social instruments for obtaining a better quality of life. It therefore follows that public leaders must hold values that are based on ethical principles and that are reflected in moral behavior. A leadership theory must include foundational ties to ethical principles if trust is to glue together leader-follower relationships.

Leaders are responsible for establishing the ethical tone of their organizations. Baumhart (1961) and Posner & Schmidt (1986a, 1986b) have contributed to my understanding of this point. Their work shows that managers in private and public organizations are most influenced by the ethics of their immediate supervisors. According to their research, many government and business executives believe that "what the boss does is O.K."

Terry Cooper's distinction between external and internal goods is also instructive for public leaders (Cooper, 1987). He explains that external goods "always become the property of some individual, and . . . the more one person has in a fixed sum situation, the less there is for others." Typical external goods include money, prestige, status, position, and power.

Cooper notes that there is no complete consensus on what constitutes the internal goods of public leaders. However, there are certain qualities that most people agree on, such as the public interest, popular sovereignty, accountability, social order, social justice, citizenship development, political equality, efficiency, and liberty. Cooper believes that a major ethical problem for the members of an organization is to maintain "the internal goods and virtues of their practice in the face of demands for personal or organizational loyalty rooted in external goods."

THE SEARCH FOR MORAL LEADERSHIP

James MacGregor Burns, in his book *Leadership* (1978), has helped me to think about how to balance the quest for external and internal goods, and how to integrate the institutional concerns that I have touched on above. His ideas provide the core for many of my views of leadership.

Two Types of Leadership

Burns's central thesis is that we need what he calls transformational leadership. He distinguishes between transformational leadership and transactional leadership. Traditional leaders approach their followers with an eye to exchanging one thing for another. Burns describes institution-bound transactional leaders as organizational parasites. They

—transact more than they administer

—compromise more than they command

—institutionalize more than they initiate

—analyze and fragment policy issues in order to better cope with them, but do not piece them back together again

—seek to limit their alternatives

—delegate thorny problems "down the line"

—accept vague and inconsistent goals (Burns, 1978, p. 406)

Transformational leaders bring life to organizations. They search out potential motives in followers, seek to satisfy higher needs, and engage the full person of the follower. Further and more critically, "the result of transforming leadership is a relationship of mutual stimulation and elevation that converts followers into leaders and may convert leaders into moral agents" (p. 4). Burns believes that his ideas can help leadership become moral "in that it raises the level of human conduct and ethical aspiration of both leader and led, and thus it has a transforming effect on both" (Burns, 1978, p. 21).

For Burns, the foundation of moral leadership is the ability to identify the power in and the sources of one's own and others' values. Power, in the positive sense as opposed to brute power, emerges as an individual chooses noble purposes and stands firm on the side of what he or she thinks is the right path to take. It is similar to what David McClelland (1975) calls the leader with a mature power motive.

Moral leadership recognizes that people respond to ends as well as to cultural influences on their individual lives. Leadership creates an elevating power when people are mobilized and shaped by a gifted leader, who is sharpened and strengthened by conflict. The result is that the values of the leader and followers can be the source of vital social change.

There are times when political and institutional inefficiencies and corruption go beyond what the public will accept. Legitimate demands are unmet. There is an increased consciousness of discrimination and injustice. In such times, people will experience the contradictions between what is and what they believe should be. The more the contradictions challenge self-conceptions, the more dissatisfaction will be aroused. Leaders can use these dissatisfactions to enact change.

Change occurs when a leader can engage prospective followers who are striving for greater understanding of their own needs. The leader makes the followers aware of present contradictions and explains how important values are being corrupted in the process. With this awareness leader and follower create a joint movement toward change.

Becoming a Transformational Leader

Burns argues that a fundamental crisis underlying leadership problems is intellectual. We cannot even agree on the standards by which to measure, recruit, and reject leadership. His efforts to remedy this gap can be summarized as follows: (1) If leadership is a relationship of leaders and followers, and (2) if leaders interact with followers in a great merging of the motivations and purposes of both, and (3) if many of these motivations and purposes are common to vast numbers of humankind in many cultures, then (4) we could expect to identify patterns of leadership behavior that (5) permit plausible generalizations about the ways transforming leaders behave.

He developed five generalizations about transformational leaders (Burns, 1978, pp. 452–56).

Collective

Transformational leaders respond to their inner motivations, stimulated perhaps by Cooper's "internal goods." As the leaders respond, they appeal to the motives of potential followers. As followers respond, a relationship emerges that joins leader and follower together into a social and political collectivity.

Dissensual

"The dynamic of political action and meaningful conflict produces engaged leaders, who in turn generate more conflict among people" (Burns, p. 454). Conflict democratizes transformational leadership. It causes leaders to create a broader field of thought, combat, and development that pushes them to search for more followers, more allies. Conflict helps to synthesize motives, sharpens common demands, and strengthens values.

Causative

The impact of transformational leadership remains long after the leader is gone. According to Burns, "The most lasting tangible act" of transformational leadership is to create something that continues to exert moral leadership and fosters needed social change (p. 456).

Morally Purposeful

The transforming leader searches for needs, raises the aspirations, helps shape the values, and mobilizes the potential of followers. Leaders and followers can use values that construct ethical principles and guide moral behavior to shape organizational and personal purposes.

Elevating

"The transformational leader is moral but not moralistic" (p. 456). Leaders engage with followers but from levels of morality that touch the unconscious needs and wants of followers. In the meshing of goals and values, both leaders and followers are raised to more principled levels of judgment.

Transformational leaders are not bound to any sphere of action. They can affect societies, political systems, policy arenas, organizations, and small groups. Their personalities reflect and shape community values. They recognize the value of conflict. They are interested in long term effects. They are bound by ethical principles. They raise individuals and communities to a higher order of moral behavior. Transformational leaders are also aware of personal fallibilities. They recognize the need to be subject to democratic constraints.

I have asserted that one cannot effectively lead in a public organization without developing a leadership theory that complements and energizes the organization. For me, the theory is not simply a prescription for behaviors that a person needs to exhibit to succeed in an organization. It is an essential element in the design of effective public social institutions.

I am partial to Burns (1978), but Neustadt (1980), Kotter (1988), and Bennis & Nanus (1985) have also contributed to my understanding of leadership. Neustadt's leader is a political person who knows how to use power, especially how to coalesce his or her own power and the power of others to achieve ends of historical significance. Bennis and Nanus tell us that power is lacking in our leadership formulations. They describe four strategies to empower leaders and to help leaders empower their followers: vision, communication, trust, and self-regard. The characteristics that comprise Kotter's "leadership factor" (for example, reputation, trust, and personal integrity) augment Bennis and Nanus.

However, Burns's transformational leader stands as an ideal to strive for, a theory that has the potential to renew each of us who are public leaders and to influence our institutions at all levels. For me, a transformational leader

- loves those he or she leads and serves
- is willing to walk into the most difficult conflict to forge values and fight for justice
- designs social institutions and implements them
- acts within a firm set of moral values that set important behavioral guidelines
- raises followers to become leaders

THE INSPIRATION OF IDEALS

Transformational leadership and the other more abstract concepts discussed in this chapter may seem lofty and useful only for academics, not practitioners. That is too bad if that is the way we think. Our origins as public leaders are important in that they separate us from the private leader. We are to serve, in the noble sense of that term. To be a civil servant is not to be subservient. It is to be inventive and creative in assuring public rights, equal recognition of each individual, and participation by those we serve in what we do.

Understanding the reasons for our institutions' legitimacy demands reflection upon constitutional rights, as well as upon the role and powers (separated and shared) of the branches and levels of government we live in every day. A healthy respect for sharing power is fundamental to our success as public administrators. But too often we employ enormous amounts of energy to secure and display power, instead of using it maturely to build for the public interest.

Dealing constantly with the tension between growth and the redistribution of resources is endemic to every public leader's job. It influences almost every public decision, and an attempt to stress one objective over the other, to the extreme, can endanger our democratic values.

Understanding how the design of organizations can influence societal wants and needs has also been posited as important for public leaders to reflect upon. Some designs can clearly subvert the public interest in favor of a set of "status quo" government services, locked in by the power of special interests. The refusal to change can endanger government's ability to make choices for the public. Clearly the self-interest of immature power holders (those who ignore internal goods) must be confronted and overcome if democratic principles are to survive.

Last, we have taken a good deal of time to articulate a leadership theory that is the linchpin for all other themes. The leader seeks to empower others as he or she transforms the present into the changed and emerging reality that lies dormant in the deepest desires of those served. Fundamental motivations for the good are searched for and found; needs are transformed into progress, creating a better place to be for all.

But who has the time for such reflection and transformation? This is the wrong question. All of us who are public leaders must reflect upon the conceptual building blocks of our public institutions. We must, because we will not act in the public interest if we do not understand how such interests are born, nurtured, and transformed in our real world. In the end each of us must be struck at the rock, so that waters flows forth. The rock is the hardness of heart that surrounds our ego. The stick of Moses is our understanding and reflection upon the themes outlined in this chapter: the truths of freedom, sharing, and community.

Our hearts are broken as self-interest flows onto the soil of our workplaces. But free of such constraining interests we can empower, lead, and make a difference as public leaders.

15

Learning from Experience

Christopher Bellavita

I asked the contributors to this book to tell me what they know about public organizations now that they would like to have known earlier in their careers. Their answers are given below. Not surprisingly, what they had to say echoes many of the ideas in the previous chapters, and thus can serve as a summary to this book.

ORGANIZATIONS ARE PEOPLE

Organizations are the socially constructed artifacts of human behavior. They are driven by the self-interest of the people in them, by power and by competition. Consequently, conflict is endemic to organizations.

Human behavior in organizations is a function of personality and the environment. If you want to understand why people behave the way they do, look at their personalities. The Myers-Briggs categories (Keirsey & Bates, 1978) provide a nonjudgmental vocabulary for understanding personality. Look also at the environmental context of their behavior, including domestic pressures, working conditions, and the organization's political, social, or physical environment.

Behavior has a significant nonrational component. People are not machines whose actions can be predicted or controlled. As a manager or leader, you should recognize that there are limits to your ability to influence other people's behavior.

THE MULTIVERSE

Public administrators operate in a "multiverse," not a universe. Organizations have multiple realities, including political reality, social reality, economic reality, legal reality, and so on. Each sphere has its own reality principles, and none of these can be wished away or ignored.

There are multiple levels of discourse in organizations. Sometimes the conversation is functional—for example, how best to get a job done. Other times it is interpretive—for example, understanding how other people are interpreting events. Discourse can concern what actions and events mean to you, or how your and your coworkers' behavior is shaped by your environment. In organizations, many levels of conversation are going on simultaneously.

The multiple realities and the multiple levels of discourse change continuously. You have to be flexible to be effective in a public organization. There are many right ways, many good ways to do something. Conversely, you can make decisions, even when there are no good decisions to make.

LEARNING

Learning is a developmental activity. It is what helps you to grow. The key attribute of an effective learner is the ability to listen: to your self, to other people, and to your experience. People learn synergistically and unpredictably from many sources.

One of the best ways to learn is to use "retrospective sensemaking," that is, to think about the theoretical implications of a significant event after it has happened. It is often difficult to think conceptually before or during action. But after the event, theory helps you make sense of what happened. It provides the conceptual tools for you to organize your thoughts.

SELF

It is important to be conscious of who you are as a human being. This means understanding your hopes, wants, and needs; understanding your personality, your values, and what you believe; and being aware of your thought processes and your moods.

To assist other people in organizations it is necessary first to know where you stand in relationship to their ideas, including what motivates you to help.

It is important to be centered at work, to collect your energies, and to bring your mind to quietness. But being centered in an organization means changing your center when you need to.

Finally, there are two kinds of people in public organizations, "human beings" and "human doings." Public organizations seem to work better if you can remain a human being while you are doing.

Bibliography

Abel, E. (1966). *The missile crisis*. New York: Bantam Books.

Adams, J. D. (ed.) (1984). *Transforming work: A collection of organizational transformation readings*. Alexandria, VA: Miles River.

Adler, M. J. (1986) *A guide book to learning for the lifelong pursuit of learning*. New York: Macmillan.

Albrecht, K. (1979). *Stress and the manager: Making it work for you*. Englewood Cliffs, NJ: Prentice Hall.

Allison, G. T. (1969). Conceptual models and the Cuban missile crisis. *The American Political Science Review, 63*, 689–718.

Allison, G. T. (1971). *Essence of decision: Explaining the Cuban missile crisis*. Boston: Little, Brown.

Appleby, P. H. (1949). *Policy and administration*. University, AL: University of Alabama Press.

Argyris, C. (1957). *Personality and organization*. New York: Harper & Row.

Argyris, C. (1964). *Integrating the individual and the organization*. New York: John Wiley & Sons.

Argyris, C. & Schön, D. A. (1974). *Theory in practice*. San Francisco: Jossey-Bass.

Argyris, C. (1982). *Reasoning, learning and action*. San Francisco: Jossey-Bass.

Astley, W. G. (1985). Administrative science as socially constructed truth. *Administrative Science Quarterly, 30*, 504–5.

Bachrach, P. & Baratz, M. S. (1962). Two faces of power. *The American Political Science Review, 56*, 947–52.

Bailey, M. T. (1989, March/April). Minnowbrook II: An end or a new beginning? *Public Administration Review, 49*, 224–25.

Bardach, E. (1987). From practitioner knowledge to scholarly knowledge and back again. *Journal of Policy Analysis and Management, 7*(1), 188–99.

Barnard, C. (1938). *The functions of the executive*. Cambridge: Harvard University Press.

Barrett, P. (1985, September). Refund? What refund? Why the IRS is screwing up. *The Washington Monthly, 17*(18), 23–32.

Bartolome, F. (1989, March–April). Nobody trusts the boss completely—now what? *Harvard Business Review*.

Baunhart, R. (1961, July/August). How ethical are businessmen? *Harvard Business Review*, 6–19 & 156–76.

Beam, G. & Simpson, D. (1984). *Political action: The key to understanding politics*. Chicago: Swallow Press.

Behn, R. (1987). The nature of knowledge about public management: Lessons for research and teaching from our knowledge about chess and warfare. *Journal of Policy Analysis and Management, 7*(1), 200–12.

Behn, R. (1988). Management by groping along. *Journal of Policy Analysis and Management, 7*(4), 643–63.

Bell, D. (1976). *The cultural contradictions of capitalism*. New York: Basic Books.

Bellah, R. N., et al. (1985). *Habits of the heart: Individualism and commitment in American life*. Berkeley: University of California.

Bennis, W. & Nanus, B. (1985). *Leaders: The strategies for taking charge*. New York: Harper & Row.

Bennis, W. G. (1971). Changing Organizations. In H. A. Hornstein et al. (eds.) *Social intervention: A behavioral science approach*. New York: The Free Press.

Berger P. & Luckmann, T. (1966). *The social construction of reality*. Garden City, NY: Doubleday & Company.

Bernstein, J. (1987). The decline of rites of passage in our culture. In *Betwixt and between: Patterns of masculine and feminine initiation*. New York: Open Court Press.

Bezold, C. (1983). *Alternative futures and the blood service system in 2025: A strategic planning workbook*. Washington, DC: Alternative Futures Associates.

Blau, P. (1955). *The dynamics of bureaucracy*. Chicago: University of Chicago Press.

Blight, J. G. & Welch, D. A. (1989). *On the brink: Americans and Soviets reexamine the Cuban missile crisis*. New York: Hill and Wang.

Bohm, D. (1980). *Wholeness and the implicate order*. London: AR Press.

Boje, D., Fedor, D., & Rowland, K. (1982). Myth making. A qualitative step in OD interventions. *Journal of Applied Behavioral Science, 18*, 17–28.

Boleman, L. G. & Deal, T. E. (1984). *Modern approaches to understanding and managing organizations*. San Francisco: Jossey-Bass.

Bolen, J. S. (1984). *Goddesses in everywoman: A new psychology of woman*. San Francisco: Harper & Row.

Bolen, J. S. (1988). *Gods in everyman*. San Francisco: Harper & Row.

Boodman, S. G. (1986, October 12). Change casts pall over mental hospital. *Washington Post*, 1, 10.

Boyatzis, R. E. (1982). *The competent manager*. New York: John Wiley & Sons.

Boyd, B. B. & Levinson, L. J. (1989). *A contextual approach to leadership development: Guidelines for program designers*. Manuscript submitted for publication.

Bozemen, B. (1987). *All organizations are public*. San Francisco: Jossey-Bass.

Brauer, C. (1987). Tenure, turnover and postgovernment employment trends of presidential appointees. In C. C. MacKenzie (ed.), *The in-and-outers: Presidential appointees and transient government in Washington*. Baltimore: Johns Hopkins Press.

Briggs-Meyers, I. (1976). *Introduction to type* (2nd ed.). Gainsville, FL: Center for Applications of Psychological Type. Pamphlet.

Brodsky, A. R. (1989, August 6). Watergate: The tapes. *The Washington Post* [Outlook section], 1.

Brookfield, S. D. (1986). *Understanding and facilitating adult learning*. San Francisco: Jossey-Bass.

Brookfield, S. D.(1987). *Developing critical thinkers: Challenging adults to explore alternative ways of thinking and acting*. San Francisco: Jossey-Bass.

Brown, D. S. (1989). Management's new goal: Concert Building. *The Bureaucrat, 18*(2).

Bryman, A. (1986). *Leadership and organization*. London: Routledge & Kegan Paul.

Buchanan, J. & Tullock, G. (1962). *The calculus of consent*. Ann Arbor: University of Michigan Press.

Bundy, M. (1989). *Danger and survival*. New York: Random House.

Burke, C. G. (in press). Themes from the history of American public administration: Rethinking our past. In Rabin, Hildreth, & Miller (eds.), *Handbook of public administration*. New York: Marcel Dekker.

Burns, J. M. (1978). *Leadership*. New York: Harper & Row.

Burrell, G. & Morgan, G. (1979). *Sociological paradigms and organisational analysis*. Portsmouth, NH: Heinemann.

Buzan, T. (1983). *Use both sides of your brain* (rev. ed.). New York: Dutton.

Caiden, G. E. (1971). *The dynamics of public administration*. Hinsdale, IL: Dryden Press.

Caiden, G. E. (1982). *Public administration* (2nd ed.). Pacific Palisades, CA: Palisades Publishers.

Califano, Jr., J. A. (1986). *America's health care revolution: Who lives? Who dies? Who pays?* New York: Random House.

Campbell, C. (1985). *Meditations with Teresa of Avila*. Santa Fe, NM: Bear.

Campbell, J. (1949). *The hero with a thousand faces*. Princeton, NJ: Princeton University Press.

Campbell, J. (1971). (ed.). *The portable Jung*. New York: Viking Press.

Campbell, J. (1972) *Myths to live by*. New York: Bantam Books.

Campbell, J. (1976). *The masks of the gods* (4 vols.). Baltimore, MD: Penguin.

Campbell, J. (1983). *The way of the animal powers*. New York: Van der Mark.

Capra, F. (1982) *The turning point: Science, society, and the rising culture*. New York: Bantam Books.

CBS Evening News (1989, July 7). New York: CBS News.

Chandler, R. C. & Plano, J. C. (1986). *The public administration dictionary*. New York: John Wiley & Sons.

Chandler, R. C. (Ed.) (1987). *A centennial history of the American administrative state*. New York: Macmillan.

Clark, D. L. (1985). Emerging paradigms in organizational theory and research. In Y. S. Lincoln (ed.), *Organizational theory and inquiry: The paradigm revolution*. Beverly Hills: Sage Publications.

Cleary, R. E. (1989, March/April). Dialogue, negotiation, and the advancement of democracy: Reflections on Minnowbrook II. *Public Administration Review, 49*, 226–27.

Clissold, S. (1979). *St. Teresa of Avila*. London: Sheldon Press.

Cohen, M. D., March, J. G., & Olsen, J. P. (1972, March). A garbage can model of organizational choice. *Administrative Science Quarterly 17*, 1–25.

Cohen, R. (1989, May 14). The evil 'I'. *The Washington Post Magazine*, 25A.

Cooper, T. L. (1986). *The responsible administrator: An approach to ethics for the administrative role* (2nd ed.). Associated Faculty Press.

Cooper, T. L. (1987). Hierarchy, virtue and the practice of public administration. *Public Administration Review*, (July/August), 320–28.

Corsini, R. & Marsella, A. (eds.) (1983). *Personality theories, research and assessment.* Itasca, IL: Peacock.

Culbert, S. & McDonough, J. (1985). *Radical management.* New York: The Free Press.

Cyert, R. & March, J. (1963). *A behavioral theory of the firm.* Englewood Cliffs, NJ: Prentice Hall.

Dahl, R. A. (1957). The concept of power. *Behavioral Science, 3*: 201–15.

Dator, J. (1981). Alternative futures and the legal system. In J. Dator & C. Bezold (eds.), *Judging the future: Alternative futures of the legal system.* Honolulu: University of Hawaii Press.

Davis, J. G. (1855). Hospital for the insane of the army and navy. *Journal of Insanity, 11,* 358–65.

Deal, T. & Kennedy, A. A. (1982). *Corporate cultures: The rites and rituals of corporate life.* Reading, MA: Addison-Wesley.

Denhardt, K. G. (1988). *The ethics of public service: Resolving moral dilemmas in public organizations.* New York: Greenwood Press.

Denhardt, R. B. (1981a). *In the shadow of organization.* Lawrence, KS: Regents Press of Kansas.

Denhardt, R. B. (1981b, November/December). Toward a critical theory of public administration. *Public Administration Review, 41,* 628–36.

Denhardt, R. B. (1984). *Theories of public organizations.* Pacific Grove, CA: Brooks/Cole.

Denhardt, R. B. (1987, Summer). The contemporary critique of management education: Lessons for business and public administration. *Public Administration Quarterly.*

Department of Defense Dependent Schools and Overseas Education Association (1983). 12 *Federal Labor Relations Authority* (FLRA), 52.

Dery, David (1986). Knowledge and organizations. *Policy Studies Review, 6*(1), August.

deVries, M. F. R. & Miller, D. (1984). *The neurotic organization.* San Francisco: Jossey-Bass.

Diamond, M. (1988). Organizational identity: a psychological exploration of organizational meaning. *Administration and Society, 20*(2), 166–90.

Diesing, P. (1976). *Reason in society.* New York: Greenwood Press.

Dooling, D. M. (1979). *A way of working: The spiritual dimensions of craft.* New York: Parabola Books.

Downs, A. (1967). *Inside bureaucracy.* Boston: Little, Brown & Co.

Drucker, Peter F. (1974). *Management.* New York: Harper & Row.

Durkheim, E. (1952). *Suicide: A study in sociology.* Boston: Routledge & Kegan Paul.

Dye, T. R. (1975). *Understanding public policy* (2nd ed.). Englewood Cliffs, NJ: Prentice-Hall.

Edinger, E. (1976, Winter). The tragic hero: An image of individuation. *Parabola, 1.*

Edwards, T. (1987). *Living in the presence: Discipline for the spiritual heart.* San Francisco: Harper & Row.

Eisler, R. (1987). *The chalice and the blade: Our history, our future.* San Francisco: Harper & Row.

Evans, M. (1986, Summer). Organizational behavior: The central role of motivation. *Journal of Management,* 203–22.

Fayol, H. (1916). *General and industrial management* (C. Storrs, trans.). London: Pitman.

Ferguson, M. (1980). *The aquarian conspiracy: Personal and social transformation in the 1980s.* Los Angeles: Tarcher.

Ferris, G. R., Fedor, D. B., Chachere, J. G. & Pondy, L. R. (1989). Myth and politics in organizational contexts. *Group and Organization Studies, 14*(1), 83–103.

Fesler, J. W. (1980). *Public administration: Theory and practice.* Englewood Cliffs, NJ: Prentice Hall.

Feyerabend, Paul. *Against method.* London: New Left Books, 1975.

Fisher, R. & Ury, W. (1981). *Getting to yes.* New York: Penguin Books.

Fox, E. & Urwick, L. (1973). *Dynamic administration: The collected papers of Mary Parker Follett.* New York: Hippocrene Books Inc.

Fox, M. (1979). *A spirituality named compassion and the healing of the global village: Humpty Dumpty and us.* San Francisco: Harper & Row.

Fox, M. (1980). *Breakthrough: Meister Eckhart's creation spirituality in new translation.* Garden City, NY: Doubleday.

Fox, M. (1982). *Meditations with Meister Eckhart.* Sante Fe, NM: Bear.

Fox, M. (1983). *Original blessing.* Sante Fe, NM: Bear.

Frederickson, H. G. (1971). Toward a new public administration. In F. Marini (ed.), *Toward a new public administration: The Minnowbrook perspective* (309–31). New York: Chandler Publishing Co.

Frederickson, H. G. (1989, March/April). Minnowbrook II: Changing epochs of public administration. *Public Administration Review, 49,* 95–100.

Freire, Paulo (1970). *Pedagogy of the oppressed.* New York: Continuum.

French, W. & Bell, Jr., C. H. (1984). *Organization development: Behavioral science interventions for organizational development* (3rd ed.). Englewood Cliffs, NJ: Prentice Hall.

Friedlander, F. (1984). Patterns of individual and organizational learning. In S. Srivastva & Associates (eds.), *The executive mind: New insights on managerial thought and action.* San Francisco: Jossey-Bass (192–220).

Fromm, Erich (1941). *Escape from freedom.* New York: Holt, Rinehart & Winston.

Fromm, E. (1964). *The heart of man: Its genius for good or evil.* New York: Harper & Row.

Frost, P. J., Moore, L. F., Louis, M. R., Lundberg, C. C., & Martin, J. (eds.) (1985). *Organizational culture.* Beverly Hills, CA: Sage Publications.

Gardner, J. W. (1981). *Self-renewal: The individual and the innovative society* (4th ed.). New York: W. W. Norton & Company.

Garfield, C. A. & Bennett, H. Z. (1984). *Peak Performance: Mental training techniques of the world's greatest athletes.* New York: Warner Books.

Gawthrop, L. C. (1984). *Public sector management, systems, and ethics.* Bloomington: Indiana University Press.

Gawthrop, L. C. (1987). Toward an ethical convergence of democratic theory and administrative politics. In Ralph Clark Chandler (Ed.), *A centennial history of the American administrative state* (189–216). New York: The Free Press.

Gazzaniga, M. (1985). *The social brain: Discovering the networks of the mind.* New York: Basic Books.

General Accounting Office (1987, August). *Senior executive service: Reasons why career members left in fiscal year 1985.* Washington, DC: Author.

Gilbreth, F. (1912). *Primer of scientific management.* New York: Harper & Brothers.

Godding, W. W. (1890). Obituary: Charles H. Nichols. *Journal of Insanity, 49,* 416–21.

Godding, W. W. (1892). *Annual report to the secretary of interior.* Washington, DC: National Archives. Record Group 418.

Goffman, I. (1961). *Asylum: The social situation of mental patients and other inmates.* New York: Doubleday.

Golembiewski, R. T. (1979)). *Approaches to planned change* (vols. 1 & 2). New York: Marcell Dekker.

Goodnow, F. (1900). *Politics and administration.* New York: Russel & Russel.

Gorelick, K. (1986a). The house that Dorothea built. *Continuing Medical Education Newsletter,* Saint Elizabeths Hospital, *3*(5), 3–9. (Available from Division of Training and Standards, Saint Elizabeths Hospital, Washington, DC, 20032).

Gorelick, K. (1986b). How Saint Elizabeths got its name. *Continuing Medical Education Newsletter,* Saint Elizabeths Hospital, *3*(1), 5–8. (Available from Division of Training and Standards, Saint Elizabeths Hospital, Washington, DC, 20032).

Gortner, H. F., Mahler, J. & Nicholson, J. B. (1987). *Organization theory: A public perspective.* Chicago, IL: Dorsey Press.

Gouldner, A. (1954). *Patterns of industrial bureaucracy.* New York: The Free Press.

Graves, R. (1966). *The Greek myths* (vols. 1 & 2). Baltimore, MD: Penguin.

Guba, E. G. (1985). The context of emergent paradigm research. In Y. Lincoln, *Organizational theory and inquiry* (79–104). Los Angeles: Sage Publications.

Gulick, L. (1937). Notes on the theory of organization. In L. Gulick & L. Urwick (eds.), *Papers on the science of administration.* New York: Institute of Public Administration.

Gulick, L. & Urwick, L. (eds.) (1937). *Papers on the science of administration.* New York: Institute of Public Administration.

Guy, M. E. (1989, March/April). Minnowbrook II: Conclusions. *Public Administration Review, 49,* 219–20.

Hall, J., Harvey, J. B., & Williams, M. (1980). *Styles of management inventory* (rev. ed.; questionnaire). Telcometrics International.

Hamilton, E. (1969). *Mythology.* New York: Mentor.

Hampden-Turner, C. (1981). *Maps of the mind.* New York: Collier Books.

Hardy, C. (1985). The nature of unobtrusive power. *Journal of Management Studies, 22,* 384–99.

Harman, W. (1988). *Global mind change: The promise of the last years of the twentieth century.* Indianapolis, IN: Knowledge Systems.

Harman, W. & Rheingold, H. (1984). *Higher creativity: Liberating the unconscious for breakthrough insights.* Los Angeles: Tarcher.

Harmon, M. M. (1971). Normative theory and public administration: Some suggestions for a redefinition of administrative responsibility. In F. Marini (ed.), *Toward a new public administration: The Minnowbrook perspective* (172–85). New York: Chandler Publishing Co.

Harmon, M. M. (1981). *Action theory for public administration.* New York: Longman.

Harmon, M. M. & Mayer, R. T. (1986). *Organization theory for public administration.* Boston: Little, Brown.

Harrison, A. & Bramson, R. (1982). *Styles of thinking.* New York: Anchor Press.

Harrison, R. (1984). Leadership and strategy for a new age. In J. D. Adams (ed.), *Transforming work.* Alexandria, VA: Miles River Press.

Haveman, R. (1987, Winter). Policy analysis and evaluation research after twenty years. *Policy Studies Journal, 16*(2), 191–218.

Havemann, J. (1988, October 10). Federal employment crisis: In some places it's arrived. *The Washington Post.*

Henry, N. (1988). The emergence of public administration as a field of study. In R. C. Chandler (ed.), *A centennial history of the American administrative state* (37–85). New York: Macmillan.

Herman, S. M. & Korenich, M. (1977). *Authentic management: A gestalt orientation to organizations and their development.* Reading, MA: Addison Wesley.

Herzberg, F. (1966). *Work and the nature of man.* New York: Crowell & Co.

Heymann, P. B. (1987). *The politics of public management.* New Haven: Yale University.

Hirschhorn, L. (1988). *The workplace within: Psychodynamics of organizational life.* Cambridge, MA; MIT Press.

Holzer, M. (1989, March/April). Minnowbrook II: Conclusions: *Public Administration Review, 49,* 221–22.

Houghton, F. (1971). *The life of Dorothea Lynde Dix.* Anne Arbor, MI: Plutarch Press. (Original work published 1890. New York: Houghton & Mifflin).

Houston, J. (1982). *The possible human: A course in enhancing your physical, mental and creative abilities.* Los Angeles: Tarcher.

Huse, E. F. & Cummings, T. G. (1985). *Organization development and change* (3rd ed.). St. Paul, MN: West Publishing Co.

Ingals, J.D. (1979). *Human energy.* Austin, TX: Learning Concepts.

I[nternal] R[evenue] S[ervice] and N[ational] T[reasury] E[mployees] U[nion] (1988). 31 Federal Labor Relation Authority (FLRA), 832.

Jackall, R. (1983, September-October). Moral mazes: Bureaucracy and managerial work. *Harvard Business Review.*

Jacobi, J. & A. Jaffe. *Man and his symbols.* Garden City, NY: Doubleday.

Janis, I. L. (1982). *Groupthink: Psychological studies of policy decisions and fiascoes.* Boston: Houghton Mifflin.

Jobes, G. (1961). *Dictionary of mythology: Folklore and symbols.* New York: The Scarecrow Press.

Johnston, W., et al. (1988, June). *Civil service 2000.* Washington, DC: Office of Personnel Management.

Joint Commission on Mental Illness and Health (1961). *Action for mental health.* New York: Basic Books.

Jones, C. O. (1977). *An introduction to the study of public policy.* Belmont, CA: Duxbury Press.

Jung, C. G. (1956). *Symbols of transformation. Volume I.* (R.F.C. Hull, trans.). New York: Harper & Brothers. (Original work published 1952).

Jung, C. G. (1958). *Psyche and symbol.* (V. S. de Laszlo, ed.). Garden City, NY: Doubleday Anchor Books.

Jung, C. G. (1962). *The secret of the golden flower* (Richard Wilhelm, trans.). New York: Doubleday.

Jung, C. G. (1968a). Archetypes of the collective unconscious. In H. Read, M. Fordhan, & G. Adler (eds.), *Collected works of C. G. Jung* (2nd ed.). (R.F.C. Hull, Trans.). (vol. [9], 3–53). Princeton, NJ: Princeton University Press. (Original work published 1934/36).

Jung, C. G. (1968b). Psychological aspects of the mother archetype. In H. Read, M. Fordhan, & G. Adler (eds.), *Collected works of C. G. Jung* (2nd ed.). (R.F.C. Hull trans). (Vol. 9 [I], 75–110). Princeton, NJ: Princeton University Press. (Original work published 1938/1954).

Jung, C. G. (1968c). The psychology of the child archetype. In H. Read, M. Fordhan, & G. Adler (eds.), *Collected works of C. G. Jung* (2nd ed.). (R.F.C Hull, trans.). (Vol. 9[I], 160–81). Princeton, NJ: Princeton University Press. (Original work published 1940).

Jung, C. G. (1968d). Concerning rebirth. In H. Read, M. Fordhan, & G. Adler (eds.). *Collected Works of C. G. Jung* (2nd ed.). (R.F.C. Hull, trans.). (Vol. 9[I]. 113–47). Princeton, NJ: Princeton University Press. (Original work published 1940/1950).

Jung, C. G. (1968e). Mandalas. In H. Read, M. Fordhan, & G. Adler (eds.), *Collected works of C. G. Jung* (2nd ed.). (R.F.C. Hull, trans.). (Vol. 9[I], 385–90). Princeton, NJ: Princeton University Press. (Original work published 1955).

Jung, C. G. (1970). Wotan. In H. Read, M. Fordhan, & G. Adler (eds.), *Collected works of C. G. Jung* (2nd ed.). (R.F.C. Hull, trans.). (Vol. 10, 179–93). Princeton, NJ: Princeton University Press. (Original work published 1936).

Jung, C. G., von Franz, M.-L., Henderson, J. L., Jacobi, J., & Jaffe, A. (1964). *Man and his symbols*. Garden City, NY: Doubleday.

Kanter, D. & Mirvis, P. H. (1989). *The cynical Americans: Living and working in an age of discontent and disillusion*. San Francisco: Jossey-Bass.

Karp, H. B. (1986). Power to the practitioner. In J. W. Pfeiffer & L. D. Goodstein, *The 1986 annual: Developing human resources*. San Diego: University Associates.

Karp, J. & Renesch, S. (1986, August 27). Shunning the job-hunt maze: Civil service loses career appeal for recent college graduates. *The Washington Post*.

Katz, D. (1974, September/October). Skills of an effective administrator. *Harvard Business Review*.

Katz, D. & Kahn, R. L. (1966). *The social psychology of organizations*. New York: Wiley.

Katz, D. & Kahn, R. L. (1978). *The social psychology of organizations* (2nd ed.). New York: John Wiley & Sons.

Kaufman, H. (1960). *The forest ranger: A study in administrative behavior*. Baltimore: Johns Hopkins Press.

Kaufman, H. (1981). *The administrative behavior of federal bureau chiefs*. Washington, DC: The Brookings Institution.

Kavanaugh, K. & Rodriguez, O. (trans.) (1979). *The collected works of St. John of the Cross*. Washington, DC: Institute of Carmelite Studies.

Kavanaugh, K. & Rodriguez, O. (Trans.) (1985). *The collected works of St. Teresa of Avila* (vols. 1–3). Washington, DC: Institute of Carmelite Studies.

Keating, T. (1986). *Open mind, open heart: The contemplative dimension of the gospel*. Amity, NY: Amity House.

Keen, S. (1988, December). The stories we live by: Personal myths guide daily life. *Psychology Today*, 42–47.

Keirsey, D. & Bates, M. (1978). *Please understand me: Character and temperament types*. Del Mar, CA: Prometheus Nemesis Books.

Kennedy, R. F. (1969). *Thirteen days: A memoir of the Cuban missile crisis*. New York: W. W. Norton.

Kets de Vries, M. & Miller, D. (1984). *The Neurotic organization*. San Francisco, CA: Jossey-Bass.

Kerenyi, C. & Jung, C. (1963). *Essays on a science of mythology*. New York: Harper.

Kilman, R., et al. (1985). *Gaining control of the corporate culture*. San Francisco: Jossey-Bass.

Kirkhart, L. (1971). Toward a theory of public administration. In F. Marini (ed.), *Toward a new public administration: The Minnowbrook perspective* (127–64). New York: Chandler Publishing Co.

Kirlin, John J. (1984). *The political economy of fiscal limits*. Lexington, MA: D. C. Heath.

Knowles, M. K. (1984). *The adult learner: A neglected species* (3rd ed.). Houston: Gulf Publishing.

Kolb, D. (1984). *Experiential learning: Experience as the source of learning and development*. Englewood Cliffs, NJ: Prentice-Hall.

Koontz, H. (1961, December). The management theory jungle. *The Academy of Management Journal*, 174–88.

Kotter, J. P. (1988). *The leadership factor*. New York: The Free Press.

Kouzes, J. & Posner, B. (1987). *The leadership challenge*. San Francisco: Jossey-Bass.

Krislov, S. (1974). *Representative bureaucracy*. Englewood Cliffs, NJ: Prentice Hall.

Kroegar, O. & Thusesen, J. M. (1987). *Type talk*. New York: Delacorte Press.

Kuhn, T. (1970). *The structure of scientific revolutions* (2nd ed.). Chicago: University of Chicago.

Laborde, G. Z. (1984). *Influencing with integrity: Management skills for communication and negotiation*. Palo Alto, CA: Syntony Publishing.

Lakein, Alan. (1975) *How to get control of your time*. New York: Peter Wyden.

Lakoff, G. & Johnson, M. (1980). *Metaphors we live by*. Chicago: University of Chicago.

LaPorte, T. R. (1971). The recovery of relevance in the study of public organizations. In F. Marini (ed.), *Toward a new public administration: The Minnowbrook perspective* (pp. 17–48). New York: Chandler Publishing Co.

Laurent, A. (1989, March 13). Authors map out the arduous road for whistleblowers [Review of *The whistleblowers: Exposing corruption in government and industry*]. *Federal Times*.

Lawler, E. E., III. (1986). *High involvement management*. San Francisco: Jossey-Bass.

Lenz, B. & Myerhoff, B. (1985). *The feminization of America: How women's values are changing our public and private lives*. Los Angeles: Tarcher.

Levine, C. H. (1980). *Managing fiscal stress: The crisis in the public sector*. Chatham, NJ: Chatham House Publishers.

Levine, C. & Kleeman, R. (1986, December). *The quiet crisis of the civil service: The federal personnel system at the crossroads*. Washington, DC: National Academy of Public Administration.

Likert, R. (1961). *New patterns of management*. New York: McGraw-Hill.

Lincoln, Y. (ed.) (1985). *Organizational theory and inquiry: The paradigm revolution*. Beverly Hills, CA: Sage Publications.

Lincoln, Y. S. & Guba, E. G. (1985). *Naturalistic inquiry*. Beverly Hills, CA: Sage Publications.

Lind, W. S. & Marshall, W. H. (1987). *Cultural conservatism: Towards a new national agenda*. Lanham, MD: University Press.

Lindblom, Charles (1959). The science of "muddling through." *Public Administration Review, 19* (Spring), 79–88.

Lindblom, C. E. (1965). *The intelligence of democracy: Decision making through mutual adjustment*. New York: The Free Press.

Lombard, J. (1987). *Archetypes in organization: Case study in the emergence and meaning of feminine and masculine archetypes in a public mental hospital*. Unpublished doctoral dissertation, University of Southern California, Los Angeles.

Long, N. (1981). The SES and the public interest. *Public Administration Review* (May/June).

Luce, R. D. & Raiffa, H. (1957). *Games and decisions.* New York: John Wiley & Sons.

Lukes, S. (1974). *Power in and around organizations.* Englewood Cliffs, NJ: Prentice Hall.

Lynn, Jr., L. E. (1987a) *Managing public policy.* Boston: Little, Brown.

Lynn, Jr., L. E. (1987b). Public management: What do we know? What should we know? And how will we know it? *Journal of Policy Analysis and Management, 7*(1).

Maeder, T. (1989, January). Wounded healers. *The Atlantic Monthly, 263*(1).

Mahler, J. (1988). The quest for organizational meaning: Identifying and interpreting the symbolism in organizational stories. *Administration and Society, 20*(3), 344–68.

Manz, C. C. (1986, July). Self-leadership: toward an expanded theory of self-influence processes in organizations. *Academy of Management Review*, 585–600.

McCall, M. W., Jr., Lombardo, M. M., & Morrison, A. M. (1988). *The lessons of experience: How successful executives develop on the job.* Lexington, MA: Lexington Books.

McClelland, D. (1975). *Power: The inner experience.* New York: John Wiley & Sons.

McCurdy, H. E. (1986). *Public administration: A bibliographic guide to the literature.* New York: Marcel Dekker.

McCurdy, H. E. & Cleary, R. (1984, January/February). Why can't we resolve the research issue in public administration? *Public Administration Review, 44*, 49–55.

McGregor, D. (1960). *The human side of enterprise.* New York: McGraw-Hill.

McGregor, D. (1966). The human side of enterprise. *Leadership and motivation.* Cambridge, MA: MIT Press.

McGregor, D. (1967). *The professional manager.* New York: McGraw-Hill.

McKelvey, B. (1982). *Organizational systematics—taxonomy, evolution, classification.* Berkeley, CA: University of California Press.

McSwain, C. J. & White, O. (1987). The case for lying, cheating and stealing: Personal development as ethical guidance for managers. *Administration and Society.*

Marini, F. (ed.). (1981). *Toward a new public administration. The Minnowbrook perspective.* New York: Chandler Publishing Co.

Marx, K. (1971). Socialism, democracy and revolution. In S. Padaver (ed.), *On Revolution.* New York: McGraw-Hill.

Maslow, A. H. (1943, July). A theory of human motivation. *Psychological Review, 50*, 370–96.

May, G. G. (1983). *Will and spirit: A contemplative psychology.* San Francisco: Harper & Row.

May, G. G. (1987). The bear the beams of love: Contemplation and personal growth. *The way, 59* (Supl. Summer), 24–34.

May, R. (1980). *The courage to create* (6th ed.). New York: Bantam Books.

Mayer, R. T. (1989, March/April). Minnowbrook II: Conclusions and reflections. *Public Administration Review, 49*, 218.

Meltsner, A. J. (1976). *Policy analysts in the bureaucracy.* Berkeley, University of California Press.

Meltsner, A. J. & Bellavita, C. (1983) *The policy organization.* Beverly Hills: Sage Publications.

Merton, R. K. (1949). *Social theory and social structure.* New York: The Free Press.

Merton, T. (1961). *New seeds of contemplation.* New York: New Directions.

Metcalf, H. & Urwick, L. (1940). *Dynamic administration.* New York: Harper & Bros. Publishers.

Miller, T. C. (ed.) (1984). *Public sector performance*. Baltimore: Johns Hopkins University Press.

Mintzberg, H. (1972). *The nature of managerial work*. New York: Harper & Row.

Mitroff, I. I. (1983). *Stakeholders of the organizational mind*. San Francisco, CA: Jossey-Bass.

Morgan, G. (1983). *Beyond method: Strategies for social research*. Beverly Hills, CA: Sage Publications.

Morgan, G. (1986). *Images of organization*. Beverly Hills, CA: Sage Publications.

Morgan, G. (1988). *Riding the waves of change: Developing competencies for a turbulent world*. San Francisco: Jossey-Bass.

Mosher, F. (1968). *Democracy and the public service*. New York: Oxford University Press.

Mosher, F. C. (1975). Introduction: The American setting. In F. C. Mosher (ed.), *American public administration: Past, present and future* (1–10). University, AL: University of Alabama Press.

Mosher, F. C. (1979). *The GAO: The quest for accountability in American government*. Boulder, CO: Westview Press.

Mueller, R. K. (1986). *Corporate networking: Building channels for information and influence*. New York: The Free Press.

Murphey, T. P. (1981). *Contemporary public administration*. Itasca, IL: F. E. Peacock.

Nadler, L. (1979). *Developing human resources*. Austin, TX: Learning Concepts.

Naisbitt, J. (1984). *Megatrends: Ten new directions transforming our lives*. New York: Warner Books.

National Academy of Public Administration (1983). *Revitalizing federal management: Managers and their overburdened systems*. Washington, DC: Author.

National Academy of Public Administration (1985). *Leadership in jeopardy: The fraying of the presidential appointment system*. Washington, DC: Author.

National Academy of Public Administration (1988, September). *The executive presidency: Federal management for the 1990s*. Washington, DC: Author.

Neumann, E. (1964). *The great mother: An analysis of the archetype*. Princeton, NJ: Princeton University Press.

Neustadt, R. (1980). *Presidential power*. New York: John Wiley & Sons.

Newland, C. A. (1984). *Public administration and community: Realism in the practice of ideals*. McLean, VA: Public Administration Service.

Nisbett, R. & Perrin, R. G. (1977). *The social bond* (2nd ed.). New York: Alfred A. Knopf.

Odajynk, V. W. (1976). *Jung and politics*. New York: Harper & Row.

Olderr, S. (1989). *Symbolism: A comprehensive dictionary*. New York: McFarland & Co.

Olson, M. (1983). *The rise and decline of nations: Economic growth, stagflation, and social rigidities*. New Haven: Yale University Press.

Oncken, William, Jr. (1984). *Managing management time*. Englewood Cliff, NJ: Prentice Hall.

OPM Backs off From RIF Rule Changes That Would Deemphasize Seniority (1982, July 26). *Government Employee Relations Report* (26), 14.

OPM Softens Stand on Pay for Performance, But Unions, Stevens Still Not Buying (1983, July 18). *Government Employee Relations Report*, (21), 1455–56.

Overholser, W. (1956). An historical sketch of Saint Elizabeths Hospital. In W. Overholser (ed.), *Centennial Papers: Saint Elizabeths Hospital*. Baltimore, MD: Waverly Press.

Owen, H. (1984). Facilitating organizational transformation: The uses of myth and ritual. In J. D. Adams (ed.), *Transforming work*. Alexandria, VA: Miles River Press.

Owen, H. (1987). *Spirit: Transformation and development in organizations*. Potomac, MD: Abbott Publishing.

Parker, L. (1984). Control in organizational life: The contribution of Mary Parker Follett. *Academy of Management Review, 9*, 736–45.

Parsons, T. (1960). *Structure and process in modern societies*. New York: The Free Press.

Pearson, C. (1986). *The hero within: Six archetypes we live by*. New York: Harper & Row.

Peck, M. S. (1979). *The road less traveled: A new psychology of love, traditional values and spiritual growth*. New York: Simon & Schuster.

Peck, M. S. (1983). *People of the lie: The hope for healing human evil*. New York: Simon & Schuster.

Perera, S. B. (1981) *Descent to the goddess*. Toronto, Canada: Inner City Books.

Performance Management System to Become Effective in April. (1986, March 13). *Government Employee Relations Report, 24*, 358.

Perrow, C. (1986). *Complex organizations*. New York: Random House.

Peters, T. J. & Watermann, R. H. (1982). *In search of excellence*. New York: Harper & Row.

Pilkington, W. (1987). *Selected determinants of managerial effectiveness*. Unpublished doctoral dissertation, University of Southern California, Los Angeles.

Pirsig, R. M. (1974). *Zen and the art of motorcycle maintenance*. New York: Bantam Books.

Pondy, L. R. (1983). The role of metaphors and myths in organization and the facilitation of change. In L. R. Pondy, Frost, P., Morgan G., Dandridge T. (eds.). *Organizational symbolism*. Greenwich, CT: JAI Press.

Porter, D. O. (1989, March/April). Minnowbrook II: Conclusions. *Public Administration Review, 49*, 223.

Posner, B. & Schmidt, W. (1986a). Values and the American manager: An update. *California Management Review, 3* (Spring), 202–16.

Posner, B. & Schmidt, W. (1986b). Values and expectations of federal service executives. *Public Administration Review, 46*, 447–54.

Pressman, J. L. & Wildavsky, A. (1973). *Implementation*. Berkeley: University of California Press.

Presthus, R. (1962). *The organizational society*. New York: Alfred A Knopf.

Prigogine, I. & Stengers, I. (1984). *Order out of chaos: Man's new dialogue with nature*. New York: Bantam.

Progoff, I. (1981). *Jung's psychology and its social meaning*. (3rd ed.). New York: Dialogue House Press.

Quade, E. S. (1975). *Analysis for public decisions*. New York: Elsevier.

Quinn, R. E. (1988). *Beyond rational management: Mastering the paradoxes and competing demands of high performance*. San Francisco: Jossey-Bass.

Radin, B. A. (1973). *Implementation, change and the federal bureaucracy*. New York: Teachers College Press, Columbia University.

Raven, B. & Kruglanski, J. (1976). Conflict and power. In P. G. Swingle (ed.) *The structure of conflict*. New York: Academic Press.

Redford, E. (1969). *Democracy in the administrative state*. New York: Oxford University Press.

Rivlin, A. M. (1971). *Systematic thinking for social action*. Washington, DC: The Brookings Institution.

Rogers, J. (1988, January). *Meeting public demands: Federal service in the year 2000*. Washington, DC: United States Department of the Treasury.

Rohr, J. A. (1987). The administrative state and constitutional principle. In R. C. Chandler (ed.), *A centennial history of the American administrative state* (113–59). New York: Macmillan.

Rose, A. (1967). *The power structure.* New York: Oxford University Press.

Sanera, M. (1984). Implementing the mandate. In S. Butler, et al., *Mandate for leadership II: Continuing the conservative revolution.* Washington, DC: The Heritage Foundation.

Sayre, W. S. (1958, Spring). Premises of public administration: Past and emerging. *Public Administration Review, 18,* 102–5.

Schaef, A. W., & Fassel, D. (1988). *The addictive organization.* San Francisco: Harper & Row.

Schein, E. (1985). *Organizational culture and leadership.* San Francisco, CA: Jossey-Bass.

Schick, A. (1966, December). The road to PPB: The stages of budget reform. *Public Administration Review, 26,* 243–58.

Schick, A. (1971). *Budget innovation in the states.* Washington, DC: The Brookings Institution.

Schön, D. A. (1983). *The reflective practitioner: How professionals think in action.* New York: Basic Books.

Schoumacher, S. & Cadden, V. (1989). Preparing your child for the 21st century. *McCall's 116*(12), 41–49.

Schumacher, E. F. (1975). *Small is beautiful.* New York: Harper & Row.

Schwartz, A. E. (1989, May 16). Motiveless malignity. *The Washington Post.*

Schwartz, P. & Ogilvy, J. (1979). *The emergent paradigm: Changing patterns of thought and belief* (Analytic Report 7, Values and Lifestyle Program). Menlo Park, CA: SRI International.

Scott, W. G. & Hart, D. K. (1976, June). The moral nature of man in organizations. *Academy of Management Journal,* 241–55.

Scott, W. G. & Hart, D. K. (1979). *Organizational America.* Boston: Houghton Mifflin.

Selznick, P. (1949). *TVA and the grass roots.* New York: Harper & Row.

Shafritz, J. M. & Hyde, A. C. (1987). *Classics of public administration* (2nd ed.). Chicago: The Dorsey Press.

Sharkansky, I. (1982). *Public administration: Agencies, policies, politics.* San Francisco: W. H. Freeman.

Simon, H. A. (1946, Winter). The proverbs of administration. *Public Administration Review, 6,* 53–67.

Simon, H. A. (1947). *Administrative behavior: A study of decision-making processes in administrative organization.* New York: Macmillan.

Simpson, F. C. (1899). Obituary: W. W. Godding. American *Journal of Insanity, 56,* 185–97.

Sims, H. P., Jr., Gioia, D. A. & Associates. (1986). *The thinking organization: Dynamics of organizational social cognition.* San Francisco: Jossey-Bass.

Singer, J. (1972). *Boundaries of the soul.* New York: Doubleday.

Smith, H. (1988, April). Power in Washington: The coup that failed and other tales. *The Washingtonian,* 142–43, 181–95.

Smith, J. K. & Heshusius, L. (1986, January). Closing down the conversation: The end of the quantitative-qualitative debate among educational inquirers. *Educational Researcher.*

Sonnichsen, R. C. (1988). Using evaluation to stimulate program change. In J. S. Wholey & K. E. Newcomer (eds.), *Using evaluation to strengthen public programs: effective strategies and approaches.* San Francisco: Jossey-Bass.

Sonnichsen, R. C. (1989). Program managers: Victims or victors in the evaluation process. In G. L. Barkdoll & J. Bell (eds.), *Evaluation and the federal decisionmakers: New directions for program evaluation*. San Francisco: Jossey-Bass.

Sorensen, T. (1965). *Kennedy*. New York: Harper & Row.

Springarn, N. D. (1956, January). St. Elizabeths: pace-setter for mental hospitals. *Harper's Magazine*, 1–6.

Stahl, O. Glenn (1971) *The personnel job of government managers*. Chicago: Public Personnel Association.

Staw, B. M. (1982). Motivation in organizations. In B. M. Staw & G. R. Salancik, *New directions in organizational behavior*. New York: John Wiley & Sons.

Steinbruner, J. (1974). *The cybernetic theory of decision*. Princeton, NJ: Princeton University Press.

Stephan, E., Mills, G. E., Pace, R. W., & Ralphs, L. (1988). HRD in the Fortune 500: A survey. *Training and Development Journal, 42*(1), 26–32.

Stephens, C. & Eisen, S. (1984). Myth, transformation, and the change agent. In J. D. Adams (ed.), *Transforming work*. Alexandria, VA: Miles River Press.

Stever, J. (1986). Mary Parker Follett and the quest for pragmatic administration. *Administration and Society, 18*, 159–77.

Stone, A. B. & Stone, D. C. (1975). Appendix: Case histories of early professional educational programs. In F. C. Mosher (ed.), *American public administration: Past, present and future* (268–90). University, AL: University of Alabama Press.

Suarez, E. M., Mills, R. C., & Stewart, D. (1987). *Sanity, insanity and commonsense*. New York: Fawcett Columbine.

Sullivan, H. S. (1940). Conceptions of modern psychiatry: The first William Alanson White memorial lecture. *Psychiatry, 3*, 1–117.

Snyder, C. (1975). *The lady and the president*. Lexington, KY: University Press of Kentucky.

Tart, C. T. (1986). *Waking up: Overcoming the obstacles to human potential*. Boston: Shambhala.

Taylor, F. (1911). *The principles of scientific management*. New York: W. W. Norton & Co.

Thayer, F. C. (1973). *An end to hierarchy and competition*. New York: New Viewpoints.

Thayer, F. C. (1981). *An end to hierarchy and competition* (2nd ed.). New York: Franklin Watts.

Theobald, R. (1987). *The rapids of change: Social entrepreneurship in turbulent times*. Indianapolis: Knowledge Systems, Inc.

Thompson, J. D. (1976). *Organizations in action: Social science bases of administrative theory*. New York: McGraw-Hill.

Thompson, V. A. *Bureaucracy and innovation* (1969). University, AL: University of Alabama Press.

Toffler, A. (1980). *The third wave*. New York: William Morrow.

Travers, P. L. (1976, Winter). The world of the hero. *Parabola, 1*.

Tulku, T. (1977). *Gesture of balance: A guide to awareness, self-healing, and meditation*. Berkeley: Dharma.

Tullock, G. (1965). *The politics of bureaucracy*. Washington, DC: Public Affairs Press.

Ulanov, A. B. & Ulanov, B. (1986). *The witch and the clown: Two archetypes of human sexuality*. New York: Chiron.

U.S. Customs Service and NTEU. (1987). 25 *Federal Labor Relations Authority* (FLRA), 248.

U.S. Merit Systems Protection Board (1989, October). *Senior executive service views of former federal executives*. Washington, DC: Author.

Vaill, P. B. (1989). *Managing as a performing art: New ideas for a world of chaotic change*. San Francisco: Jossey-Bass.

Valle, R. S. & Eckartsberg, R. (eds.) (1989) *Metaphors of consciousness*. New York: Plenum.

Vanier, J. (1978). *Community and growth*. New York: Paulist Press.

Vocino, J. & Rabin, J. (1981). *Contemporary public administration*. New York: Harcourt Brace Jovanovich.

Volker, Paul, et al. (1989). *Leadership for America: Rebuilding the public service*. National Commission on the Public Service: Washington, DC.

von Franz, M.-L. (1964). The process of individuation. In C. G. Jung, von Franz, M.-L., Henderson, J. L., Jacobi, J., Jaffe, A. *Man and his symbols*. Garden City, NY: Doubleday.

von Franz, M.-L. (1972). *Patterns of creativity mirrored in creation myths*. Dallas, TX: Spring Publisher.

von Franz, M.-L. (Speaker) (1986). *The way of the dream*. (Film). F. Boas (producer). Toronto, Canada: Windrose Films, Ltd.

Vukelich, D. (1988, December). Pay raise critical to keeping best managers, group says. *The Washington Times*.

Waldo, D. (1981). *The enterprise of public administration*. Novato, CA: Chandler & Sharp.

Waldo, D. (1984). *The administrative state: A study of the political theory of American public administration* (2nd ed.). New York: Holmes & Meier.

Wehr, D. (1987). *Jung and feminism: Liberating archetypes*. Boston, MA: Beacon Press.

Weick, K. E. (1979). *The social psychology of organizing* (2nd ed.). Reading, MA: Addison-Wesley.

Weimer, D. L. & Vining, A. (1989). *Policy analysis: concepts and practice*. Englewood Cliffs, NJ: Prentice Hall.

Weintal, E. & Barlett, C. (1967). *Facing the brink: An intimate study of crisis diplomacy*. New York: Charles Schribner's Sons.

Welch, J. (1982). *Spiritual pilgrims: Carl Jung and Teresa of Avila*. New York: Paulist Press.

White, J. D. (1986, January/Febuary). On the growth of knowledge in public administration. *Public Administration Review*, 15–24.

White, L. D. (1926). *Introduction to the study of public administration*. New York: The Macmillan Company.

White, O. F., Jr. (1969, January/February). The dialectical organization: An alternative to bureaucracy. *Public Administration Review, 29*, 32–42.

White, O. F., Jr. (1971). Administrative adaptation in a changing society. In F. Marini (ed.), *Toward a new public administration: The Minnowbrook perspective* (59–83). New York: Chandler Publishing Co.

White, O. F., Jr. (1983, April). *A structuralist approach to organizational action*. Paper presented at the Annual Conference, American Society for Public Administration, New York City, NY.

White, O. F. & McSwain, C. (1983). Transformational theory and organizational analysis. In G. Morgan, *Beyond method: Strategies for social research* (292–305). Beverly Hills, CA: Sage Publications.

Whitmont, E. (1969). *The symbolic quest: Basic concepts of analytical psychology*. Princeton, NJ: Princeton University Press.

Whitmont, E. (1982). *Return of the goddess*. NY: Crossroad Publishing Co.

Wholey, J. S., et al. (1970). *Federal evaluation policy*. Washington, DC: The Urban Institute.

Wilber, K. (1977). *The spectrum of consciousness*. Wheaton, IL: Theosophical Publishing.

Wilber, K. (1983). *Eye to eye: The quest for the new paradigm*. Garden City, NY: Doubleday.

Wilber, K. (1984). *A sociable god: Toward a new understanding of religion*. Boulder, CO: Shambhala.

Wildavsky, A. (1964). *The politics of the budgetary process*. Boston: Little, Brown.

Wildavsky, A. (1976). The once and future school of public policy. *The Public Interest, 38*.

Wildavsky, Aaron (1979). *Speaking truth to power: The art and craft of policy analysis*. Boston: Little, Brown and Company.

Wildavsky, A. (1984). *The nursing father: Moses as a political leader*. Birmingham: University of Alabama Press.

Wilkins, A. L. (1983). Organizational stories as symbols which control the organization. In L. R. Pondy, et al. (eds.), *Organizational symbolism*. Greenwich, CN: JAI Press.

Will, G. (1989, April 30). They went "wilding." *The Washington Post*.

Willoughby, W. F. (1918). *The movement for budgetary reform in the states*. New York: D. Appleton & Co.

Wilson, W. (1887, June). The study of administration. *Political Science Quarterly, 2*, 197–220.

Wolf, J. (1988–1989, Winter). The legacy of Mary Parker Follett. *The Bureaucrat*, 53–57.

Wood, A. (1926). The social philosophy of Mary Parker Follett, *Social Forces, 4*, 759–69.

Yankelovich, D. (1981). *New rules: Searching for self-fulfillment in a world turned upside down*. New York: Random House.

Young, A. M. (1976). *The reflexive universe*. Mill Valley, CA: Robert Briggs Associates.

Young, G. (1977). *Effective management*. Philadelphia: Dorrance and Company.

Yukl, G. (1981). *Leadership in organizations*. Englewood Cliffs, NJ: Prentice-Hall.

Zaleznik, A. (1970) Power and politics in organizational life. *Harvard Business Review, 48*, 47–60.

Zilboorg, G. (1956). The unwritten history of an inspiration. In W. Overholser (ed.), *Centennial papers: Saint Elizabeths hospital*. Baltimore, MD: Waverly Press.

Index

About the Editor and Contributors

CHRISTOPHER BELLAVITA received his Ph.D. in Public Policy from the University of California, Berkeley, and has published articles and books on organizations and on public policy. He has worked for federal, state, and local governments, is a consultant to several public organizations; and has taught at the University of California and the University of Southern California.

BARBARA BERTSCH BOYD is the manager of the Human Resources Development Institute, U.S. Department of Health and Human Services. She is responsible for the design and implementation of executive, management, and other employee development programs. She has been with the department for fifteen years, during which time she has worked for the Social Security Agency, the Office of Human Development Services, the former Office of Education, and the U.S. Public Health Service. She is a doctoral candidate in public administration at the University of Southern California.

ARTHUR A. CIARKOWSKI is the Chief of the Prosthetic and Monitoring Devices Branch, Food and Drug Administration. He was a chemist and a biomedical engineer before joining FDA, where he has been employed for ten years. He is a public administration doctoral candidate at the University of Southern California.

NANCY J. EGGERT has been an attorney with the National Labor Relations Board since 1973. She has also worked with many organizations involved with adult literacy, community development and organizational transformation. She is completing her doctorate in public administration.

FRANK D. FERRIS is the Director of Negotiations, National Treasury Employees Union. Ferris has been a public administrator for 18 years, in positions with the union, the Internal Revenue Service and the University of Missouri. He is currently completing his doctorate in public administration.

JUDITH M. LOMBARD is an employee development specialist for the Food and Nutrition Service, U.S. Department of Agriculture. Lombard received her DPA from the University of Southern California in 1988. For twenty years she was a mental health specialist at St. Elizabeths Hospital, U. S. Department of Health and Human Services.

PAUL B. LORENTZEN is an adjunct faculty member at the University of Southern California, Washington Public Affairs Center. Lorentzen was a public administrator in the federal government for 32 years. During his career he progressed from a management intern in the Civil Service Commission through various positions in the Departments of Commerce and the Interior. He is the past president of the Federal Executive Institute Alumni Association. He earned his public administration doctorate in 1984.

FRANK J. NICE is a Captain in the U.S. Public Health Service. He has been a public administrator for 16 years. Since 1981 he has been a branch and program administrator in the National Institutes of Health, Neurology Institute. He is also the Chief Pharmacist administrator for the National Boy Scouts of America Jamborees. He is a doctoral candidate in public administration at the University of Southern California.

WILLIAM F. PILKINGTON is the Health Director of the Cabarrus County Public Health Department in Concord, North Carolina. He began his career in 1974 as a policy analyst for the governor of North Carolina, became an assistant director of a health systems agency in 1977, and assumed his present position in 1981. Pilkington received his public administration doctorate from the University of Southern California in 1987.

PATRICK J. SHEERAN is a public administrator in the Office of Population Affairs, U.S. Department of Health and Human Services. He has been a public administrator for over 25 years, and has served in the Office of the Secretary of Defense and in the United States Air Force. He received his doctorate from the University of Southern California in 1986.

RICHARD C. SONNICHSEN is the Deputy Assistant Director, Inspection Division, Federal Bureau of Investigation. He has been a Special Agent of the FBI for 25 years, and has held management positions in the Bureau for the past 16 years. Sonnichsen is a doctoral candidate in public administration.